TARDIS Eruditorum: An Unofficial Critical History of Doctor Who

Volume IV: Tom Baker and the Hinchcliffe Years

Philip Sandifer

ERUDITORUM

PRESS

To Alex Reed, who I think of when I think of gothic horror.

Acknowledgments

First and foremost, to First and foremost, to my wife, Jill Buratto, who puts up with me far more than is strictly speaking necessary.

Second, as ever, to James Taylor for the phenomenal cover art. And, in his debut acknowledgment, Chris O'Leary for his careful copyediting. Anything in the book that makes sense is to his credit, and anything that isn't is probably because I mucked about with it.

And, of course, to the readers and commenters who have shaped the book's development. I am phenomenally proud of the community that has formed around *TARDIS Eruditorum*, and profoundly grateful for their support.

Table of Contents

A Mad Man with a Blog (Introduction)

Why hello there! It looks like you bought a copy of the fourth volume of *TARDIS Eruditorum*, which I, as the writer, thank you for, because that probably means you have given me money. (If you haven't given me money and downloaded this off the Internet, on the other hand, I hope you enjoy it and will consider not stealing future volumes.)

In the unlikely event that you have no idea what book you're holding, let me explain to you, generally speaking, how this book works. First of all, here's what it isn't: a standard issue guidebook to Doctor Who. Those looking for the nitty-gritty facts of Doctor Who can probably get a decent sense of them by inference, but that's not what this book is for. There are no episode descriptions, cast lists, or lengthy discussions of the behind-the-scenes workings of the show. There are dozens of books that already do that, and a fair number of online sites. Nor is this a book of reviews. For those who want those things, I personally recommend the *Doctor Who Reference Guide*, *Doctor Who Ratings Guide*, and *A Brief History of Time (Travel)* – three superlative websites that were consulted for basically every one of these essays.

What this book *is* is an attempt to tell the story of Doctor Who. Not the story of how it was made, or the overall narrative of the Doctor's life, or anything like that, but the story of the idea that is Doctor Who, from its beginnings in late 1963 to . . . well, early 1977 in the case of this book, but there's more to come. Doctor Who is a rarity in the world – an extremely long-running serialized narrative. Even rarer, it's an extremely long-running serialized narrative that is not in a niche like soap operas or superhero comics – both provinces almost exclusively of die-hard fans. Doctor Who certainly has its die-hard fans (or, as I like to think of you, my target audience), but notably, it's also been, for much of its existence, absolutely mainstream family entertainment for an entire country.

What this means is that the story of Doctor Who is, in one sense, the story of the world from 1963 on. Politics, music, technological and social development, and all manner of other things have crossed paths with Doctor Who over the nearly fifty years of its existence, and by using Doctor Who as a focus, one can tell a story with far wider implications.

The approach I use to do this is one that I've, rather pompously I suppose, dubbed psychochronography. It draws its name from the concept of psychogeography – an artistic movement created by Guy Debord in 1955 and described as "the study of the precise laws and specific effects of the geographical environment, consciously organized or not, on the emotions and behavior of individuals." More contemporarily, the term is associated with writers like Iain Sinclair, who writes books describing lengthy walking tours of London that fuse his experience with the history of the places he walks, weaving them into a narrative that tries to tell the entire story of a place, and Alan Moore, who does the same thing while worshiping a snake.

Psychochronography, then, attempts the same feat by walking through time. Where walking through space involves little more than picking a direction and moving your feet rhythmically, walking through time without the aid of a TARDIS is a dodgier proposition. The easiest way is to take a specific object and trace its development through time, looking, as the psychogeographers do, at history, lived experience, and the odd connections that spring up.

And so this book is the first part of a walk through Doctor Who. The essays within it wear a lot of hats, and switch them rapidly. All involve a measure of critical reading (in the literary theory sense, not in the complaining sense) of Doctor Who stories to figure out what they are about. This generally means trying to peel back the onion skins of fan history that cloud a story with things "everybody knows." But it also involves looking at the legacy of stories, which often means looking at that onion skin and trying to explain how it got there. No effort is made to disguise the fact that the first appearance of the Daleks is massive for instance, but on the other hand, the book still looks carefully at what their initial impact might have been.

This approach also means looking at how a story would (and could) have been understood by a savvy viewer of the time, and at how the story can be read as responding to the concerns of its time. That means that the essays tend to be long on cultural context. And, in the end, it also means looking at how I personally interact with these stories. This book has no pretense of objectivity. It is about my walking tour of Doctor Who. I try to be accurate, but I also try to be me.

To fully grab the scope of the topic, in addition to the meat of the book – entries covering all of the Doctor Who stories produced in Tom Baker's first three seasons (that is, the Philip Hinchcliffe years) – there are four other types of entries. The first are the Time Can Be Rewritten entries. One peculiar feature of Doctor Who is that its past is continually revisited. The bulk of these came in the form of novels written in the '90s and early '00s, but there are other examples. At the time of writing, for instance, Big Finish puts out new stories every year featuring the first eight Doctors. These entries cover occasional highlights from these revisitations, using them as clues to how these earlier eras are widely understood.

The second are the Pop Between Realities, Home in Time for Tea entries, which look at popular media and culture to build context for understanding Doctor Who. These entries usually crop up prior to the bits of Doctor Who they're most relevant for, and provide background and points of comparison for the show as it wrestles with the issues of its many times.

Third, there are the You Were Expecting Someone Else entries, which deal with spinoff material produced concurrently with Doctor Who but that, inevitably, has some significant differences from the approach of the televised material. These exist to give a broader sense of Doctor Who as a cultural object and, perhaps more importantly, because they're kind of fun.

Finally, there are some essays just thrown into the book version as bonuses. These mostly consist of me slogging my way through some established fan debate about Doctor Who and trying, no doubt fruitlessly, to provide the last word on the matter.

It's probably clear by this point that all of these entries began as blog entries on my blog, also called *TARDIS Eruditorum*. This book version, however, revises and expands every entry, as well as adding several new ones – mostly Time Can Be Rewritten entries, but a few others.

To this end, I should thank the many readers of the blog for their gratifying and edifying comments, which have kept the project going through more than one frustrating stretch. I should also thank the giants upon whose shoulders I stand when analyzing Doctor Who – most obviously Paul Cornell, Martin Day, and Keith Topping for *The Discontinuity Guide*, David J. Howe, Mark Stammers, and Stephen James Walker for the Doctor handbooks, Toby Hadoke and Rob Shearman for *Running Through Corridors*, and Lawrence Miles and Tat Wood for the sublimely brilliant *About Time* series, to which this book is a proud footnote.

A final note – although I have expanded and revised the essays in this book from their original online versions, I have not attempted to smooth out the developing style of the entries. Much like the show it follows, this project has evolved and grown since its beginning, and I did not wish to alter that.

But most of all and most importantly, thank you, all of you. But most of all, thank you, dear reader. I hope you enjoy.

Pop Between Realities, Home in Time for Tea (*The Tomorrow People, The Uncanny X-Men*)

A problem with the book versions of *TARDIS Eruditorum* is that they introduce discontinuity where none existed. On the original blog, the entries spanning Planet of the Spiders to The Ark in Space form a fairly clear line of thought addressing the Jon Pertwee/Tom Baker transition. In books, however, the first essay of the four is cut off from the rest, exiled in Volume Three. So to recap, I ended my book on the Pertwee era by noting that Planet of the Spiders, his final story, was my first Doctor Who story ever, on a VHS tape containing it, Robot, and The Ark in Space. This book begins with the traditional interstitial post between Doctors, ostensibly on something other than Doctor Who, but really there as a sort of opening act in which themes for the next chunk of essays are introduced.

To wit: upon its first appearance, under the editorial eye of David Whitaker, the TARDIS was explained via a metaphor of television in which the Doctor justifies his ability to fit a very large room inside a small box on the grounds that the same thing is accomplished via television. Aside from the role this moment plays in setting up the strand of alchemical and mystical thought I've traced through eleven years of Doctor Who thus far, this speaks to another crucial metaphor: that of the rabbit hole.

Of course, strictly speaking, if you're going to talk about connections between Doctor Who and children's literature in that Victorian tradition (and as I said in Volume Three, there are very good reasons to talk about those connections), the TARDIS owes more to the work of CS Lewis, who, as I never get tired of pointing out, died the day before Doctor Who premiered, almost exactly an hour before the Kennedy assassination, and eight hours before Aldous Huxley. But the basic concept is the same either way: the TARDIS is the very first image we had of Doctor Who, where Ian and Barbara fall out of the world.

Of course, that's any Doctor Who fan's first image of Doctor Who. That's what shows like it are. Rabbit holes that we fall into. I don't mean this according to the utterly banal logic of "suspension of disbelief" whereby we imagine ourselves endlessly in made-up places. I mean something much more literally. For me, on a weekend afternoon in September of 1992, I fell out of the world. I put a tape into the VCR, and when it was over I was not the same person anymore. I imagine you have had some similar experience.

Speaking on his blog after The Doctor's Wife aired, Neil Gaiman explained why he wrote the episode, saying, "I like mythologies, and I knew what a Dalek was and what planet it came from, or what TARDIS stood for when I was five, before I knew who Thor or Anubis were." This is, more or less, exactly it. The significance of Doctor Who, first and foremost, is an entire mythology and system of storytelling that has been unspooling through my brain for over twenty years now.

This is the way of fandom. Anyone who lives and breathes in geek culture has their rabbit holes: the books or movies or television shows that grabbed them and began exerting gravity in their minds. Usually the gravity is a subtle thing. It's not that we embark on major life decisions out of a commitment to fandom, but that our fandoms cast a shadow over our lives. How many of my Christmases would have had a completely different tenor had most of the presents not been Doctor Who themed? How would my honeymoon with my ex-wife have gone had we not planned it around seeing David Tennant in *Hamlet*? How would middle school have gone if the bullying I got for liking something as weird as Doctor Who had focused on something else?

This last one is, perhaps, the most interesting. Most of our rabbit holes, after all, are generational affairs. Each generation has its narrative subcultures. Mine has its Transformers fans, its *Labyrinth* fans, its *Baby-sitters Club* fans, but the one thing my generation in America conspicuously lacks, or, at least, lacked before now, is any significant number of Doctor Who fans. This is not surprising. I was seven when the series was cancelled and in the wrong country. It was not something many people were going to get into, except by the odd vector I did—their parents happened to love it, and the love caught.

Even then, the series of events that led to my Doctor Who fandom feels odd. It comes down to, I suppose, the fact that my mother never does anything halfway. So when she and my father got into Doctor Who, of course they got a mammoth run of Target novels, of course they bought the Peter Haining 20th Anniversary book, of course they taped huge swaths of episodes. And when I got into the show, of course my mother bought a multi-region VCR so she could have access to more Doctor Who tapes. It's not even that my family was particularly posh—we do fine for ourselves, and we're a damn sight luckier than a lot of people. It's just that my mother has that essential geek trait—the one that obviously passed onto me, given that I'm the sort to attempt an insane book like this—of maniacal completeness.

So I ended up, in a real sense, falling out of the world. Fall out of the world with something of your culture—even something a bit obscure—and you're fine. But 1970s British science fiction shows were not exactly socially advisable obsessions in the suburban public schools of early 1990s America. Out of both time and place, my life of being a freak was well set out for me.

In this regard, at least, I was actually more suited for the other rabbit hole on offer for the British children of 1974: *The Tomorrow People*. Of the many iterations of "ITV's answer to Doctor Who," *The Tomorrow People* stands out as the one that people have the most fondness for. Certainly it's the longest-running - the show debuted during *Planet of the Daleks*, and its last episode aired midway through *The Armageddon Factor*. And on top of that it had a lousy nineties revamp, which, unlike Doctor Who's lousy nineties revamp, actually managed to last three series, followed by, in 2013, an equally lousy American revamp.

Unfortunately, it's crap. This is a common phenomenon affecting most of the "ITV's answer to Doctor Who" attempts, so it can't really come as a surprise. The problems with *The Tomorrow People* are numerous. First of all, it is a textbook example of falling between two stools. *The Tomorrow People* has two ideas, one of which is brilliant and the other one of which is, at least, not bad. The latter concept is a gang of plucky kids who fight various alien menaces. This is not, obviously, the most original idea for children's sci-fi television ever devised, but we surely haven't seen the last successful implementation of it even in 2014, so it's tough to complain too much.

Yet even by the meager standards of this idea, *The Tomorrow People* falls short. Every single actor in its debut story, The Slaves of Jedikiah, is excruciatingly bad, with both Sammie Winmill and Stephen Salmon being particularly gruesome. Admittedly neither were retained for the second series, so it's entirely possible that as of Season Two the quality of acting suddenly skyrockets. The general consensus is that it doesn't, however. And frankly, the problems go a lot deeper than two poor child actors, especially because it's not likely that any actor could do well delivering the lines expected of this cast. Add this to a set of effects that make the show look like the low-rent Doctor Who knockoff it is and you have, well, a recipe for unfortunate things.

Let's face it: clearly nobody was expected to tune into *The Tomorrow People* for its vivid depictions of bold and original sci-fi concepts. The show's appeal was much more basic: it was one of the most unabashed and unapologetic panders to the geek mindset ever. See, it turns out that some kids are special kids who are the secret future of the human race and have superpowers: Homo Superior.

The problem is that *The Tomorrow People* tries to have it both ways. A story about special teenagers who, while hated and feared by the larger society, try to help it and save it is a good idea. But the basic appeal is the real-world setting—the fact that these are teenagers who go through recognizable problems of kids, only here amped up with superpowers. This is basically the concept of the first three seasons of *Buffy the Vampire Slayer*. So the one thing you absolutely *shouldn't* do is have the main cast be a bunch of cardboard cut-outs going on a bunch of space adventures that utterly lack any meaningful connection to the real world.

For the first five minutes or so—even the first episode, by and large—there's a crackling sense of potential to the whole thing. The first few scenes are gorgeously shot, and there's a taut, gritty feeling to the show. Yes, it all goes to hell in a hand basket quickly, but it's just enough that you can see how *The Tomorrow People* might have served as a rabbit hole, and why people would have genuine affection for it today.

Especially because that central premise is so good, and, if we're being honest, because *The Tomorrow People*'s execution of it was so flagrantly a metaphor about homosexuality that I can't even bring myself to use the phrase "gay subtext" here because it's such an egregious misuse of the word "subtext." This has been analyzed at length by other critics, but basically: realizing you're different from everybody else, and that you have to keep it a secret from your parents while you hang out with other people who are "different" like you and wear oddly skin-tight clothing? Yeah.

And in this regard, at least, *The Tomorrow People* deserves credit for getting there in 1973, given that its most obvious

American counterpart took two more decades to even start to hint at that connotation, having previously inexplicably believed itself to be about the Civil Rights Movement. I am, of course, alluding to Marvel Comics' *X-Men* franchise, which, although it debuted in 1963, didn't really become its most famous and beloved form until 1975 with the publication of *Giant-Size X-Men* #1, and, a few months later, the beginning of British expat Chris Claremont's sixteen-year run writing the comic.

Unlike *The Tomorrow People*, which I never saw as a child and for which I don't imagine I'd have had any particular fondness, the *X-Men* were, for a time, one of my rabbit holes. I was a voracious comics fan from about 1991 to 1994, and the *X-Men* were my favorite line. Part of this was simply that they were everybody else's favorite. But as the saying goes, some works are unjustly forgotten, but nothing is unjustly remembered. To be a mass success on the scale that the *X-Men* were, and still are, requires some genius.

Reading Chris Claremont's *X-Men* comics makes it clear where that genius lay. The X-Men are, in every regard, what *The Tomorrow People* flails helplessly at being. Claremont's major skill as a comics writer was his ability to wed soap opera character dynamics to the action genre of the comics. In other words, a Claremont book is generally about emotional drama playing out over multiple issues of people punching giant robots. And it's great. My *X-Men* comics consisted of the books coming out in the early 1990s—which were horrible, barely intelligible, and not written by Claremont anymore even though his successors tried to ape his style—and of selections given to me by my uncle from his comics collection, which spanned the mid-to-late 1980s. The former made minimal sense even if you did have all of the issues, whereas the latter was a hodgepodge of random issues that rarely, if ever, included entire storylines.

Despite this, it was easy to fall in love with the books simply because it was impossible not to love at least one of the characters. The X-Men, particularly under Claremont, was a massive ensemble cast of extremely likable and fun characters. The actual stories of the future of humanity being hunted and oppressed were fine, but they were, quite frankly, just excuses to read about Nightcrawler or Kitty Pryde or Storm. It was a soap opera dressed up so young boys would read it and my God, did we read it.

But oddly, Claremont never really shone anywhere else like he did on *X-Men*. Something about that property and his writing fit together perfectly. He was at his best on *X-Men*, which didn't truly work until he took it over. And even then it was a time-limited phenomenon - virtually everyone will agree that Claremont was past his peak by the mid-1980s. No - there is, it seems, something about the mid-1970s and the image of outsider teenagers - a moment where the cultural zeitgeist embraced that idea.

(Although oddly, the intersections between *X-Men* and *The Tomorrow People* are largely unremarked upon. Mark Millar finally acknowledged the debt when he named his first arc of Ultimate X-Men "The Tomorrow People," and *The Tomorrow People*'s premiere has an charming coincidence in which the psychiatric hospital at which part of it is set is named "Claremount." But beyond these obvious and minor intersections, the two topics are oddly separate. It's tough to argue that Claremont was influenced by *The Tomorrow People*, as he'd long since emigrated to the US, and Marvel's UK distribution was not such that *The Tomorrow People* could rip off American superhero comics easily.)

But then again, this makes sense. The term "homo superior" was, after all, borrowed from David Bowie's 1971 "Oh! You Pretty Things," one of the great songs of glam rock. Glam, also covered extensively last book, had as one of its central images the starchild: a child of the future who heralded a concrete shift in the tenor of the culture. This idea was terribly big in 1973, when *The Tomorrow People* debuted in the same month as Bowie's *Aladdin Sane*. But this turned out to be glam's peak, and both *The Tomorrow People* and the X-

Men would outlive the subculture that spawned them by years.

The result was a legion of glam fans—starchildren giddily embracing their specialness—who were suddenly and abruptly cast out by mainstream culture. It was, in other words, the exact right time for stories about special but persecuted teenagers. This may be the point where glam rock drops out of the narrative but its heritage survives in things like *The Tomorrow People* and *The X-Men*, which provided needed rabbit holes for the dispossessed starchildren to burrow into and wait for the next cultural wave. Millions of them, glued to their television sets or their comic books, a future waiting to explode.

It would, I suspect, be very difficult to do a project like this with *The Tomorrow People*, whereas it would be almost trivial to do it with the X-Men. Then again, one of them is a rabbit hole I went down, and the other isn't—of course it's easier to do my rabbit holes than someone else's. And, of course, there are countless other rabbit holes out there, and not all of them for children.

But there is something substantive in this transition as well. Glam was a subculture with one eye on the future in a way that its successors aren't. *The Tomorrow People* and *The X-Men* are the last flourishings of that futurism. But Doctor Who is about to take a very different approach. Unlike the other prominent rabbit holes of its time, Doctor Who goes somewhere other than the future. And in doing so, as we'll see, it ends up on the one hand securing its own future, and on the other hand destroying it.

Philip Sandifer

Where There's Life (*Robot*)

It's December 28, 1974. Mud are "Lonely This Christmas," and apparently a lot of people care and are buying their single to make them feel less alone. After three weeks of this Mud finally plummets down the charts as people realize Christmas has been over for a while, and Status Quo's "Down Down" takes the number one spot. Also in the charts are Barry White, Bachman-Turner Overdrive, Gloria Gaynor, Disco Tex and the Sex-O-Lettes (I promise I did not make that up), and The Wombles, who make their fifth and final top ten placing.

Since Pertwee's regeneration, the 1974 FIFA World Cup has happened, sans England, but with Scotland, so that's nice and frustratingly rarely mentioned when people decide to list England's failure to qualify as a reason why the Heath government fell. Richard Nixon resigned, kicking off a brief intermission from the rise of the political right that his 1968 election marked. Haile Selassie was deposed in Ethiopia, Ceefax began in the UK, and Ali defeated Foreman in the Rumble in the Jungle. More tragically, the Birmingham pub bombings took place, killing 21 and injuring another 182. The exact cause is under some dispute, with the IRA being widely blamed, a Marxist splinter group called Red Flag 74 trying to take the blame despite probably not being responsible, and a group of Irishmen known familiarly as the Birmingham Six ultimately being arrested and, after some truly spectacular police corruption, convicted and sent to prison for sixteen years.

While during this story, the British government abandons another attempt at a Channel Tunnel, *Wheel of Fortune* debuts, and Lesley Whittle, a 17 year old heiress, is kidnapped by Donald Neilson. Also, International Women's Year is kicked off in the UK, which I note not because I'm particularly enamored with commemoration-style politics like that but because I haven't cited a lot of news stories that point to the degree to which these are golden years for feminism, so I figured I should.

I, of course, am still off in 1992, in the basement. I think, though I honestly don't remember vividly, that I actually marathoned that entire tape in one day, so while we've jumped over six months in world history since *Planet of the Spiders*, I'm pretty sure from my perspective we've had lunch. Still, this is perhaps advantageous: it's not clear that there is any story to date in Doctor Who more suitable for watching when you are A) ten, and B) have no idea what the show is supposed to be like than Robot.

Robot is, by necessity, an odd duck. By convention, Doctor Who has, for the past few seasons, banked an episode across seasons. So The Time Warrior was actually made immediately after The Green Death, and Carnival of Monsters immediately after The Time Monster. The effect of this was that, following Planet of the Spiders, Barry Letts had one more story to do on his contract, and so the opening story of Season Twelve was produced at the end of Season Eleven with a production team staying on from the Pertwee era.

On top of that, Terrance Dicks managed to persuade Robert Holmes that there was an active tradition of hiring the outgoing script editor for the first script of the new editor's tenure. (To be fair, this had actually happened for several of the previous outgoing script editors, although the claim that it was a conscious tradition was perhaps self-serving) But the result was, by most sane standards, unfortunate: instead of getting a big, impressive launch, the Tom Baker era begins with a retread of the already-tired Pertwee era.

It's not that this is a huge problem. The Pertwee era was massively popular, and massively popular things on the decline are still quite popular. Were the Tom Baker era wall-to-wall Pertwee retreads it would have been bad. That it starts with one is essentially just an odd historical detail.

If you want to approach it from a question of quality, we get about what we'd expect based on the preceding five years. In what is actually his first solo credit for a story, Dicks smashes out an *Avengers* story in which the John Steed role split between the Doctor and Harry Sullivan. Letts finds some new ways to misuse CSO. Everyone finds bold new ways to have horrifying politics, this time treating the environmental movement with suspicion and feminism with disdain. (What's particularly strange and disturbing is the fact that the bad guys include both sexist men and repressed and clearly-intended-to-be lesbian women, with nothing in between.) All of these things are absolutely true. They are also, however, beside the point. Because what this story is about is far more important and superficial than all of that.

There is something of a devil's bargain in the casting of Tom Baker. The main brief for a new Doctor was that the BBC wanted an eccentric. For a while the part was expected to go to an elderly actor (hence the creation of Harry to fill the old Ian/Steven/Jamie role in the expected absence of Pertwee's physicality), but eventually Bill Slater, Head of Drama at the BBC, pointed Letts towards Tom Baker. Slater was seemingly impressed with, well, Baker's craziness. The problem with casting someone for their craziness, however, is that, well, they're a bit crazy.

So throughout the Tom Baker era, lurking in the background, or sometimes in the foreground, is the fact that Baker was frequently a profoundly ungracious actor who stole scenes and sabotaged co-stars with reckless abandon, and who was prone to petulant sulking when he didn't get his way, despite the fact that his ideas were often self-evidently idiotic. To say that this caused problems from time to time is an understatement. (This was by and large a slowly developing thing: Baker started out gracious and got less so, with the stories that reflect poorly on him not really beginning until around Lis Sladen's departure. It's also important to note that he got on well with a number of his co-stars, most obviously Lalla Ward, fraught as that situation may have become, and that those with whom he'd had a poor relationship at the time have since largely reconciled with him. It's also worth noting that the person who is by far nastiest about Baker is Matthew Waterhouse, about whom nobody says anything nice.)

This would be easier to fault if there weren't so many occasions when Tom Baker salvaged a scene or an entire script through sheer charisma. Baker was exceptionally good at winning over the audience and he knew it. (He knew his limitations as well, freely admitting that he was a performer, not an actor.) And for all that his tenure is peppered with anecdotes of his ungraciousness or, towards the end, overt cruelty towards his co-stars, no small portion of that was motivated by his absolutely correct belief that a fair share of the audience was watching the show purely for him, and that they considered scenes in which the Doctor isn't talking as being actively inferior to ones in which he is.

All of this stems from one very simple reason: Tom Baker is gobsmackingly charismatic. From the moment he opens his eyes in Robot, he is all charm. He has several things going for him. First is that Terrance Dicks, lacking any clear idea of where this Doctor was going (and perhaps more to the point, lacking any real investment in that question), just wrote him as funny. The first episode's scenes featuring the Doctor are almost all played for comedy, including set pieces such as him trying to prove his fitness to Harry or endlessly changing clothes for the Brigadier. Oddly, some of the credit here then has to go to Patrick Troughton. Not knowing where Baker's Doctor is going and forced to differentiate him clearly from

Pertwee, Dicks takes the most obvious route available and just writes for Troughton at several points, figuring that since Pertwee distinguished himself from Troughton, returning to Troughton would in turn distinguish this new Doctor from Pertwee.

This is most obvious in the scene in which the Doctor and UNIT go to question Professor Kettlewell, who remains adamantly prickly in response to the Brigadier. So instead the Doctor proceeds to butter him up, praising his work and his genius for a minute or two before suddenly dropping his voice and telling Kettlewell to fill him in on the robot. It's not a trick Pertwee would ever use, and it's clearly derivative of how Troughton would seize an authority that wasn't his to befuddle people and get his way.

Indeed, Baker's take on the part clearly owes considerable debt to Troughton. In the Kettlewell interrogation scene, Baker opts to stand behind Kettlewell for a conversation, literally lurking on the periphery of events in a way reminiscent of Troughton's performance in *Tomb of the Cybermen*. But there's a bombast and excess in Baker's performance that Troughton would never have gone for. Troughton stayed at the periphery of events to hide, keeping himself underestimated and unnoticed. Baker, on the other hand, is carrying a massive "I am lurking on the periphery of things waiting to make my move" sign. This is the moment where Troughton's approach, which until now had been an oddity among three very different types of Doctor, becomes the baseline against which all other Doctors are defined.

From a viewer's perspective, it's wonderful. And what it comes down to, in the end is Baker. As I suggested above, you can get away with constantly mugging for the camera if you are, in fact, colossally likable.

And my God, Tom Baker is. I fell in love with him watching the episode. He was funny and charming and as soon as he did the bit about unsinkability and the Titanic I knew that I wanted to see more of him. I didn't feel that about Pertwee after Planet of the Spiders. He wasn't unlikable as such—it wasn't like anything about his portrayal of the Doctor made me root against him. But he didn't have the immediate head-over-heels charisma of Tom Baker.

Part of this, if I am being honest, is a matter of what does and doesn't work for geeks. Another theme that will appear in earnest during the Tom Baker years is the emergence of Doctor Who fandom as an organized and coherent force. It's not just that the show had now been around for long enough to acquire a fandom; it's subtler than that, and it has to do with the question of rabbit holes. Part of why fandom started to crystallize in the Tom Baker years was that Tom Baker was unusually well-poised to be liked by geeks. Because Tom Baker played what is, in many ways, one of the fundamental fantasies of a socially ostracized smart person. He's adored precisely because he's clever.

Previous Doctors were valued for their intelligence, yes. And previous Doctors were adored. But William Hartnell was adored because he was kind and paternal. Troughton was adored because he was mercurial and silly. Pertwee was adored because he was dashing and manly. Baker is adored because he's clever. This is close to Troughton, but it's distinct. Whether clever in a humorous sense or clever in a "solves-problems" sense, Baker is the first Doctor whose intelligence is overtly the source of his leading-man charm. This is what the scene in the fourth episode in which he disarms the computer is about. Here Baker delivers straight-facedly a lengthy monologue about how difficult his task is, and then smiles widely as he does it anyway. In other words, what's charming about him is that he was clever enough to do the terribly difficult thing.

If I'm being honest, it's what I loved about Baker at age ten. And it was enough to make this episode seem like a revelation after Planet of the Spiders. But for more established audience members, it was a sign that the nature of the show is about to change in a big way. The decision to have Baker start off with key parts of Pertwee's supporting cast in place is a sound one, though not for the reason you'd expect. The normal logic of a decision like this is to ease the new guy in. Having old pros like Nicholas Courtney and John Levene around helps distract from any stumbles as Baker finds his way into the part. It's the reason the Daleks were used for Troughton's debut, it's (rather unfortunately) why the Rani comes back for Sylvester McCoy's debut, and, more modernly, it's why Harriet Jones, Jackie, and Mickey all come back for Tennant's debut.

Instead, what we get is something more oddly transformative. All of the normal props of a UNIT story are put into place, yes, but Baker just acts them off the screen. Part of this is his sheer charisma, but part of it is owed to Baker's conscious decisions to look at UNIT and the work he's doing with mild disdain, and to visibly want to run off and shirk responsibility. Pertwee's Doctor would want to avoid doing something for the Brigadier because something else interested him more, but Baker seems to want to do anything just so long as he doesn't have to work for somebody. Some of this is Dicks' doing as well—the decision to have the Doctor seem willing to abandon Sarah and just run off speaks volumes about how little the new Doctor cares about the day-to-day affairs of Earth. (Though it's a gambit, given how likeable Sarah Jane is and Baker makes some deft decisions to avoid hurting his likability.)

The result is that *Robot* seems in a real sense to continue a thread from Planet of the Spiders and kill off the Pertwee era at its most fundamental level. Here UNIT are ruthlessly shown to be surplus to requirements. The Doctor doesn't care about them anymore, and the Doctor wins us over with such utter charm that we take his side and find ourselves looking down on the Brigadier. By being turned slightly against the tenets of the Pertwee era, it becomes easier for us to invest in the beginning of the Baker era. This is sensible: even if the UNIT era was in decline, it was still massively popular. Demonstrating its obsolescence is a risky strategy, but one that pays off.

This is also the time to say goodbye to both Barry Letts and Terrance Dicks. While both will return a few more times, this is the end of their continual tenure and of the phase of the program made to their image of it. Consider this a belated addendum to Volume Three, where I was exceedingly hard on both at times. Despite my frustrations with them, however, both are rightly beloved and honored by fandom. If I may briefly discourse on their legacy, then, I would say this:

There are two ways to improve a television series. The first is to make the show good more often. The second is to make the show bad less often. Some production teams on Doctor Who have aspired to the first: both John Wiles and Peter Bryant clearly came in hoping to make the show do more impressive things. Barry Letts and Terrance Dicks, however, are of the second school. And this is something easy to miss when watching the Pertwee era. Tat Wood points it out in the *About Time* entry on Planet of the Spiders by observing how bizarre the standard criticisms of the show would seem to somebody coming off of Spearhead From Space: there's yet again too many gratuitous chases and action scenes? What? From the show that did The Space Pirates last year?

But it's actually bigger than that. Letts and Dicks pulled the baseline quality of the show up to the point of where its best episodes had been when they took over. Under Letts and Dicks, even the two lowest points of Pertwee's tenure were at least as good as their nearest equivalent Troughton episodes, and even something like Invasion of the Dinosaurs—a business-as-usual piece in which everybody was on autopilot—is about on par with a Troughton-era masterpiece like The Invasion. Dicks's ability to spin an engaging adventure yarn in his sleep consistently keeps any script from bottoming out too badly. And, as we're seeing him off, we should also reiterate his massive contribution to childhood literacy in the form of his Target novelizations.

As for Letts, he's far and away the best technical producer that the series had since Verity Lambert. Most obviously, he brought in huge innovations in how stories were made. He moved to doing two episodes as a block over two weeks with two straight days of filming, instead of making one episode every week that shot one day a week. It got so that stories were shot entirely in order of location, and it became so organized that stories could air out of production order, something Doctor Who had never come close to doing under any previous producer. In the past, there was sometimes a mere week between an episode's production and transmission. Under Letts this reliably became months. And he did all of this while managing the transition to shooting in color.

The result is a series that's consistently interesting, consistently shows new and exciting things, and is consistently entertaining. It's a series that firmly and unequivocally deserves to be recognized as a classic of its era, a series that is, in production values and basic quality, miles better than its closest competitors, which we've looked at in previous volumes and found wanting.

That's not something that comes through on an episode-by-episode approach, where the individual weaknesses shine through. But taken as a whole, and not dissected with the critic's scalpel, the Letts/Dicks era is amazing in its ability to hit the B+/A- level week in and week out. That's not something many shows can do. And it explains why so many people love the Pertwee era. Letts and Dicks produced five years of a show that people wanted to be on the air just because of how much they loved watching it. In a very literal sense, that's why the show is still on the air.

So as we move into the Hinchcliffe era that forms the bulk of this volume, let's reflect, one last time, on how strong a show Philip Hinchcliffe inherited from Letts. Now let's see the wondrous things that Hinchcliffe and Robert Holmes do with it.

Monsters are Real (*The Ark in Space*)

It's January 25, 1975. The Tymes, a Philadelphia soul group, are at number one with "Ms Grace." This is a genre that had been growing in the US for a while, and here it spills over to the UK. In return, David Bowie slips over to the US and records *Young Americans* - which he's just putting the finishing touches on now. *Young Americans* is his version of a soul album - an album that would spawn his first number one single in the US, "Fame," which merely hits 17th in the UK. It lasts one week before giving way to Pilot, a splinter group of the Bay City Rollers, with "January," which stays on top for the remainder of this story. Gloria Gaynor, Marie and Donnie Osmond, The Carpenters, Helen Reddy, and Wigan's Chosen Few also chart.

In real news, the Weather Underground bombs the US State Department, hurting absolutely nobody and generally continuing their reputation as the fluffy bunnies of the terrorist world. An earthquake takes place in Haicheng, China, killing over two thousand people, but here the real news is that it did so as expected, being as it was the first ever successfully predicted earthquake. An unsuccessful attempt to partition Cyprus following last summer's Turkish invasion of it takes place. And, for our purposes most interesting of all, Margaret Thatcher defeats Edward Heath to become the new leader of the Conservative Party. This will end well for everybody.

While on television, we have a legend. It is not that The Ark in Space is the best story of the Hinchcliffe era. It's not. But there are a handful of points in the history of Doctor Who when an episode airs that clearly marks a sudden leap forward in quality: a point where you can basically say that nothing that has come before is quite this good. The tendency I've discussed before whereby storytelling techniques get ever savvier and lead to a general trend of improvement for all television helps make this happen, but the point remains: watching The Ark in Space, it is clear that we have just moved to an entirely new sort of show. The show hasn't shown hostile and alien environments like this in years. Monsters like the Wirrn, which are conceptually horrifying instead of being based around a compelling visual, are unthinkable in the Pertwee era. The first episode, a functional three-hander in which the Doctor, Harry, and Sarah just explore the space station, is unlike anything since The Underwater Menace.

In this regard, what's most striking about the episode is that it's so much grimmer. Not since Terror of the Autons has the series made such a concentrated and extended effort to be scary. In *Autons*, the fear was wedded to a sense of the spectacular and the emerging glam aesthetic (the last time the show spent a lot of time being scary for its own sake was The Wheel in Space.) But here, all of a sudden, Doctor Who is all about fear, and more specifically about lingering in moments of fear. I'd say "again," but that would obscure things somewhat. Even in the Troughton era, at the height of the golden age of monsters in season five, the show didn't go for this sort of unrelenting horror. The nearest equivalent, Fury From the Deep, is downright cuddly in comparison to this. This is Doctor Who as a horror movie. (Indeed, it's Doctor Who as *Alien*, albeit several years early.)

On top of that, there's a new sort of pessimism to this story. In the Pertwee era, the future was either not going to happen because we would destroy ourselves, or it would happen and be awesome. There was very little middle ground.

If the future had humans in it, it would be good. On one or two occasions you'd get a slight hybrid—the future where the Earth is crap but everywhere else is good. But here we get a strange new approach: a future in which humanity has survived, and where the Doctor paces around making speeches about the indomitable nature of humanity, but where everything is grimy and dangerous and not at all sexy. A future, in other words, in which humanity survives but life remains full of drudgery and toil.

It's worth noting that part of this tonal shift comes not from moving forwards, but rather from moving backwards. One of the most interesting things about the story is that its first episode has no characters aside from the TARDIS crew. The last time this happened was The Mind Robber, itself a special case where an extra episode had to be hurriedly tacked on. Before that was The Space Museum. And there's a sense of a return to first principles behind the camera as well. Although the script for this story is credited to Holmes, it's actually a full rewrite of a John Lucarotti script, Lucarotti having all but defined a particular style of historical adventure during the Hartnell years.

The down side of this is that really selling the episode requires putting Sarah in the refrigerator - quite literally this time. Lis Sladen has only twenty lines in an episode with only three characters, and several of those are just shouting "Doctor!" or moaning "where am I?" This probably has less to do with the usual division of labor whereby the companion gets in trouble and the Doctor rescues her, and more to do with the fact that there are actually two companions here (another move back to pre-Pertwee approaches), one of whom is on his first adventure. Accordingly, it's more interesting to have the more clueless Harry around for the Doctor to explain things to while the more experienced Sarah goes and gets into trouble. But it's still a shame to see Sladen marginalized. (Though to be fair, in episode four she gets her best moment on the series to date, so it works out.)

But all of this points towards a larger refocusing going on here: a turn towards an aesthetic of discomfort instead of comfort. There are only three Pertwee stories (The Curse of Peladon, The Mutants, and Carnival of Monsters, if you're one of those sorts who need to know) in which the show doesn't leverage a familiar element (generally the Master or UNIT) to introduce us to the world of a given story, and two of those depend on unseen Time Lords sending the Doctor on a mission. Pertwee rarely landed anywhere in which the point is how strange and unusual the place is. Even if we confine ourselves to his non-terrestrial adventures, the majority use a familiar or returning element to ground things. But here things change. Even though The Ark in Space is the only one of the five stories shot in its recording block not to feature a returning concept, the ones that do return are often twisted and changed into new shapes, as we'll see in both Genesis of the Daleks and Revenge of the Cybermen. And this forms a transition as we move to a stretch of stories that are reliably about strange and alien environments again.

The Ark in Space isn't just a turn away from the familiar, however; it's a turn towards revelling in unfamiliarity. The whole point of the first episode is that the space station is a strange and scary place. This is an older and more visceral aesthetic than the comparatively simple aesthetic of the glam spectacle. The heart of the glam spectacle—the pop commodity—is a relatively modern invention that depends upon mass media to function in the first place. But with The Ark in Space we revert suddenly to the more primal aesthetic of the grotesque.

The grotesque is an odd category, best treated as a special case of the sublime. I'll just go ahead and offer one of my favorite quotes, from Immanuel Kant's *Critique of Judgment*, on this:

Bold, overhanging, and, as it were, threatening rocks, thunderclouds piled up the vault of heaven, borne along with flashes and peals, volcanoes in all their violence of destruction, hurricanes leaving desolation in their track, the boundless ocean rising with rebellious force, the high waterfall of some mighty river, and the like, make our power of resistance of trifling moment in comparison with their might. But, provided our own position is secure, their aspect is all the more attractive for its fearfulness; and we readily call these objects sublime, because they raise the forces of the soul above the height of vulgar commonplace, and discover within us a power of resistance of quite another kind, which gives us courage to be able to measure ourselves against the seeming omnipotence of nature.

In other words, the sublime is a sense of safe fear. Kant later compares it to the fear that a righteous man would have in the presence of God: the righteous man knows that God loves him, but is still afraid of God because God is worthy of fear. The grotesque works along similar grounds - it is scary and repulsive, but it is also contained so that we are drawn to it despite its unnerving nature. This is one of the major aesthetics of the Hinchcliffe era. Which brings us back to the subject of fear, and of lingering within fear.

I can talk about this first hand for The Ark in Space. Because of the three stories on that first VHS tape of Doctor Who, this was the one that really grabbed me. Largely, as it happens, because it scared the pants off of me. I knew it was great. I endlessly hoped for a return of the Wirrn. But I always managed to find a reason to watch something else when I was looking for Doctor Who to watch, because this one, good as it was, freaked me out. It was at once my favorite story and the one I could not bring myself to rewatch.

Part of this is production. The Ark in Space has some of the most laughable special effects to date, with several parts of the Wirrn very obviously being bubble wrap spray painted green. Most obvious is a scene at the start of Part Three in which Kenton Moore, as Noah, has to stare in horror at his hand, which is transforming into a Wirrn's hand. And he is very obviously staring at green spray-painted bubble wrap that has been wrapped around his hand. It looks ridiculous. Or, at least, it should.

But somehow, it doesn't. Moore acts the hell out of the scene, grappling with the hand with utter conviction such that you don't notice the hand, you notice the horror and agony of the actor. It's actually one of the great triumphs of cheap effects in Doctor Who and a textbook case of what I have previously called invisible effects. The point of the effect is not to be noticed, and it works far, far better than green bubble wrap has any right to do, cementing one of the basic rules of invisible effects: if everybody acts as though they believe the green bubble wrap is terrifying, it will be.

This gets at the real reason this story is scary, which is the confidence with which it leaves things unsaid. Here we get to the heart of how scary children's television—a subgenre that Doctor Who in Seasons Twelve through Fourteen is basically the pinnacle of—works. Neil Gaiman once remarked of his novel *Coraline* that it is far too scary for adults, but just right for kids. One of the fundamental trickinesses of children's horror is that most adults are terrible at evaluating it. This is because adults tend to assume that children dislike being upset and disturbed. From an adult perspective, it's easy to see how this mistake could be made, particularly if you have to put the scared kid to bed afterwards.

The result of this is that people imagine that there is some sort of firm line for a given child, one side of which is fine and the other side of which is too scary. Which is rubbish. There's a whole grey area between "totally fine" and "too scary." And children's entertainment thrives in that grey area. Almost every truly classic piece of children's entertainment that's remembered vividly by adults decades later is something that's disturbing but isn't so disturbing as to be completely unmanageable. Put another way, traumatizing children is good. It's also worth noting that children are very, very good at managing their own trauma levels. It's very rare for a kid to sit through something that's too grown-up and too scary for them. The result is that, by and large, children can be trusted with scary media.

This is what the entire "behind the sofa" image is actually about. The sofa serves as a physical interface for managing how disturbed one is. In practice "behind the sofa" is a phrase to be taken non-literally—most kids do not and did not actually crouch behind the sofa. Instead, children engage in a more internal version of this same negotiation between fear and pleasure. Central to this is also the phenomenon we settled way back in Volume One about how cliffhangers work. All television, but Doctor Who especially, is based around anticipation. It sets us up so that we think we know what is going to happen, and then plays with and on our expectations. The sofa is really a metaphor for how that works; we crouch down behind it and peer up over it as part of our re-evaluating of how OK everything is or isn't going to turn out, using the sofa to manage our level of fear.

In these terms, The Ark in Space is a triumph. It delights in creating large and anxious stretches to mess with viewer expectations and tease them with the prospect of something terrible happening. But more time is spent on the possibility of the terrible thing than on the terrible thing itself. The horror of the Wirrn is left shown but not told. Lawrence Miles and Tat Wood suggest that this works according to an age line—that the people who are old enough to understand the true horror of the Wirrn are also old enough to know it's just men in rubber suits. But this assumes a much more rigid line than I'm inclined towards, and, perhaps more to the point, a much more rigid line than I experienced.

Rather, the Wirrn are clearly disturbing in a way that is slightly hard to quite articulate or nail down at a young age. If you are too young to intuitively grasp that what makes the Wirrn horrifying is that they give you the experience of being eaten alive and slowly converted into one of them simultaneously, that's fine, because you can still tell that these monsters are terrifying in a way that previous monsters haven't been simply by how everyone acts towards them. The gruesome explanation is held back to be read between the lines, but the consequences of that expectation are on clear display.

In particular Tom Baker handles this well, playing against the charismatic bravado he usually projects by having the Doctor appear genuinely afraid of the Wirrn at times. This is a trick he uses throughout the Hinchcliffe era to great effect, but it's remarkable when seen in only his second story, albeit his third filmed. The result is a story that manages to achieve one of the true pinnacles of children's entertainment: something that disturbs children just enough that they remember it for their whole life, but not so much that they don't enjoy it.

And, of course, the standard tropes of the Baker years are on display here too. While Baker is still easing into the role and isn't completely comfortable yet, his performance is perfectly pitched for this. He's still charismatic and fun to watch, and provides a helpful anchor of safety in amongst all the scares. On the other hand, his ability to instinctively make the Doctor seem alien and strange is miles ahead of any of his predecessors which ratchets up the alienating quality of the story.

And, of course, massive credit goes to Robert Holmes, who understood this well. Most obviously there's the scene in Part Four where the Doctor berates Sarah for her incompetence in order to motivate her. It's a truly stunning moment. On the one hand, it reaffirms that this Doctor is socially aware and clever in a way that his predecessor wasn't - that he's someone who understands people well enough to manipulate them. Pertwee had social status, but Baker has social ability, which allows him to manufacture status. Yet he's also cruel in a way Pertwee's Doctor would never be, and Troughton's Doctor only was in extreme cases. Holmes has an intuitive sense of how well Baker can sell the alien nature of the Doctor without endangering the audience's sympathies, and he goes to town with it.

Even with only two Doctor Who stories, both of which I'd watched earlier in the day, under my belt, this story carried a tangible sense that a truly incredible thing was beginning. This was the story that made Tom Baker's era my favorite (at least until I discovered that there was a Doctor beyond Colin Baker, the last Doctor referenced in any of the books my parents owned). And though there were no more Baker episodes in my parents' collection, between their extremely thorough set of Target novelizations and the VHS releases I eventually discovered (which at the time heavily favored Hinchcliffe-era Baker stories: eight of the sixteen Hinchcliffe stories were out on VHS in the US when I started buying tapes), it was easy to have a childhood defined by this era of Doctor Who. More to the point, watching The Ark in Space, it was clear to me, as it had been to millions of kids in 1975, that I wanted my childhood defined by this.

And so it was. For all of us.

Transmitting Matter

A commissioned essay for Sean Williams

One of the most curious moments of technology in all of Doctor Who comes when Sarah Jane Smith gets a change of clothes when she's teleported within Nerva Beacon. There are, from a pragmatic perspective, a couple of ways this could be handled. It's certainly possible that at some point dressing robots pick over her unconscious body before putting her in the cryogenic cell. This, however, is terribly unpleasant to even think about. It's far more likely that the change of clothes is a by-product of the matter transmitter.

This requires us to briefly think about matter transmitters. The canonical way they work is that they dismantle your atoms, then reassemble them elsewhere. Thus it isn't hard to, while reassembling you, make a few alterations—for instance, to ditch your '70s outfit in favor of a nice, consistent white sci-fi jumpsuit.

All of this opens a wealth of complications, however. For instance, it makes little sense to actually convert all of your atoms into energy and then send that energy. It's much more sensible to just take some details about your atoms and send the data, then have a machine on the other end assemble you according to the instructions. The problem, as countless critics have pointed out, is that what this really means is that the transmitter disintegrates and kills you, and then builds a clone of you in a separate location with your old memories.

It also suggests that we should firmly be in a post-scarcity society. Matter transmitters are never shown to have a supply block of material akin to what's used for 3-D printers or other technology of that sort. They appear to find the necessary matter lying around, conjuring people out of thin air. Any technology that can take a pattern and use it to constitute something as complex as a human being with all its memories and thoughts intact should have no problem solving world hunger, constructing infinite amounts of free housing, and generally doing away with all material problems with society.

This impacts something like *The Ark in Space* more than one would think. We see that Nerva Beacon is held together with screws and made up of individual panels, as though it has been built. But if you have matter transmitters there's absolutely no reason why you shouldn't be able to just construct an entire space station out of a solid piece of material. For that matter, why cryogenically freeze people? Wouldn't it be easier to just disintegrate the entire population of Earth and rebuild them when the flares pass, thus not leaving any bodies that might, you know, get eaten by giant insects? In fact, why is death even a thing? It should be possible to just reconstitute someone's body in a younger and healthier form.

All of these questions are, within the broader universe of Doctor Who, lampshaded brilliantly by Lawrence Miles's novel *Down* (from the Virgin New Adventures line), suggesting that the implications of this are quietly covered up by major corporations, but this is clearly a case of making fun of sci-fi conceits and not a serious effort to think through the implications of the technology. Because, of course, the actual implications of matter transmitters are completely series-destroying. If you have technology of that level, you're off in Iain M. Banks's Culture novels, not in any sort of normative sci-fi realm.

And this isn't even the end of the implications. Matter transmitters strongly imply that consciousness is an entirely mechanistic process—that all of our thoughts and memories consist only of material components that reside in our skulls. All notions of the soul or of an afterlife are destroyed by matter transmitters. Or, alternatively, matter transmitters understand the soul and can transmit that too, a prospect whose theological implications as big as its economic ones. Either way, we have another rabbit hole that the series simply cannot afford to explore because it would subsume its actual premise.

It is helpful to remember that matter transmitters are not, in fact, pieces of technology. Rather, they are narrative contrivances. The transmitter in *The Ark in Space* is there only to solve a couple of plot problems, and it doesn't actually have any function beyond that. Likewise, the transmitter at the end is really just a bridge to get from *The Ark in Space* to *The Sontaran Experiment* and little more. Which is what matter transmitters have been, in televised sci-fi at least, from the beginning. They really are just genre tropes, and even when you get into savvy modern usage of matter transmitters as in *Silence in the Library*, it's really just playing with the genre tropes of matter transmitters and "downloading people into computers" with little to no thought about the actual material practice.

For the most part this is because matter transmitters are a classic case of bringing a thermonuclear device to a knife fight. While they're present in sci-fi to eliminate tedious "getting from point A to point B" sequences, they have implications far, far more wide-reaching than the problem they're designed to solve. The result is a classic bit of story matter: something that really only makes sense as a plot device instead of as an object existing in a world that just happens to not be real.

Still, what might we accomplish if we decide to go looking for other ways that matter transmitters might work? After all, of the stories discussed so far, only *Silence in the*

Library seems like it outright has to depend on disintegration-based transportation, and that purely because it can stash Donna in a computer temporarily.

One oft-proposed option is that matter transmitters might work by bending space and time or through clever tricks with quantum entanglement. Lawrence Miles and Tat Wood fret over the implications this has for Earth's timeline (since it appears Earth has the technology as early as the 21st Century, but apparently abandons it later), but in truth the difficulties are no worse than any other attempt to get Doctor Who's future history to cohere.

Casual wormholes have their own sets of problems, though they're probably slightly less ridiculous in their implications than trivially making new matter out of nothing. Certainly this seems likely to be the sort of technology in play by the 51st century in stories like *The Girl in the Fireplace*. But punching holes in the fabric of space and time is usually suggested to be a rather bad idea. *The Seeds of Death* comes close to suggesting a limiting factor; the T-Mat system there clearly runs along existing lines, suggesting permanently opened wormholes instead of just punching through the universe every time you want to move something, a decision that would, in terms of Doctor Who, probably settle things down a bit.

But this still gets wibbly for *The Ark in Space*—surely it's not worth constructing a wormhole just to move people around a dinky little space station. That's ludicrous overkill. Then again, *Doomsday* suggests that a very similar sort of technology leads to global warming, and you could maybe suggest that excessive use of matter transmitters is why the Earth is having such trouble by the time of *The Ark in Space*. (This line of thought also lets you whip up an absolutely fabulous continuity theory about why the Doctor arrives at the wrong time on Nerva Beacon in *Revenge of the Cybermen* and how it squares away the question of how to reconcile Mondas-style and Cybus-style Cybermen, but that's another essay and another book.) Still, on the whole technology that lightly damages the entire space-time continuum is perhaps preferable to one that causes casual disintegration, and it's actually a claim that makes sense in light of the claim that the Time Lords transcended the technology.

On the other hand, the Time Lords do pose a problem here. We've seen them flip out over seemingly more minor technology, so if teleporters are really punching nasty and dangerous holes all over space and time one would think they'd be stepping in and getting them banned. If they're willing to get their hands dirty over a silly little miniscope, after all, enforcing a ban on matter transmitters for the purposes of protecting the space-time continuum seems sensible. And yet they don't worry about it. Perhaps more damningly, they describe a "transmat beam" (the Doctor's specific term) as being a "simple mechanical device," suggesting something far more mundane than wormholes.

Indeed, *The Ark in Space* through *Genesis of the Daleks* makes it very clear that there's some sort of "beam" being transmitted. It doesn't seem to be a simple data transmission either, as there's no reason you'd need a specific type of beam for that—if you're just reducing the human body to data, you could send it in any format. Indeed, the Doctor's claim in *The Sontaran Experiment* that the beam is "oscillating" makes it explicit that this is an analog signal, not a digital one. That is, of course, in practice because *The Sontaran Experiment* was made in 1975 and digital signals weren't really a thing yet, but it still suggests a specific type of beam.

Could it be that at some point in the future a new type of energy or signal was discovered that had the practical effect of allowing easy matter transmission? It seems to be the implication, with this type of energy being a simple toy for an advanced species like the Time Lords. How this would work is certainly obscure, but so is a lot of what passes for science on Doctor Who.

But even given all of this, the clothing change in *The Ark in Space* is still a problem. Which means that the biggest problem with matter transmitters turns out to be creepy undressing robots. Go figure.

On Your Television Screen, You Can Do What Seemed Impossible (*The Sontaran Experiment*)

It's February 22, 1975. Steve Harley and Cockney Rebel are at number one with "Make Me Smile (Come Up and See Me)," and continue to be through to the next week. The Carpenters, Helen Reddy, and Johnny Wakeland and the Kishasa Band also chart.

In the US, Daylight Savings Time kicks off two months early to deal with the ongoing energy crises that defined the 1970s. A fleeing IRA member fatally shoots a chasing London police officer, setting off most of what you'd expect. The IRA member, Liam Quinn, went on to a several-decades long career as a cause célèbre. The Movement 2 June, an anarchist group allied with the Baader-Meinhof Gang, kidnaps a West German politician, managing to secure the release of five of their members from prison doing so because, unlike the Weather Underground, they were actually good at being terrorists. A massive tube crash at Moorgate station kills 43 people. And, on the day the second and final episode of this story airs, Aston Villa defeats Norwich City in the Football League Cup, now known as the Capitol One Cup.

While on television, it's The Sontaran Experiment: the only two-part Doctor Who story between 1965 and 1982. This alone should raise some red flags from our perspective, in that the story clearly doesn't quite fit with the normal order of things. Doctor Who, in the period we're talking about, does four and six part stories. This is the only Doctor Who story from 1972-1981 that's not either four or six episodes long, and one of three between from 1966 to 1981.

The previous two-part stories had relatively straightforward reasons behind them. The Edge of Destruction existed to fill out an initial thirteen-episode order on the cheap, while The Rescue existed because it was the first time the show had tried introducing a new character, and they wanted a small and character-centric story for it. Given that both were written by the incomparable David Whitaker, both fulfilled a clear narrative function—indeed, both are far closer to the single-episode stories of the modern series than to the rest of the classic series. The Sontaran Experiment, however, does not have nearly so lofty a set of goals: its storytelling is minimal and ill-paced, its narrative ambitions are modest at best, its reason for existing entirely technical.

Part of this due to the writers. Giving this story to the veterans Bob Baker and Dave Martin made sense from a script editor's perspective, but there are major problems with the decision. Baker and Martin are best at coming up with weird ideas and at their weakest in the specific mechanics and craft of scriptwriting. A two-episode story necessarily prioritizes having one or two ideas in a carefully-crafted script. It is, in other words, a poor match.

The result is something that feels like it was written as a four-parter, and then presented with the first episode as written and the second episode a condensation of the rest of the story. All of this seems to have been done to maintain the traditional first episode cliffhanger of the monster reveal. A monster, of course, who is named in the title of the story. And while I recognize that the monster reveal cliffhanger isn't based on surprise but anticipation, such anticipation doesn't justify the awkward structure here. As for ideas, basically all Baker and Martin have is to recast Lynx from *The Time Warrior* as Styre and have him play Josef Mengele. Miles and Wood make a stab at selling this story as really being about debates over winter heating allowances, but it's a stretch, and I say that as someone who turned the last Baker and Martin story into a postmodern Blakean odyssey.

All of this comes perilously close to missing the point, however, because in a lot of ways this is actually an episode that almost begs to be called not-actually-canon or some similar phrase, simply because it has more in common with the material in the You Were Expecting Someone Else entries than it does with actual televised Doctor Who. I mean, sure, it was transmitted on BBC1 over two weeks in between The Ark in Space and Genesis of the Daleks, but that's just about the end of the similarities. This is a production experiment - a test to see if something works. And it doesn't quite, but the results are, in their own way, interesting.

The first thing to know is that Robert Holmes hated six-parters. There are good reasons for this, as we've complained about padded six-parters far more than we've praised their pacing. Holmes, unsurprisingly, noticed the problem, and one of the first things he did upon taking over was try to figure out how to get rid of six-parters. His first attempt at that was to try to sever them into a four-parter and a two-parter.

The obvious problem with this is that six-parters were money savers. This is why they decreased in frequency in Seasons Two through Four as the show established itself, and then increased as the Troughton era hit budgetary problems. A six-parter gives you two extra episodes out of the same sets and props. Splitting it into two stories means you lose all those savings. Which is why Terrance Dicks stuck with the format despite its problems; abandoning two six-parters to create another four-parter was expensive. But Holmes, aided by recent developments in television technology and a clever understanding of how Doctor Who is made, was able to come up with a plausible solution. This solution, as I said, didn't quite work, largely because this story is rubbish, but it's still historically significant.

But to understand how that worked, we need to take another digression into how Doctor Who was made. We talked back in the Robot essay about how Barry Letts changed the way Doctor Who was made, moving from the original model of rehearsing and shooting an episode in one week to rehearsing and shooting two episodes in two weeks. This had major benefits for the program: sets had to be struck half as often, they suffered less damage, and you had considerably more leeway, enabling a producer to plan shoots further in advance. However, this only governed the studio days. Location filming was a different beast.

Ah, yes, location filming. I didn't make a lot of that as it slowly crept into Doctor Who. As you might imagine, in the original week-an-episode model, location filming, which required a separate shoot, was a pain in the ass. Generally it involved taking the cast from rehearsals for the previous story to do the location shoot for the next story. By the Pertwee era this had smoothed out, but location shoots still, for obvious reasons, were a different chunk of filming from studio shoots.

Holmes's brilliant idea, then, was to take a six-parter and split its location and studio elements into making a studio-bound four-parter and an all-location two-parter, so that the location shoot ended up being the shoot for one entire story. This continued to save money on sets while still allowing the discarding of a six-parter. With a little more cleverness like recycling some equipment from The Time Warrior and bringing back the Sontarans, you could have the extra story cost basically nothing compared to a six-parter.

This also explains why Baker and Martin got the job. Because a fiddly, requirement-heavy script like this is one you give one of your old-hand writers. Recall that Barry Letts hired Robert Holmes when he got a bright idea to only pay actors for two weeks while getting four episodes of material out of them, thus creating Carnival of Monsters. So Holmes, when he had a similar idea to this, needed an old pro. Unfortunately, the Pertwee era was not long on old pro writers of any quality. There were basically two. One of them, Malcolm Hulke, had by this point decided to leave the program in favor of novelizations. The other was Robert Holmes himself.

I say all of this to point out that the bench for writers is really quite thin right now. The other writers from the Pertwee era to have experience from past eras are... idiosyncratic to say the least. Brian Hayles, who Holmes never commissioned, had generally required extensive rewrites. Louis Marks is quite good, but only did one Pertwee story. Terry Nation... is Terry Nation. That basically leaves Baker and Martin, previously our zany experimental ideas men, to become trusted lieutenants. For Holmes, they become the new Malcolm Hulke: the writers you can trust to deliver what you ask for. And so they get the brief.

Yet all of this would still be impossible if it weren't for a big change in technology: video cameras have gotten small enough to use on location. The Sontaran Experiment is not actually the first story to take advantage of this: that was Robot, which used it to do CSO effects outside. But it's the first one to take advantage of an obvious consequence of this: you can shoot a story entirely on location now without paying outrageous amounts for the film stock. This subverts one of the basic codes implicit in color television production up to this point: the film/video divide.

Previously, location work was shot on film, studio work on video. Each one looked very different, in ways that are intuitively familiar even to viewers who haven't had the difference pointed out to them. The easiest places to see the difference are in any scene in the Pertwee era where characters move from outdoors to indoors and back again (it's harder in the Hartnell and Troughton eras because surviving episodes there survive on film transfers). The bits in The Time Monster and The Sea Devils in which people look out windows are particularly clear. Interior spaces, being studio sets, are shot on video, but as soon as a character walks to the window and looks out and the camera moves to being outside looking into the window, it switches to film. Visually speaking, the basic difference is the texture. Video looks much smoother and high resolution, whereas film looks grainier, and has fewer frames per second.

Ironically, despite this difference, film is the one that feels more expensive to viewers, since it's the dominant medium for, well, films. (This is so prevalent that when *The Hobbit* used a higher frame rate that made it look more like video people complained that it looked "cheap.") So the film/video divide signifies a couple of things. Film cameras, being lighter, were traditionally used for location work, so film suggests "real place" in a way video doesn't. And film's texture is associated with more expensive productions. So the decision to shoot a given scene on film or video isn't just a technical decision - it says a lot about the content of the story. This gives rise to the trick of using film in the studio - something done for The Curse of Peladon to make the arrival sequence outside the citadel feel as though it's happening in a real place instead of in a studio.

The basic reason for this is simple: video cameras were too heavy and unwieldy to take on location. Now in 1975, you could shoot locations in video. This has its own set of advantages, namely that you can make a real place feel like a BBC studio. (Miles and Wood point out a particularly inept failure to take advantage of this in an instance where the production team found a location that looked like a Doctor Who corridor that was a mile long, then failed to shoot it on video, thus making it obvious that it was a location instead of a jaw-droppingly good studio set.) More to the point, this marks a fundamental shift in the grammar of television, because suddenly the film/video distinction stopped being as much of a clear signifier as it used to be because the film/video location/studio divide was broken down.

This is the start of a much longer road one that leads to the dominant television production strategy outside of the United States in 2011—what's called filmification. Basically, this means you shoot something on nice, cheap video, then apply some digital filters that make it look more like it was shot on film. So in other words, there's now something approaching a universal style for television (and, for that matter, for movies, which are almost all shot digitally these days too).

But this progression also gets at the fundamental difference between film and video in the first place - the issue of detail. But even this is a complex issue. In and of itself, for most of the time during which Doctor Who was made, film does look better than video in an absolute sense—that is, the level of detail offered by 35mm film exceeds that offered by a video camera. (Film can be upgraded to high definition, whereas video not originally shot in high definition can't.) But film, in terms of television, is never seen in and of itself—it's always converted, often several times, to create a broadcast signal. Whereas video gets far fewer conversions in its road to broadcast, and so ends up looking sharper on broadcast. But, equally crucially, sharper is not always an advantage: the softer colors of film look better to a lot of viewers.

But by 2011, all of this is basically moot, since film is increasingly giving way to digital video wholesale. This is basically because of the shift towards high definition television—a shift that, even though it didn't directly affect Doctor Who until 2009, is still crucial to its return because it hastened the development of a single visual aesthetic for film and television.

In 1975, of course, with The Sontaran Experiment, all of this is in the future; even Doctor Who's conversion under John Nathan-Turner to an all-video production is still more than a decade off. But video cameras made suitable for location filming was still a crucial development towards the overall conversion to video with film-like effects as the standard approach for more and more of the world. Consider this story Doctor Who checking out the technology and seeing what it meant for how they could make the show (as opposed to using it for one obvious stunt, which is why it appeared in Robot—so Barry Letts could have one last throw at disastrous CSO by using outside video cameras to do the CSO of the giant robot). And while they don't try this precise trick again for a while, this is still Doctor Who trying out a host of production techniques that it will continue to use over the remaining fourteen years of the classic series as well as the history of the series in general. It's an artifact from a technological transition.

So yes, as a story, it's filler—a new producer trying things out, and marking time between The Ark in Space and the next essay, and giving Baker an opportunity to ease into the part, since it was filmed before The Ark in Space. Mind you, Baker failed spectacularly to take the opportunity to ease in, breaking his collar bone in an ill-judged stunt and having to be replaced, not entirely convincingly, by Terry Walsh for large swaths of it. An unimportant story, in other words, but in no way a pair of unimportant or uninteresting episodes.

The Face of the Devil Himself (*Genesis of the Daleks*)

It's March 8th, 1975. Telly Savalas is at number one with "If," which, in layman's terms, means that the star of *Kojak* is at number one with a spoken word cover of a Bread song from 1971. This unlikely state of affairs lasts for two weeks before the Bay City Rollers clean things up with "Bye Bye Baby," holding #1 for the other four weeks of this story. Mud, Johnny Mathis, Barry White, Guys 'n' Dolls, and The Sweet also chart.

In real news, the UN proclaims International Women's Day, the *Rocky Horror Picture Show* debuts on Broadway, Bobby Fischer concedes his world chess championship title to Anatoly Karpov by refusing to play against him, and Bill Gates founds Microsoft. In bigger events, the Vietnam War moves towards its conclusion as North Vietnamese troops close on Saigon. Operation Babylift, an attempt to evacuate children from Vietnam, gets off to a terrible start as the first plane crashes, killing 138. Rio Di Janeiro becomes the capital of Brazil after the state of Rio Di Janeiro merges with Estado de Guanabara. And the body of Lesley Whittle, the teenage heiress kidnapped back during Robot, is found.

While on television... I mean, what is there to say. It's Genesis of the Daleks. The latter three words of which are wholly unimportant. There are a handful of stories in Doctor Who history that can be shortened to one word titles where the title is not the monster. But if you talk to a Doctor Who fan about "Genesis," they know what you're talking about, and it's not Peter Gabriel's old band. This story is flat-out one of the most iconic stories of Doctor Who. Given that our approach to the series is tinged with the alchemical, and that we do take an actively mystical view of the series at times, we must tread with some care here. This is, if you will, a piece of sacred ground in the psychochronography of this territory.

It's not that the story is without flaw. Under the hood, it's still very much a Terry Nation story, with all the attendant problems. But for the first time in a decade, it's also a Terry Nation story with all the attendant benefits. His knack for adventure, his ability to keep a plot moving, his ability to create properly scary villains, all of that is firmly in play here. Even the things that can be hit or miss—his tendency towards tedious moralizing—end up working here, albeit as much because the actors are top notch as anything else. On top of that David Maloney, the director here, is on fire, using everything he learned about Daleks from the spectacularly dull Planet of the Daleks and using it for more interesting purposes.

And then there's the aspect of this story in legend. For my first year or so as a Doctor Who fan, there was no story I wanted to see more. Not the Romana stories, not any of the missing stories, not even Terminus. (Yes, really. I was desperate to see Terminus. We'll get there.) Between the novelization (a solid Terrance Dicks effort) and the audio (a cut-down version that I owned on a two-tape combo release with the Sixth Doctor audio Slipback), this was a story I knew by heart before I ever watched it, and when my mother got me the region-free VCR that opened up the British VHS releases to me, the Sontaran Experiment/Genesis of the Daleks combo-pack was just about the first one I got her to buy me for it. (I believe it and City of Death were my first two British tapes) And this isn't unusual—everybody recognizes this story as totemic. No, what's unusual is that this one deserves the hype.

Last time, I complained bitterly that Nation was just blithely trusting that people wanted to see Daleks and that the Daleks were enough of a justification that you didn't need to try to sell a story beyond the very fact of their presence. Here, however, he's forced out of that. Because the story demands that the Daleks have a mythic presence (otherwise who cares about their origin?), Nation is pushed into the Whitaker style of treating the Daleks as mythic creatures and building up to their eventual unleashing. Ever since Evil of the Daleks the Daleks have been trotted out in bland, generic ways. But here they're played with restraint, taking on a totemic role that looms over the story. It's the first story since 1967 to manage that, and the last one until 1988. And it has to be that way. It's the Genesis of the Daleks.

We never get, of course, Genesis of the Time Lords. Nor Genesis of the Doctor. Nor will we ever. We can't, frankly - the moment where any such absolute determinism can be imposed upon the prehistory of Doctor Who's "canon" is long since past. The closest thing, in all likelihood, is The Doctor's Wife, which is almost, but not quite, Genesis of the TARDIS. This is the only Genesis you can do - the only time you can tell the secret origin of the series.

After all, the Daleks have never been reducible from Doctor Who. Try as we might, we in the end have to return to the theme that played out over the opening stories of the series. The show only becomes Doctor Who proper once four concepts are in place: the Doctor, the TARDIS, the companions, and the monsters. And the Daleks are the ones who establish what monsters are. They are the ones who set up one of the tent-poles of the series, and in one sense every other monster in the series is just an expansion or a variation on something the Daleks do in the original Nation or Whitaker stories. The Cybermen are the Daleks with unfeeling extermination turned up to eleven, the Ice Warriors are just a variation on the small core of Daleks struggling to survive, and the Silence are just Whitaker's alchemical Daleks for a new generation. Even the Master is just a sexier version of the Dalek shouting "I AM YOUR SERVANT" in Power of the Daleks.

Let us fix them, then, at the center of the narrative. This is, after all, their story. This story repeatedly defines them as creatures of pure survival. But let's be precise. There is something explicitly Darwinian about the Daleks, who survive by being stronger than other races. But it's a very odd sort of Darwinism, because one of the most basic tenets of Darwinism is explicitly rejected: evolution. This is admittedly probably mostly due to the fact that Terry Nation doesn't understand evolution, but regardless, the premise of the Daleks is that they are apparently the final form of evolution for the Kaled people.

In other words, the Daleks are a point of stasis—a thing that does not change. They are, to use someone else's phrase, being without becoming. They avoid even death—the ultimate and most primal form of becoming. They are an unchanging insistence on their own survival. But what's crucial is that this stasis is still wedded to an explicitly Darwinian view of how the strong survive and the weak must die.

And so, in their incubator room, the Daleks seethe and hate. But mostly, they exist. Not yet in their travel machines, it's true, but they exist. Their fixed, Newtownian sleep has begun. It is very easy to misphrase this—to talk about their history beginning, or of the first steps taken along a familiar narrative arc that will in time lead us to Spiridon and Vulcan and Mechanus. No. These things will happen, it is true, but there is no arc here. No story. The Dalek timeline is just that: a defined, fixed line.

(As with many things that are truly great about Doctor Who, this too descends from Whitakerrian alchemy. The Daleks were always contrasted primarily with the Doctor's mercurial nature under Whitaker. This simply codifies it in a new way.)

And then he appears. A nameless, terrible thing that seems to just drop out of the sky to tear down their world.

Never before—not even in the most cavalierly anarchic moments of the Troughton era—have we seen the Doctor in a way that fits that description quite like this does. Here he shows up for the sole and explicit purpose of destroying the world. Not just disrupting it or changing it or sprucing it up by removing an injustice. You can't do that with the Daleks. The Daleks simply are. Ontologically. They are not changed or disrupted, and to be changed or disrupted is, for them, death—the antithesis of what they are. No. All you can do is destroy them. And that is what this nameless, terrible thing sets out to do.

Why? The circumstances, after all, are a bit odd. The Time Lords make their first appearance in over two years, calling for an act utterly unlike any they have advocated before. In the past, the Time Lords have stressed their refusal to interfere, sending the Doctor only on missions that seem to preserve the general arc of history. But the Daleks do not pervert that as such. After all, the idea behind the arc of history is that history naturally and inherently progresses towards certain kinds of outcomes. All well and good. The nature of the Daleks is that they are, apparently, what history progresses towards. They are the final form of Kaled history, accelerated by Davros so that they can become the final form of the universe. In an odd sense they seem almost perfectly compatible with the Time Lords. Both are, after all, fundamentally concerned with the motion of history.

And yet the Time Lords try to destroy them. Remember, the Time Lords are not a factionalized race as of yet. At present, they appear to be a hegemonic society, with their renegades exiled and wandering the universe. And so we are hard-pressed to pawn this off as a black ops project run by the Celestial Intervention Agency, as fan lore tends to. Watching this in 1975, it would be hard to get around the claim that the Time Lords are acting as a whole here, not least because the Celestial Intervention Agency is still two seasons out.

Why, then? To some extent, it's easiest to suggest that there was some turning point in The Three Doctors. In that story the Time Lords face unceasing fixity in another context and see their society wholly reformed based upon it as they switch from powering themselves from a black hole to powering themselves from a supernova. But even before that, there is some intuitive sense that the Time Lords and the Daleks are incompatible and must be enemies. The Time Lords, after all, are not guardians of the endpoint of time, but of the motion of history—the continual advancement of it. The Time Lords, if they are guardians of the dialectic of history, are guardians of change. The Daleks are creatures of stasis. Of course they fight. One is the process and the other is the result.

And of course The Doctor is the one who is sent to take care of it. The Time Lords and the Daleks may be opposed, but it's the mercurial, ever-shifting Doctor who is the true and absolute antithesis of the Daleks. This is, after all his show, and they're his arch-nemesis. And it is in this context that we can finally look at the big moral speeches of this story. The two big ones, of course, are the Doctor asking Davros what he would do with a virus that could destroy all life, and the Doctor's "have I that right" agonizing over whether to destroy the Daleks.

The first thing to note is that almost everyone praising these two monologues should probably stop. Not that they're bad monologues—they're not. It's just that nobody praises them for the reasons they're good, and a fair number of people praise them for things that aren't actually good at all. The "have I that right" speech is particularly galling: on its own, it's just the Doctor going through one of the most basic ethical hypotheticals in existence—the "would you kill Hitler" debate. On top of that, the initial reason he gives for not destroying them—that it would make him no better than the Daleks—is on the face of it absurd. By any remotely sane ethical standards short of outright pacifism (which the Doctor clearly does not believe in), destroying the Daleks is clearly the right call. There exist ethical systems that would preclude blowing up the Daleks, but it's very hard to argue that the Doctor as we've seen him to date follows any of them. (Tellingly, Sarah—who has secured by this time a firm position as the one who expresses the audience's point of view and thus as a real conscience of the show—is adamant that he should blow them up.)

So it's tough to treat the "have I that right" speech as some high point of ethical debate within the series, at least in the most obvious sense. And yet it's also tough to just declare that one of the most beloved sequences in Doctor Who is crap. I mean, I'll admit, I have always thought the sequence was a bit overlong for a recitation of such a blazingly clichéd ethical debate. But it's not bad. It's well-acted enough. It's just not as interesting as people want to make it, or at least, not in the way they try to make it.

The speech makes more sense, however, when coupled with Davros's (on the surface far more compelling) monologue about the virus. Davros himself is a complex character; he's mostly an overt counterpart to the Doctor among the Daleks. Being a Terry Nation creation, he's a bit old fashioned—there's that Hartnell-era signifier of both of them being scientists and thus, apparently, inherently reasonable people. But in this story, his role is really limited to that of a foil for the Doctor—something played up by the fact that he is, in practice, the scientific advisor to a military operation. On top of that, he's played brilliantly by Michael Wisher,. But his end—being gunned down by the Daleks for being inferior to them—is essentially inevitable, and it's not until he improbably reappears in the next Dalek story that he really becomes Davros as we know the character. (Actually, in this story he's hampered in part by the fact that his henchman is played phenomenally. Even though Wisher is by far the best actor to take on Davros in the classic series, he still can't keep all his scenes from getting stolen by Peter Miles.)

But all the same, the central tension of this story is clearly the ethical debate between the Doctor and Davros. So let's see if we can find something more fundamental in it than this business of pacifism. Clearly the two monologues are at the heart of it. Since Davros's speech comes first, however, we should treat the Doctor's speech primarily as a response to it. And it's fairly clear - Davros's speech is about attaining godhood. So when the Doctor asks if he has the right, the question seems to be less about the right to kill the Daleks and more about the right to set himself up as having that kind of power—the right, in short, to be a god.

It is this right that he recoils from—the right to refashion history to his will. It is in this regard— not the genocidal regard—that the Doctor views destroying the Daleks as making him like them. Were he to destroy them, he would be moving from the chaotic churn of history to a fixed, determined sequence of events chosen by him. He doesn't refuse to kill them; he refuses to take authorship of them.

This reading brings us to one of the biggest continuity questions in Doctor Who. Even to those who discount the idea of Doctor Who canon—and I largely do—this is impossible to ignore. Simply put, to what extent does this story retcon the history of the Daleks? One school of thought holds that it is a full retcon: *Genesis of the Daleks* completely overwrites the previous history of the Daleks, and is not a secret origin but a do-over. It certainly could be, but as a second school of thought maintains, quite reasonably, this story does not introduce any more problems to established Dalek history than Terry Nation's ham-fisted attempt at continuity did in The Dalek Invasion of Earth. (Which he manages to further bungle here with a bewilderingly almost but not quite totally wrong recap of what is clearly meant to be that story.) In this view the Doctor makes no change to Dalek history, all is right with the world, and there's only ever been one Dalek timeline.

Aside from the fact that this is the school of thought that eventually spawned John Peel's legendarily awful novel War of the Daleks, this second theory is blatantly contradicted by the end of the story. The Doctor says he delayed the Daleks

Philip Sandifer

by a thousand years. (Tellingly, the people who ignore this unequivocal line are often the same ones who insist that Evil of the Daleks is sacrosanct and must always be the final Dalek story, despite the fact that the Daleks are explicitly shown to survive in it.) Imagine the Nazis trying to invade Russia and failing in 1942. Now imagine the Nazis—i.e. the same tanks and planes—trying to do it in 942. (Or, within Doctor Who, imagine Remembrance of the Daleks set in 963. Edgar the Peaceful is totally wicked.) Clearly a thousand-year delay is enough to cause massive changes to the entire future. This story unambiguously declares that established history is being altered, and the degree of change we are told about explicitly (never mind any butterfly effects, of which there are many plausible ones) is sufficient to be a credible explanation for any continuity error between an episode before this and an episode after this. Delaying the rise of a particular army with particular capabilities a millennium is a massive shift in history. And we're explicitly told that is what happens. There's no way to argue around this being a complete rewriting of the universe.

So clearly history is changed. But to what extent? Well, frankly, that's not a particularly interesting question. Because in terms of what this story is about, the extent doesn't matter. Consider precisely what the Doctor does in the climax of the story. Clearly when he goes back to destroy the incubator room, he knows he is not ending the Daleks but merely delaying them. More to the point, this judgment seems based on things he's seen since the "have I the right" number. In other words, it is presumably because he realizes the Daleks now exist and cannot be stopped as such. It's only after this realization that he goes back to blow them up, and similarly it's only then that he seems to come to his conclusion that the Daleks will somehow be a force for good. The easiest explanation for this seemingly strange behavior, to my mind, is that he has come to realize that there is something he can do to the Daleks that is worse than merely killing them. He can change them. He can rewrite them.

Later lore, and in this case I am inclined to accept it, is that this story is the opening battle of the Time War. And this is why. The Daleks—the unchanging, fixed point and the end of all things—are changed. They are rendered mutable. It is difficult to imagine a more egregious slight. But more to the point, this satisfies the stated mission of the Time Lords perfectly. The Doctor has discovered a fundamental weakness of the Daleks: they can be changed. They are still subject to history. They are subject to being written. This is what "time can be rewritten" means. It is the battle cry of the Time War itself—the statement that the very understanding of a species' history can be altered. All understanding and thought—the entire understanding of what a culture is—can be rewritten. Not destroyed, or killed, or even harmed. Just... given a rewrite. Which is, in its own way, even more terrifying.

In many ways, then, the story Genesis is most similar to is the supposed end of the Daleks: Evil of the Daleks. Evil of the Daleks observes that the Dalek factor is in a fundamental sense inferior and subject to the human factor. Genesis expands on this: the Daleks are subject to the forces of history—forces that are, in Doctor Who, overtly humanist. The human factor destroys them not just at the end, but at the beginning. This exists with one foot firmly in the classical ethical tradition that Terry Nation, Terrance Dicks, and David Whitaker all belonged to—one where there are big, important morals to be learned about the world. But *Genesis* has another foot elsewhere, which makes it far sharper and more brilliant than the ethics of the series to date.

But let's switch gears for just a second.

All of this gets coupled with the fact that everyone on the production team here that wasn't in the giant clam department is at the top of their game, and you have what almost deserves to be called the series premiere of a new Doctor Who. Aside from all the big ideas this story has, it's just terribly, terribly good. The Letts era, as we discussed, brought the floor of quality up dramatically, so that below par for the Letts era was miles above par for the Troughton era. That's not really true of the Hinchcliffe era, which, when it's off its game, is often miles out in left field making you wonder how it even contrived to screw up in that particular way.

But the Letts era never quite produced its iconic classic. That's ultimately one of the maddening things about it—every story either fails to do anything extraordinarily well, or also manages to do at least one thing extraordinarily poorly. It never quite had the day where everything went right. For a long time everybody assumed it was The Daemons, but then that story became widely available and we realized that, no, it was as flawed as all the other Sloman scripts. The closest the Letts era had to everything working at once was ostensibly Inferno, where, yes, everything did go right, except that A) the series had no idea what it was doing in Season Seven and thus everything going right is still confused and a bit lackluster, and B) Ambassadors of Death also had everything go right, only with a better script.

But as we talked about last time, what television was has been changing tremendously over the last five years. Just on a technological level, Doctor Who is a completely different show in 1975 than it was in 1970. And it's been so long since the show aced it like this that *Genesis* ends up being an outright redefinition of the show: it's the first definitive classic for so long that it becomes a definitive classic of a whole new show.

In other words, this story is the equivalent of The Daleks itself. *The Daleks* is why the show survived—because it landed a massive hit right out of the gate. Without that, it probably wouldn't have made it. The series debuted with An Unearthly Child, but its moment of emergence into brilliance was *The Daleks*. Now Hinchcliffe and Holmes baptize it again, for the color era. This is how it works. To really make yourself a definitive Doctor Who, you've got to nail a Dalek story. If your Dalek stories aren't top notch, people will always ask questions of your era. So this is it. This is the big one.

But there's this sort of wonderful overlap of big moments here. Hinchcliffe is making his grand, iconic statement—his massive, glorious classic where he unabashedly tries to just make something that people will call the best Doctor Who story anybody has ever made. And he's making it with a story about rewriting the fundamental tenets of Doctor Who.

Consider the concept of an imaginary space, in which ideas have some sort of form and coherence, and in which they are capable of interacting—metaphors, say. Characters that represent ideas—things that can talk, but are not really people so much as symbols for, say, Nazi Germany and Josef Mengele. (Not that there are any of those in this story.) So at what point, when you have something that you have lent a notion of coherence to, and something that has some sort of animus, do you declare that an idea is alive? That it can think? That it is conscious?

Some stories might just be big enough to do that. "What if our thoughts could think for themselves," as someone said once. Certainly if any are, Doctor Who is. There is no concept of ideas that are conscious beings that would exclude Doctor Who. And if it is, it has to be taken very seriously as one.

Genesis is where Doctor Who becomes postmodern. And in 1975, this is a very big deal. Postmodern literature is really just emerging as a term, as people finally start noticing that what was previously a bunch of things on the fringe is looking increasingly like a coherent movement worthy of an ism. We've traced some of the bits of this as it began to emerge in previous volumes - the essay on *International Times* in Volume One, or the ones on *The Atrocity Exhibition* and glam rock in Volume Three. But right around here, people started to notice that this was a thing, and dubbed it postmodernism. So to be a sterling example of it on BBC One, a story watched by millions and beloved for generations, is quite a feat in 1975.

Because what happens here is that Doctor Who explicitly destabilizes its own central concept. It takes one of its fundamental pillars—the Daleks—and casually knocks it down. But it doesn't do this in a glib, retconning sort of way. It does it by crashing another one of its pillars into the first. The Doctor's mercurial nature runs smack into the Daleks' absolute fixity, and only one walks out alive. Previously the Doctor had only defeated the Daleks. Now he's defeated the very idea of them.

And so here the nature of what a monster in Doctor Who is changes. Where before monsters were reliably some real world fear extrapolated, here they become fear itself. They become the idea of fear and of darkness, or at least, manifestations thereof. This is the essential evolution from the Pertwee era to the Baker era—the equivalent of The War Games's demand that the Doctor learn to invest in real people. Now the Doctor fights ideas instead of just green things.

In this regard we harken back to the observations I made about The Mind Robber in Volume Two. Because for the first time since that story, the Doctor is acting as much like a Story Lord as a Time Lord. The Time Lords seem, more than at any other point in the series, like creatures that might actually be connected to the Land of Fiction—even appearing in an explicit homage to Bergman's *The Seventh Seal*. And so we get one of Doctor Who's most impressive tricks for the first time. Because the series is a mythology in its own right—an idea with immense power—and a series with a protagonist who rewrites mythologies.

So it rewrites its own mythology. It demonstrates that time can be rewritten. And it demonstrates that by time we mean our very history and identity. Time can be rewritten. We can be rewritten. And, most terrifyingly and wondrously of all, Doctor Who can be the author.

Once again, everything has changed.

Changing Dalek History For Dummies

The question of how much, if at all, *Genesis of the Daleks* retcons previous Dalek stories is thorny, to say the least. For one thing, it fundamentally alters the nature of Dalek stories. Every Dalek story after *Genesis* utilizes Davros, where none before it did: even when Daleks who are not under Davros's control are introduced, they're just a faction of classic-style Daleks opposing the Davros-ruled ones. The new series improves things a bit by mostly focusing on Daleks without Davros, but nevertheless there's an enormous narrative pressure to let *Genesis* mark some sort of fundamental change to the Daleks, if only because, well, it was a fundamental change to the Daleks.

Within the narrative the suggestion is that the Daleks were set back a thousand years. As we noted, this should be a big deal, but on the other hand, the Daleks are these days portrayed as unstoppable terrors who can wipe out any force short of the Time Lords, such that being a thousand years further along when you meet them just isn't that helpful. We could probably just allow that most Dalek stories happened as we saw them, but with the date nudged a thousand years forward. For many this doesn't matter: the post-apocalyptic wasteland of *The Daleks* would probably work no matter when the Thal/Dalek war took place. Stories like *The Power of the Daleks* and *The Evil of the Daleks* in which the Daleks are time travellers are similarly easy to deal with; moving the

Skaro sections of *The Evil of the Daleks* a thousand years forward doesn't affect the story a lick.

Similarly, the future history timeline is sufficiently sketchy that moving *Planet of the Daleks* from 2540 to 3540 just isn't a huge deal. To use Lance Parkin's chronology, this moves the story from being set roughly around the same time as *Earthshock* to being set around the same time as *Terminus*. Again, little has to actually change for this.

Still, two stories present potentially interesting consequences. The first is mainly frustrated. *The Dalek Invasion of Earth* is a story where it should matter that it's moved forward. Simply put, the 2157 date that's standardized for that story is consciously near-future, to the point where *The Dalek Invasion of Earth* doesn't make any move to portray Earth as being or having ever been a space empire. A handful of later stories shoot down the idea that Earth doesn't have a space empire in 2157 to hell, but in a scrap between keeping *The Dalek Invasion of Earth* or *Nightmare of Eden*, most people are going to pick the former, and not without reason. Nevertheless, the intention of *The Dalek Invasion of Earth* is clear—it's supposed to be a relatively near-future Dalek invasion. (Indeed, *Genesis of the Daleks* seems to present an alternate date for it as the year 2000. The story itself directly refutes this, but it would have made things so much easier.)

But if you push the date for the Daleks invading Earth back a thousand years you end up firmly in the "earth as Empire" period of Doctor Who's future history, and there's really no turning back from that. It might not be a big difference to the Daleks (although to be fair, Earth seems to do all right whenever it encounters the Daleks in this period, so it's plausible they could have repelled the invasion), but it should be a huge one for the humans given the disastrous effects of the Dalek invasion.

The thing is, Doctor Who repeatedly reasserts the reality of *The Dalek Invasion of Earth*. It's confirmed in *Remembrance of the Daleks*, and tacitly confirmed in *The Stolen Earth* when the Doctor ominously mutters about someone trying to steal the

Earth before. This latter reference gives us our way out, however, because there's a compelling ambiguity. The Daleks didn't so much try to steal the Earth in *The Dalek Invasion of Earth* as, you know, drive it around like a space Cadillac. The instance where the Earth was actually stolen is *The Mysterious Planet*, where it's the Time Lords who nick it. You can, in other words, decide that the business of Earth-stealing is wrapped up in the Time War, and that the Daleks in *The Dalek Invasion of Earth* are Time War combatants trying to make off with the Earth before the Time Lords do something dire with it two million years later.

The problem is that the Daleks in *The Dalek Invasion of Earth* are crap Daleks who still rely on static electricity, a problem that's always been a bugbear in Dalek history. But if we assume that the details of the story have changed, you actually get a much simpler life. (It's notable that the Daleks in *Genesis of the Daleks* have no static electricity problems to speak of. The Doctor's intervention may well have established that as the new normal, thus ironically strengthening the Daleks.) So if we decide that *The Dalek Invasion of Earth* is actually a Time War battle now we can keep it in the same year and get everything to make sense.

More interesting is *The Chase*, a story that shouldn't have any issues given that it's another Dalek time travel story. But let's consider the possibility that the Daleks strike at the Doctor a thousand years later in his personal timeline: a move that you don't have to make, but that you can certainly justify under the logic of a thousand year shift (time travellers rarely seem to interact with each other at dramatically asynchronous points in their timelines, after all). Determining the Doctor's age is a mug's game, but nobody's going to fault you that strenuously if you decide that the Time War takes place about a thousand years after *The Chase* for the Doctor. This feels oddly appropriate for *The Chase*, and you can even keep it as a Hartnell story by deciding the Daleks are playing their own version of *Genesis of the Daleks* and trying to take the Doctor out before he becomes a serious threat to their plans.

You'll notice a pattern here—any discussion of how *Genesis of the Daleks* alters Dalek history is pre-empted by the fact that the Time War provides another huge rewrite of Dalek mythology and of how the Daleks function such that any discussion of Dalek history will run smack into it and have to take it into account. It's certainly possible to read any number of Dalek stories as having been battles in the Time War, but again, at that point you're not really talking about *Genesis of the Daleks* anymore.

And you're certainly not explaining the problem of why the Daleks get obsessed with Davros afterwards. But wait a moment: what would have happened to Davros if not for the Doctor's intervention? Certainly in every other story in which a paranoid mad scientist creates an evil race to conquer the universe the answer is "he'd have been murdered by his creation," just as he is here. But it's easy to believe he could have lasted longer than he did, since the Doctor's presence speeds up the initial activation of the Daleks before it sets them back a thousand years.

This could explain the absence of Davros from any pre-*Genesis* stories: the Daleks in those stories had firmly gotten over Davros before killing him, whereas after *Genesis of the Daleks* Davros has been killed essentially "too soon," and the Daleks have become obsessed with reincarnating him—a problem that persists right up through to *The Stolen Earth*. This newfound obsession with their creator can even be used to explain things like the Emperor's ascension to godhood in *The Parting of the Ways*, and makes for a relatively concrete and meaningful dent to Dalek history for *Genesis of the Daleks*. The Doctor hasn't materially slowed them down so much as he's saddled them with a mad scientist creator they're all obsessed with. In the end, the change to history offered by *Genesis of the Daleks* is exactly what it looks like: Davros himself.

Tiny Metal Minds (Revenge of the Cybermen)

It's April 19, 1975. The Bay City Rollers are at number one with "Bye Bye Baby," which lasts for two weeks before Mud overtake them with "Oh Boy," an a cappella cover of an old Buddy Holly song, which also lasts for two weeks. Peter Shelley, The Goodies, 10cc, and, in the highest concentration of Tammy's ever seen in the top ten, Tammy Wynette and Tammy Jones all chart as well.

While in real news, the Red Army Faction takes over the West German embassy in Stockholm, then promptly inadvertently blow themselves up, leading to West Germany changing to a "we don't negotiate with terrorists" policy, and to an unexpected tightening in our ongoing "who were the best 1970s terrorists" contest. That's about all that happens in these four weeks. Well, that and the Vietnam War ending. But that's nothing, right?

While on television, we have Revenge of the Cybermen. On the surface, this is straightforward: a story commissioned under Letts and made under Hinchcliffe, written by Gerry Davis, a writer who was frankly rubbish even in his prime, and thus desperately rewritten by Robert Holmes in a not-entirely-successful effort to salvage it. It's a lackluster story of the sort that new production teams do in their first year. And that's not a completely unfair reading of it. But for once, it's instructive just how this story gets snared between the Letts and Hinchcliffe approaches and in particular how it follows (and more significantly fails to follow) from the doors blasted open by Genesis of the Daleks.

Letts, for his part, had been trying to bring the Cybermen back for a while. This is not surprising—one of the ways in which Letts dramatically evolved the show was in how it actively and savvily manipulated and engaged with audiences and audience expectations. Occasionally this backfired, as with the dropping of the dinosaurs from the episode title for the first part of Invasion of the Dinosaurs, or the shoehorned Daleks in Day of the Daleks, but more often it led to tour de forces like the reveal of the Daleks in Frontier in Space. So of course he would have gone for bringing back the "other classic monster," and Letts was savvy enough to have a good angle on how to do it as well: hire back one of the writers who had done that monster last, and who was also still a respectable television man (Davis was only three years out from the very good *Doomwatch* here) to do it so that the story feels nice and nostalgic.

But neither Hinchcliffe nor Holmes are particularly enamored with nostalgia and classic monsters. In fact, after this and the next story, they basically don't use nostalgia as a major story appeal again until The Deadly Assassin, and that's as much a stark break with the past as a nostalgia trip. So it's not quite a surprise that the Hinchcliffe era balks at doing a straight nostalgia piece. But all the same, they don't get nearly enough credit for resisting the temptation.

Because, honestly, think about it—you inherit the brief to bring back the Cybermen. You have a writer who is familiar with Troughton-style base under siege stories. You have a new Doctor that is easily described by lazy people as being funny again like Troughton was (never mind that this was never actually what was going on with Troughton's Doctor, nor quite what's going on with Baker's). You have a shiny space station set you built for The Ark in Space and are reusing here. And the show hasn't done a proper base under siege since The Seeds of Death six years ago. It is, in other words, very easy to just do an old-fashioned base under siege and be done with it.

Given that, it's genuinely impressive that Holmes had the good sense to forcibly rewrite this script into something else (and this after fully rewriting *The Ark in Space* and doing at least some major work on *Genesis of the Daleks*). And what we end up with is not so much a nostalgic story as a story that is about nostalgia, and that just happens to use the Cybermen to make its point.

Because the thing Holmes's rewrite on the script is firmly aware of is that the Cybermen are crap. Because, let's all be honest here, they are. Yes, they were brilliant in The Tenth Planet as Qlippothic parodies of humanity. But it's been all downhill ever since, due in no small part to Innes Lloyd and Gerry Davis deciding that the Cybermen would just get slotted in as "the new Daleks" when Terry Nation took the Daleks and went home. This was by far the worst thing ever to happen to the Cybermen, who were intriguing enough to have probably come back on their own otherwise. Because they were unambiguously replacement monsters. They weren't the new Daleks. They were the half-assed replacements for the Daleks, and everybody knew it. This is what everybody who complains that the Cybermen are always poorly used misses—that poor use of them has been a tradition since 1967.

And the brilliance of Revenge of the Cybermen is that it admits this, Holmes writing a story in which rubbish B-list villains are a necessity. The characters openly talk about how they thought the Cybermen had died out years ago—which, in point of fact, they had, having not appeared since 1969. The Doctor calls them a bunch of pathetic tin soldiers. But, perhaps more importantly, the story does nothing to undermine the Doctor. The Cybermen show up with a ludicrously dumb scheme and the Doctor foils it without ever seeming to take the Cybermen even remotely seriously. None of this would work with any other monster, but because the Cybermen always carry a vague whiff of disappointment and of the show settling for the second choice, they're perfect for this. (It would be going just a bit too far to suggest that there's a stroke of cleverness in having the Cybermen actually be the lame follow-up to Genesis of the Daleks, but it's terribly tempting.)

The result is a story that largely seems to be mocking the very idea of doing a Cybermen story in 1975, and attacking the idea of living in the series' past. In this regard it actually picks up neatly on the themes of Genesis of the Daleks. Here the Doctor really is confronting an idea first (nostalgia for the series' past) and a monster second. The story doesn't reduce into an allegory about politics or a practical moral lesson. It reduces into a story about stories, memory, and nostalgia. And this is interesting in several ways.

First of all, it's the first time the series has been this brazen in telling fans of its history to sod off. Throughout the Letts era the series attempted to redo its own classics, whether bringing back Terry Nation-style Dalek stories or redoing UNIT classics from earlier seasons in later ones. It generally tried to improve on the classics, but it was still fundamentally trying to recreate the past.

But for the first time since The Highlanders the series is doing a story that does not try to recreate the past so much as it tries to mock it. And this alone explains some of the flak this story gets. It certainly makes *Revenge of the Cybermen* a terribly inappropriate choice for an initial video release. (Supposedly it was chosen by a fan poll. Nobody actually believes this, with theories ranging from the actual winner of the poll being Tomb of the Cybermen, which was still missing, to the probably more credible theory that the Cybermen featured heavily in The Five Doctors, which debuted a month after the VHS of this came out, and this was the only complete Cybermen story available. Frankly, I suspect it was process of elimination—the BBC wanted to release a Baker story, and they wanted a classic monster. Genesis of the Daleks is too long for one tape, Destiny of the

Daleks is too recent and too wretched, and that basically leaves Revenge of the Cybermen.)

But a series wrapping up its twelfth season and airing its 397th-400th episodes frankly has to decisively break with its past sometimes. Being beholden to nostalgia when there's that much history to wax nostalgic about is a disaster. And before a successful mining of the series' past—including, let's be honest, the Cybermen's next appearance—can happen, the series first has to firmly show that it's brave enough not to cling to its past. After the stories filmed for Season Twelve, that's basically what the series does for the next five seasons, which feature only three "returns to the past" among them. And frankly, the abandonment of that practice in favor of fandom-friendly nostalgia is arguably the thing that eventually dooms the show.

But there's something to be said for the decisive and definitive break as well. Especially with a story like this, which begs to be dragged backwards into nostalgia. Left to their own devices, this isn't a story that would appear in the Hinchcliffe era. Stuck with it, however, Hinchcliffe and Holmes take the other route—doing a story that shows why ditching UNIT (which at this point it's clear the series has done) doesn't mean going back to the show as it was before UNIT came along. Which, after five straight years in which at least two stories a season were UNIT-based, is actually probably a good idea. Hedging against straight Troughton nostalgia makes a lot of sense, especially with such an ostensibly Troughton-esque Doctor in place.

The other thing to note is that while Holmes's rewrite obviously declines to take the Cybermen seriously, that doesn't mean he treats them unfairly. Actually, part of the cheeky thrill of this story comes from the fact that Voga is unrepentantly a wandering planet that has the same relationship with Mondas that Mondas has with Earth. Even the choice of gold for the substance that is fundamentally lethal to the Cybermen feels like an homage to their original alchemical roots. (Though the attempt to pretend that there's a reason for this involving breathing is unfortunate. Especially because the real reason is obviously unrepentant alchemy involving the solar power represented by gold contrasting the lunar silver of the Cybermen.) The story also consciously invokes both Tomb of the Cybermen (via the Cybermats) and The Moonbase (via the Cybermen plague). It's unapologetically a greatest hits compilation of past Cybermen stories. Which only turns up the volume on the story's steadfast refusal to treat the Cybermen seriously. It's as if every idea of the Cybermen has been dug up, put on display, and found wanting.

The problem with this reading is that, ultimately, not even Robert Holmes can quite find a way to polish Gerry Davis's writing into something that's remotely acceptable. Even if he manages to slant the story to be an extremely bitter joke about how rubbish the Cybermen are, he runs smack into the problem that he can't get Voga to work. Admittedly, Voga was as much Holmes's idea as Davis's, but it's still shambolic. All of Holmes's best aspects—his ability to paint interesting regular characters—desert him here, and he's left with Vorus and Tyrum, who are just the same pair of interventionist/warlike and isolationist/pacifist aliens that apparently govern every planet in the universe and have since *The Sensorites.*

And this is a real problem. Skewering the Cybermen only works if you can present a credible alternative. In practice, the show does this with the stories on either side of it (though the next story is a "shaking off the past" story in its own right), but there's not actually a credible alternative within this story. The only thing more rubbish than the Cybermen turns out to be the Vogans. The saving grace is Kevin Stoney as Tyrum. Stoney, having previously impressed as Mavic Chen and Tobias Vaughan, here gets his one shot at a good guy, and he's as impressive with his face completely obscured by a prosthetic as he is without it. In particular, take his decision to give Tyrum an accent that signals his age and experience. This is an obvious trait of the character, but the decision to communicate it via a detail of British culture, accent, as opposed to the more obvious choice of just playing the character as aloof and imperious, is a delightful one. It's a rare case of using a non-received pronunciation accent for a character who is more powerful, as opposed to less.

But Stoney is the only good thing that can be said of the Voga cast. And that's still one more good thing than can be said of the Nerva Beacon crew. And with those elements gone on walkabout, the decision to turn on the Cybermen comes off not as a triumphant rejection of nostalgia that continues the thread from Genesis of the Daleks but rather as yet another disappointing element of the story. It's only when you look closely that you realize that the Cybermen are actually supposed to be rubbish—it's just that everyone forgot to make sure their rubbishness a meaningful contrast with everything else in this story.

But even still, we're faced with a story with its heart in the right place and a show that's trying very hard to find a way to simultaneously return to its past glory and avoid being a remake of a late 60s sci-fi show starring Patrick Troughton. And, of course, when considered in production order, it all makes much more sense. This story may feel like a damp squib after the triumph that was Genesis of the Daleks, but in practice it was in fact the warm-up for Genesis, shot right after The Ark in Space so that the set could be re-used. Having shown that Doctor Who can turn its back on the past with this story, moving into an epic invocation of the past as a means to plow into a new future seems like the logical next step. *Revenge of the Cybermen* is a story that establishes clearly that the show is on its way to something impressive. Unfortunately, that something impressive arrived before its herald.

Philip Sandifer

Pop Between Realities, Home in Time for Tea
(*Survivors*)

In one corner, we have Doctor Who running, with considerable vigor, away from the legacy of the Pertwee era. Not just in the sense of moving into a postmodern aesthetic instead of a glam one, or in the sense of its massive and definitive breaks with its history. The distancing exists in a broader sense: the transition we're following is in part a swerve away from the materialism of the Pertwee era. The series is turning from the immediate concerns of the world back towards a realm of ideas and stories. The first great era of social realism in Doctor Who, which began roughly with The Macra Terror, is flickering to a close and we're still more than a decade out from its next real rise.

With *Survivors*, then, Terry Nation walks pointedly in the other direction: a science fiction series based almost entirely on social realism. A series that is 100%, unabashedly about the ethical issues seemingly raised in The War Games, and for that matter about the ones raised by The Daleks, in which the Doctor pointedly declines to stick around for the business of rebuilding. This is the polar opposite: a series in which rebuilding is the entire focus.

It is, of course, a disaster. It's tough to call this a surprise. I mean, looking at Terry Nation's Doctor Who scripts, cutting social realism is not what you'd call his wheelhouse. He's king of the tedious moralizers. Genesis of the Daleks is a great script, yes, but that's because he successfully uses the twin mythic giants of the Daleks and Nazi Germany to cover up the fact that Kaled society is astonishingly lazily designed and that the centuries-long war on Skaro is between two domed cities which are within walking distance of one another and have hilariously lax security. Yes, *Genesis* is very good, but what's good about it is very obviously not that it depicts a remotely sane or realistic view of society.

And now he's tackling a series where the entire idea is a probing and realistic view of society. The premise is straightforward: an overwhelming majority of the world's population drops dead of a pandemic and the survivors have to try to preserve human society. It is, in other words, a sort of prototypical *Deadwood*—a story about how civilization establishes itself and deals with its most basic problems like providing food or security. In other words, it's a story that demands the exact opposite of what Nation has proven himself good at.

In light of this, it's actually surprising how many good bits there are scattered throughout the show. Or, at least, it could be taken as surprising. Actually, for all Nation's inadequacies in portraying civilization, there are things Nation is good at that turn out to be very useful here. Most obviously, Nation has always been one of the best Doctor Who writers at the job of crafting situations of physical and material danger. To my surprise when reading *About Time*, I learned that apparently the scene at the start of Genesis of the Daleks in which the Doctor steps on a landmine is widely hated. Which honestly baffles me, as to my mind it's a scene that captures one thing that Nation is among the best at: the ebb and flow of immediate danger. What's great about the landmine scene is that it's not the sort of problem we expect to see the Doctor dealing with, and even though we don't really think Harry is going to accidentally set it off, watching him carefully wedge rocks under a mundane, real-world military weapon is startling and visceral in a way that the series hardly ever is without Nation.

What it comes down to is that Nation is clearly steeped in a tradition of science fiction that values a dashing and endlessly-pragmatic male action hero—the sort of Robert Heinlein tradition, if you will (though in Britain it would really be the Dan Dare tradition). He is, in fact, far more steeped in that tradition than anyone else working on Doctor Who, and it shows. And it's a subtle thing, but this helps *Survivors* tremendously, because it means that he can at least write extremely engaging sequences about characters struggling with mundane issues of survival.

It also helps that a post-apocalyptic world is a world suitable for writing Terry Nation characters, and he proceeds to pack the cast with various iterations of hardened pragmatists. This helps cover up the fact that Nation is at sea writing much of anything other than hardened pragmatists. The result is that, as with the premiere of *The Tomorrow People*, *Survivors* at first crackles with energy. The first episode in particular, with its relentless march towards global catastrophe, is stunningly bleak.

Two problems soon emerge. The first is that eventually Nation finds himself marginalized by the show. The other writers on it are quite capable, so this isn't a complete disaster, but it does mean that a bit of *Gilligan's Island* syndrome sets in. Where Nation is happiest leaving everybody struggling and scraping by, other writers steadily drag the show towards being little more than a post-apocalyptic soap opera. They're aided by the show's heavy use of outdoor videotaping that recodes scenes that would normally seem cinematic as looking like studio-bound dramas. At times it's only the lengthy speeches about the future of humanity that usefully distinguish *Survivors* from *Emmerdale*.

The second problem, actually, is the show's fondness for lengthy speeches about the future of humanity. Nation has always been a bit of a moralizing windbag, but in and of itself, this isn't any more of a problem for *Survivors* than any of his other quirks. Stirring speeches about the future of humanity are, in the end, something a show like this should have. That's all well and good. The problem isn't the incessant moralizing. It's the fact that Terry Nation—and indeed the writers of *Survivors* at large—are all terrible people.

It's become a cliché that one of the major faults of *Survivors* is that it's excessively middle class. What this argument basically means is that, mysteriously, the overwhelming majority of people who survive the plague are white and middle class. And this is absolutely true. The series has virtually no racial minorities whatsoever. The working class characters who appear are all generally untrustworthy schemers. The series is unambiguously a fantasy about the ability of middle class English people—and it's clearly English people—to muddle through adversity. And the belief of the series is very clearly that it is just the middle class people of English ancestry that are the proper muddlers. The working class and the proper nobility just get in the way and risk endangering the glorious English ability to muddle.

It's horrid, and while you can say much about the dubious ethics of the Pertwee era, particularly in dealing with the Welsh (which *Survivors* has trouble with as well), at least Malcolm Hulke never allowed crap like this to happen. But the complaint that *Survivors* is too middle class suggests that the ethical/political problems with *Survivors* are confined to this one area. And I should hate to give the false impression that the problems with this show are less jaw-droppingly deep than they are.

Let's start with the bewildering idea the show has that, following a pandemic, rural living would be preferable to urban living. Now it's true that within a pandemic, urban areas are disasters because of the increased spread of germs. But if you assume small bands of survivors, cities are in fact great. Yes, there's an immediate sanitation problem of tons of dead bodies, but this is a sanitation problem across the planet, and one the series appears to discretely sidestep as the large piles of corpses seem to vanish about five minutes into the second episode. Perhaps more importantly, though, in reality the matter would be, if not trivial to handle, at least predictable: there would be mass incinerations. Even *Torchwood: Miracle Day* understood that.

But more important is the show's bizarre idea that cities would be disastrous and to be avoided. When it finally gets around to dealing with London in its second season, London turns out to be disease-ridden and dying out, despite the fact that, unlike most settlements, it has things like hospitals full of medical supplies. But more than that, this idea ignores the fundamental role cities play in the rise of civilization. I mean, we've talked about the nature of London on this blog before. London is not unaccustomed to massive social collapses. It does fine, as major cities do, because major cities are not simply dropped randomly onto landmasses: they're built up at sensible geographic locations near major resources.

On top of that, there are huge numbers of resources in cities. In *Survivors*, people are living in part largely on scavenged supplies and yet they mysteriously don't favor living in areas that are full of supplies. And shelters. Plus, there are, you know, other people there. Since global infection appears to have happened, meaning that all survivors either have immunity to the disease or survived it, cities are still going to have more people than anywhere else. And yet there's a ludicrous amount of time in the show spent by people wandering the countryside being disappointed that they can't find anyone else instead of going into a bloody city where they're actually likely to find some. If you want to, you know, build a functioning community - as the people in *Survivors* ostensibly do—going to a city that has an actual population is probably a good idea. Because the fact of the matter is, short of a zombie apocalypse in which the cities are populated by undead hordes, cities would be absolutely crucial centers of recovery.

But ultimately, and this is the real problem with *Survivors*, the show is not actually about the practical matters of survival, except inasmuch as they provide fodder for speeches. It's about the moral issues of survival. This starts to be clearest in the second episode, in which we meet Arthur Wormley, a former union president, who sets up a barbaric regime of capital punishment in the name of reconstructing government. What's wrong with Wormley, in the show's judgment, is twofold. First, he has the wrong priorities— being interested in building big institutions instead of a proper Blitz-style muddling. But second, and seemingly more important, at least in terms of how he's presented to us as a character, he's a union man, and thus apparently inherently corrupt and power mad. I'm not really sure how to craft a sentence that adequately captures my disdain for this.

So *Survivors* isn't about surviving. It's about what sorts of people are the best people, and what sorts of people aren't. Its plot lines aren't about the material experiences of survivors at all—that's just window dressing for what amounts to ethics lessons about which sorts of people are secretly fascists or criminals who are just waiting for an opportunity, and what sorts of people are good god-fearing Brits who are the sorts of people that helped us win the war. Which is a problem both because Nation and the other writers have a horribly classist (and frankly racist and sexist, albeit mostly tacitly in both of those) view of who the best people are, and because the vision of survival offered has nothing to do with the material conditions of the world. It's a story of rugged survival in which the conditions in which people are trying to survive are irrelevant.

In this regard, the moral nadir of the show has to be the much-discussed episode Law and Order from its first season. Let's take a moment and look at the sheer and dizzying lows to which this episode strives. The basic premise of the episode is simple enough: there is a murder within the settlement that the characters have founded, and the characters must identify the murderer and settle how to handle the crime. The audience knows full well that the murderer is Tom, the scheming Welshman (played, of course, by Talfryn Thomas, the BBC's default Welshman of the 1970s, who previously appeared in both The Green Death and Spearhead From Space). But the camp assumes it's Barney, the other working class person, who is also mentally disabled.

There are, of course, the obvious class issues involved in having the two working class people be the ones who are suspected or guilty. But this is only the beginning! First of all, right before Tom rapes and murders his victim, two other characters talk about May Day and the ancient practice of human sacrifice. This scene is explicitly symbolic, coming directly between when Tom first attacks his victim and when we find out that he's killed her. So it's unambiguously the case that the rape and murder is, at least in part, because Tom is a Welshman and thus closer to these pagan roots and their barbarism. (Entertainingly, Nation—who did not write Law and Order—is Welsh.)

Then comes the actual trial and decision to execute Barney. In the decision to convict, the vote is 6-3, with the people voting to acquit being either women or Tom. In the decision to execute, however, with the exception of Abby, the short haired and most boyish of the female characters, the votes against execution are precisely the same female characters and Tom. So women are intelligent in that they do not fall for Tom's framing of Barney, but are soft and unable to do the hard work of following through on the consequences. Plus, apparently, they're most similar to people with guilty consciences.

Then comes the drawing of lots for who has to carry out the execution. This is possibly my favorite (by which I mean the most appalling) moment, based purely on who has to draw lots. Namely the men, All of the women—even Abby— are spared having to do this. This is just about the least sane way imaginable to decide who has to execute Barney. They do not, for instance, pick only people who actually voted for execution. They do not excuse Tom, who, in the eyes of the characters, both doesn't think Barney did it and doesn't want to execute him—he's on the hook for executing him. Nor is it just out of some belief that men, being stronger and more physically capable, are better executioners. Because the character who uses a wheelchair, who is possibly not the best executioner available, also has to draw. No. It's the flat-out sexism of "men have to draw, women don't."

And yet we're still not up to the worst part. No, no. After Barney is killed, Tom finally confesses. At which point the two lead characters, after the male lead informs the female lead that she's just a figurehead and he's really in charge, decide that Tom's skills are too useful and they have to let him live and not tell anyone he was the real killer. In other words, the mentally disabled—who are, of course, dangerous and prone to murderous rampages—ought be subject to a more rigorous justice system than people who have more useful skills. It's more OK to rape and murder someone if you're useful and the useless are subject to execution in a way others aren't. And notably, nobody is given a voice to dissent here. This is the show's final judgment—that Tom can't be executed like Barney, because Barney was stupid and useless and Tom is useful.

This, in a nutshell, is what's wrong with *Survivors*. Because it's so disconnected from the material consequences of its premise, and its ethics are ultimately based entirely on the society it ostensibly burns down at the end of the first episode, it comes up with an ethical system that is both incoherent for the circumstances and morally indefensible.

And what's worst is that, like the last piece of jaw-dropping moral bankruptcy we saw, it's not overt. It's not that *Survivors* is made by moustache-twirling villains, any more than *Moonbase 3* (to use an example from the previous volume) was. Rather it's a systemic problem. The BBC of the mid-70s wasn't good enough for socially realist science fiction. It tried, and it even had some successes, but ultimately, at this moment in time, the limits of what, culturally and aesthetically the BBC could do were such that they weren't capable of taking the next steps in social realism at the time. They weren't capable of doing genuinely good female characters, or diverse casts, and TV writing hadn't gotten sophisticated enough to do issues stories without tedious and often very bad speeches.

And fine. This happens sometimes. The old generation of writers like Terry Nation and Terrance Dicks are, at this point, starting to reach the limits of what they can do in this area, and the next generation isn't quite good enough to pick up the torch yet. Essentially what we need is for the generation who was influenced by JG Ballard and David Bowie to grow up. And until then, social realism, for a bit, at least, is going to duck back under the water and bide its time until people who can help evolve it come along. We'll see it again later. But for now, we need to bid it a necessary farewell.

Forms Into Other Patterns (*Terror of the Zygons*)

It's August 30, 1975. The Stylistics are at number one with "Can't Give You Anything (But My Love)," one of the many Philadelphia Soul songs to chart in the UK and not the US. They are unseated by Rod Stewart's "Sailing," which is not even the most famous very bad song with that title. It still lasts the remaining three weeks of this story. KC and the Sunshine Band, Gladys Knight and the Pips, Roger Whittaker, and Mike Batt with the New Edition all also chart.

In the only two months since Doctor Who was last on our screens, there's been a bit of a kerfuffle between the US and the Khmer Rouge in Cambodia, the deadliest motorway accident in UK history, a referendum resulting in the UK staying in the European Community, and the release of the Rockefeller Commission's report that concluded and made public at least some of just how evil the CIA had been being lately. This was the first of three major studies into the CIA in about a two year period that began to scratch the surface of how upsettingly bad things were with the CIA. Most of these revelations were strenuously opposed by officials in the Ford administration, most notably some guy named Donald Rumsfeld, whose political career was surely brought to an end by such a brazen attempt to cover up staggering abuses of power. There's also the Pine Ridge Indian Reservation shoot-out, the disappearance of Jimmy Hoffa, and the sentencing of the Birmingham Six.

While during this story's transmission, the IRA bombs the London Hilton, Rembrandt's *Night Watch* is slashed up by a vandal, and the two and a half weeks in which everybody tries to kill Gerald Ford take place.

It has, you may notice, been a short break since *Revenge of the Cybermen*. This is where Doctor Who moves to the third of what will be five major transmission schedules. Originally the show ran basically from the end of summer to the beginning of the following summer, occupying forty weeks of the schedule. Then, when the episode count was cut to twenty-six with the switch to color, it became a roughly Christmas-to-summer run. Now, in order to deal with what everyone at the BBC is assuming is going to be the juggernaut of Gerry Anderson's *Space: 1999* (we'll get there), Doctor Who moves to a fall through spring run with a brief break for Christmas - a run, I should note, that characterises how Series Seven of the new series worked as well.

Since this was done to compete with an ITV show, this move is the only time Doctor Who has jumped around the calendar by shortening the gap between seasons rather than by lengthening it. And the first consequence of that is that *Terror of the Zygons*, which was supposed to close out Season Twelve, instead got pushed forward to lead off Season Thirteen. This is not entirely to the story's advantage. The story is very obviously, as all of the Hinchcliffe-contributed stories in Season Twelve basically were, about breaking from the past of Doctor Who. And in this regard, *Terror of the Zygons* performs a necessary function, because frankly, UNIT was enough of a major (and enjoyable) part of what Doctor Who was from 1970-74 that it couldn't just be dropped with *Robot* and never seen again.

So equally clearly, the "correct" structure here is to end Season Twelve with the last nostalgia piece and then start Season Thirteen off with the no-more-nostalgia approach that basically guides the rest of the Hinchcliffe era. Instead there's a slight sense with *Terror of the Zygons* that we're just sort of stalling for time. On the other hand, given that there was a massive sense of that with *Revenge of the Cybermen*, this is still progress. And it's equally true that moving *Terror of the Zygons* away from *Revenge of the Cybermen* probably softened the sense that the show has no ideas beyond redoing its old ideas that might have set in from an uninterrupted sixteen-week run from *The Sontaran Experiment* to this. *Terror of the Zygons* and its reputation, in all likelihood, benefit considerably from its separation from the rest of the Season Twelve material, both on original transmission and in terms of how VHS/DVD/Target novelization releases turn the series into a disconnected anthology series. But either way, the decision to taper off UNIT within the series instead of pulling the plug abruptly is the right call, and the necessities of scheduling made this the only way to do it.

Anyway, for every person who views *Terror of the Zygons* as a frustrating retread there are two or three as many who view it as one of the best stories ever. This is a bona fide classic. Which isn't surprising—it's got enough Pertwee DNA to appeal to the Pertwee-era fans, but is still unmistakably a Baker story. And so it manages to win over fans of the two most popular eras of the classic series, and has a solid director and a well-done villain to boot. We also, coming off a run of stories I'd seen at least once and often several times prior to starting this project, get one that I got to come to fresh.

See, going into the Hinchcliffe era for the blog, there were only three stories in the whole era which I'd neither seen nor read the novelization of. Only the 1980s stories were more familiar to me. (Though here I should note, for readers less familiar with the nature of pre-2005 Doctor Who fandom, that not having seen a story and not knowing a lot about it are two very, very different things. The difficulty in obtaining large swaths of the classic series meant that in practice Doctor Who fans have scads of opinions on things they've never seen, which is why *The Gunfighters* is canonically the worst Doctor Who story ever despite not even being close to that.) One of the stories I'd never seen—*The Android Invasion*—is not exactly surprising, given that it didn't have an early video release and was generally seen as the nadir of the era. But the other two are both massive classics, and one of them was *Terror of the Zygons*. (The other, to spare people guessing, is actually *The Talons of Weng-Chiang*.)

There's nothing much to this—I had the tape, but somehow never got around to watching it, and the one time I tried I got distracted, lost the plot, and gave up. It happens. But as a result, this was one of the two opportunities *TARDIS Eruditorum* gave me to be genuinely surprised by a classic Hinchcliffe-era story and to make sure fond memories of decrepit armchairs and adjusting the tracking on my VCR aren't getting in the way of my being fair to stories. And my God. *Terror of the Zygons* is even better than the classic that fans make it out to be. This is a thing of utter beauty.

In terms of the standard narrative of Doctor Who's history, as we said, *Terror of the Zygons* is the farewell to UNIT—the Brigadier's last story until he was reinvented as "the character every Doctor has to meet" in 1983. But *Terror of the Zygons* isn't merely the last UNIT story: it's a story that is about killing off that format. So what we have is a brutally honest critique of the Pertwee/UNIT era and its conventions. The lynchpin of this critique is the same thing that it was in *Robot*: Tom Baker. But whereas *Robot* was written as an ultra-traditional and frankly overly cautious UNIT piece and then redeemed by Baker's manic charisma, *Terror of the Zygons* is clearly written with the deluge of charm that Baker will inevitably provide firmly and unequivocally in mind.

Whereas before it was mostly Baker's emphatically enthusiastic acting that upstaged UNIT, here the entire script contributes to that process. The Pertwee era was full of stories where the Doctor was called in to investigate strange goings-on at some sort of energy project. And while Pertwee bristled at it, he bristled at everything the Brigadier told him to do. Here, however, Baker gets an extended complaint about the smallness of this issue. We're told from the start that this isn't worth the Doctor's time. And for once the reason isn't "this doesn't need me," it's that the Doctor just doesn't care about oil as an issue in the first place. The Doctor, in other words, has largely concluded that UNIT is beneath him.

It's not merely UNIT that's under attack here: the entire logic of Pertwee-style invasion stories comes in for critique. The Doctor starts by mocking UNIT, but by the end he's equally ruthless in mocking the Zygons and their plan, leading to some of the best dialogue of the story. He's similarly dismissive of the Duke of Forgill's authority and class, which comes tantalizingly close to mocking the class structure that Pertwee's entire characterization was based around. Pertwee may have subverted the class structure by being a drag version of the upper class dandy, but the drag style of subversion still basically validates the underlying social structure. Baker, on the other hand, seems to have no time for or interest in the entire social structure. He doesn't care about British class politics enough to try to "pass" in his interpretation. If he attempts to mimic them at all, it's purely as overt mockery.

But it's the Zygons that really end up making this story. Miles and Wood, among other critics, quite wrongly suggest that the Zygons are undeveloped and flat monsters saved by good design. While it's true that the designers on this hit it out of the park, complaining that the Zygons are underdeveloped misses the central and hilarious joke of the story. Consider the fact that Broton and the Duke of Forgill are both played by John Woodnutt. This makes sense, given that for the bulk of the story the Duke of Forgill is actually being impersonated by the Zygons. Woodnutt, who is a very solid actor, makes the intelligent decision to make sure that his performance differs slightly when he's playing Forgill and when he's playing Broton-as-Forgill. But what's more striking is that he makes sure his performance differs when playing Broton-as-Broton and Broton-as-Forgill, even when Broton-as-Forgill is not trying to fool anyone into thinking he's Forgill. As Broton-as-Broton, he is a fairly static, hissing

Doctor Who monster. But when he transforms into Forgill he becomes a James Bond villain. In other words, when he changes into human mode he also changes the flavor of his evil scheme, suggesting that Broton seriously believes that in order to conquer the Earth, he needs to dress up like a James Bond villain.

Thought of this way, the Zygons' entire scheme makes sense. Because otherwise, quite frankly, using the giant cyborg sea monster on whose lactic fluid they depend to attack oil rigs and an energy conference as a way of taking over the Earth is a strange and dangerously stupid scheme even by the standards of Doctor Who monsters. It's one of the few schemes that one can imagine calling in the Cybermen and the Master as consultants and being told "well, it's a bit overly complicated, isn't it?" But it's entirely sensible when you assume that the Zygons learned everything they know about conquering the Earth by watching Pertwee-era Doctor Who stories. Certainly it helps explain why they attack an energy conference, which is possibly the archetypal thing for aliens to attack in the Pertwee era, being simultaneously a futuristic energy installation and an international gathering of highers-up, and thus hitting both standards at once.

It's particularly strange for Lawrence Miles to miss this, as he basically ended up using the idea for the Remote in his Pertwee-including novel *Interference*. But it makes sense, given how much the Zygons' scheme is a collage of Pertwee standards done with the same not-quite-right style that characterized his drag action hero. Scotland gets treated with the same cavalier stereotyping that previously plagued Wales, but this time there's a tongue-in-cheek feel as opposed to a callous-condescension-towards-struggling-mineworkers feel (helped significantly, it must be said, by the fact that there are multiple actual Scotsmen working on this, Robert Banks Stewart included, giving it a feel of a loving parody more akin to Torchwood's take on Wales than *The Green Death's*). There's a whiff of Von Danikenism (that old Pertwee favorite) to the idea that the Loch Ness Monster has an alien cause, but the actual explanation—squid people living in Loch Ness and drinking the monster's lactic fluid— is just a bit too weird to take seriously. Von Danikenism here becomes less something that's cool in and of itself as an excuse for absurd contrasts so that the show can do a story that's got evil alien duplicates, werewolves, and the Loch Ness Monster and have it come off.

Which is also to say that we're firmly in postmodernist territory again, with the basic dynamic of juxtaposition that has always been a part of Doctor Who being ramped up to eleven. In the past the juxtaposition worked in one of two ways: either you put ordinary people in strange circumstances where they don't belong, as the show did in its first episode, or you put the Doctor into an existing genre and watch him subvert it. A story like *Terror of the Zygons* is much more of a mash-up, where a plethora of genres are sutured together by the basic weirdness of the Doctor. In the past, this was something that only Robert Holmes really did, and now that he's in charge it quickly becomes the norm.

This is, of course, a natural extension of those earlier and simpler juxtapositions. The juxtaposition has been the basic narrative building block of Doctor Who since its first shot. But the nature of the juxtapositions has evolved from juxtaposing Doctor Who with something else to using Doctor Who as an occasion to bring together disparate existing genres. So in this story we have mysterious monsters in the highlands, doppelgängers, and a traditional alien invasion all co-existing. Then on top of that we get a Doctor who is even more mercurial and anarchic than Troughton was - one who doesn't merely skulk on the edges of scenes, but who regularly stands in odd places while simultaneously dominating the frame, remapping entire spaces around himself. Now the Doctor is able to provide a sort of running commentary on the absurdity of his own show. Eventually (mostly in the next volume) this will start to get out of control, but at this point, at least, it's a tremendous breath of fresh air.

Despite however excessive it may get, this is the stuff Baker is absolutely best at. His highlight in this story is fondling the rather suggestive-looking Zygon controls. But he also, in this story and others, displays an amazing talent for pulling a somewhat inscrutable and puzzled expression when he's doing a reaction shot to a dodgy effect, as if he's vaguely appalled by the effect as well. This is particularly helpful here given that the Skarasen is an infamous disaster. But it's also an interesting updating of Troughton's old tendency to look out of television screens. Baker has a similar power to defy and control the medium he's presented in. Not only does he make frequent eye contact with the camera that emulates Troughton's peering, but he also seems to look at things within the narrative with the perspective of someone outside the narrative. Troughton's Doctor was in some ways the audience's agent inside the narrative, but Baker's is nobody's agent—a force that stalks the liminal space between audience and narrative, commenting freely on both.

What's really striking, however, is how much this goes beyond the merely superficial. There are a lot of easy-to-do parodies of the Pertwee era, but *Terror of the Zygons* avoids almost all of them. This isn't a parody of Pertwee: it's a critique. The Pertwee era isn't, for the most part, being mocked for dodgy CSO and an obsession with hovercars. It's mocked for not understanding 1970s Britain, for its poor handling of rural culture, its appalling misunderstanding of global politics, or just its sense of scale. In *Robot*, when the Doctor suggests that of course the US, Russia, and China gave their nuclear codes to the UK for safe-keeping, since otherwise they'd be giving them to foreigners, it's a fun grace note—one of Terrance Dicks's cleverest lines, but ultimately a side joke. Here that joke becomes the entire point of the story. This is a story about the fundamental absurdity of aliens using the Loch Ness Monster to attack Margaret Thatcher (and they explicitly do attack Thatcher as opposed to Harold Wilson). The entire story is about how utterly stupid the story is. It is, in effect, a snide comment about the lousy politics of the Pertwee era, and by dint of that ends up being the most successful political commentary of the UNIT era. What's truly amazing is that all of this is done lovingly (in much the same way that Robert Banks Stewart is self-parodying his own Scottish heritage). The show goes out of its way to have this story not only be a scathing critique of the UNIT era but to also be the best UNIT story in memory. It's not just mocking the Pertwee era, it's surpassing it.

Although David Maloney has for the most part become Doctor Who's most accomplished visual stylist, having Douglas Camfield behind the camera is still a major improvement over anyone else available. The UNIT members are solid as ever, with Courtney proving adept at positioning the Brigadier both as a thick object of ridicule and as a noble man who is at times horrified by the things he sees in his world. The designers are, as previously stated, fantastic. And for all of Pertwee's reputation as the physical Doctor, the fact of the matter is that Baker is actually far better than Pertwee was at scenes of running around, giving an amped up and visceral feel to the action scenes that the show hasn't had since Action by Havoc was still a novelty. (It's also worth making the off-handed suggestion that the common image of an alien grabbing Baker's shoulders and him collapsing in pain is a parody of Venusian Aikido, though we could just as easily treat it as Baker's version of the Pertwee Death Pose.)

The production values equal or better past UNIT stories, which makes the undermining of them all the more effective. Not every Hinchcliffe story will be this well-made, and they won't always have to be in order to work, but given the sheer sacredness of the cow being slaughtered here, everyone had to bring their A-game, and they did. This is a story that was either going to be an enduring classic or a mean-spirited train wreck. Mediocrity was never in the cards for it. And with everybody making sure to capture the appeal of UNIT stories as vividly as they express their critique of it, it landed solidly on "classic." Which, notably, means that for this production block of five stories (everything since *The Ark in Space*), three of them were unambiguously classics.

The only thing that can really be called a major flaw is the decision to write Harry out. Despite his reappearance in *The Android Invasion* and his lengthy career of writing some of the best Target novelizations, this is where Ian Marter's involvement with televised Doctor Who basically reaches its endpoint, and it's a massive pity. Between the added flexibility given when you have two companions (and thus the ability to follow three plot lines, reducing padding) and Marter's genius comic timing in his repartee with both Sladen and Baker, having Harry around has dramatically improved every story he's appeared in.

Robert Holmes, apparently, fought for his retention, but Hinchcliffe, in a decision he later came to regret, ordered him written out anyway. But Marter's importance to the development of Doctor Who is crucial despite his short run. He's the missing link between Ian and Rory in the understanding of the reluctant male companion (Moffat has cited the Doctor/Sarah/Harry crew as his inspiration for bringing Rory on as a regular, in fact). This is, unfortunately, his weakest appearance since *Robot*, and you can virtually feel the character slowly slipping from being a full-on companion to being a character on the level of Benton, even reverting to wearing his military uniform partway through the story. But Ian Marter is still great, as he always is with Doctor Who— especially when he came back as, surprisingly, one of Target's best novelizers. And he deserves a very fond farewell.

Civilizations of Pure Thought (*Planet of Evil*)

It's September 27, 1975. Rod Stewart sails on at number one. He sinks, and David Essex arrives to demand "Hold Me Close." Pop music may be a fickle mistress, but the people of the United Kingdom obey and keep him at number one for the next three weeks. Art Garfunkel, Showaddywaddy, Leo Sayer, The Four Seasons, and ABBA all also chart.

In real news, The Spaghetti House siege takes place in London. This is mostly just a sensationalist news story to fill the yawning gap between the first two episodes of *Planet of Evil*, but as it involves Marxist black nationalists holding up an Italian restaurant and staying for six days and has no fatalities, it's hard not to be charmed. The "Thrilla in Manilla" happens, as does a bombing outside Green Park Tube Station, and, in the US, the first episode of *Saturday Night Live*.

In the Pertwee era, Doctor Who intruded into its audience's lives by using the familiar as its setting—unfolding dramas in real places, and creating allegories for current events. But the central turn of the Hinchcliffe era, as we've said, is that the Doctor fights ideas now. Doctor Who has taken a very cerebral turn (to use that word in its literal sense for once). It's not telling stories about the world around the viewer anymore. Instead it's telling stories about the world inside the viewer.

So instead of making allegories and allusions to the real world, it embeds itself in the viewer's world according to an altogether subtler logic. By great fortune, the move to an autumn/winter schedule for Doctor Who moves it into darker and colder evenings. *Planet of Evil* went out just as the sun was setting in most of England, and later in the season stories will go out firmly after dark. But the change involved here is about far more than light levels.

I live in New England, and at the time of this writing (October 2011) the last week or two has been marked by that sensation of cold the moment you set outside. Not the frigid and despairing cold of winter, although that's worth discussing in its own right, but an altogether more pleasant cold. It is a cold that causes the body to draw inward, to huddle inside of itself slightly. One becomes more aware of one's self; of the crunching of leaves underfoot and the swirl of scents and spices that seem to waft continuously through the air. The trees are just peaking, though to be honest, this year they're nothing impressive to anyone who has lived through twenty or more of these. It has been a rainy and nasty fall, and that in turn made the trees drop leaves early, turning to nothing more interesting than a ruddy yellow before they fall. Even still, there were enough leaves on the trees that the early snowstorm we got at the end of the month brought branches down, knocking power out for most of the state, giving the mediocre season one final, crowning indignity. But this is no matter. A visually beautiful fall is a luxury, but is not necessary. One does not live in New England for the good falls. One lives here for all of them.

Or at least, I do. I won't lie. Fall is my favorite season, and I'm delighted that one of my favorite eras of Doctor Who is falling into it; they are astonishingly well suited to each other. The pleasure of fall is that sense of drawing inwards. It is a fundamental aspect of the season - the sense of harvest. To harvest means to gather and bring in—to take the outside world into yourself. Autumn is inherently a time of introspection. The autumnal world is one that makes you aware of how you occupy space, of how you move about through it. The cold brings the edge of one's interior life into sharp relief. This is also, then, a time for fear. Awareness of the boundaries of the self makes clear the idea that there are things that cross those boundaries, or powerful things outside of those boundaries.

The most explicit thing that becomes visible in this map of the world is change and death, which are in autumn both inexorably linked and breathtakingly gorgeous. It is winter, of course, that is the true and stark contemplation of death. Only the frigid blast of a chill that must be protected against to survive—the extended act of living amidst something that will quite literally kill you if you don't do something about it—can quite qualify as an extended contemplation of death. But fall has its own relationship with death. Unlike winter, it doesn't exist within the land of the dead, but rather alongside it, peering into it. And from its exterior perspective death is beautiful. Which makes fall the natural place for a celebration of horror. When else in the year could Halloween possibly fall? Beautiful death is the paradox inherent in any enjoyment of horror.

So fittingly Doctor Who, as it moves to autumn transmission, becomes itself autumnal. This is the first time that Doctor Who has been so tightly tuned to its transmission dates. In the Hartnell and Troughton eras, the show was basically always on, and in the Pertwee era it ran as a straight shot at the start of every year, tied more to the logic of the television event than to any seasonal logic. But Hinchliffe's Doctor Who is intensely autumnal, sticking closely to a horror tone that melds naturally into the cold and the dark, and, equally importantly, into the introspective realm of ideas.

Planet of Evil is not one of the highlights of the Hinchcliffe era. Since the era has so many very bright highlights—seven of its sixteen stories, not always completely deservingly, make the top 20 list in the most recent comprehensive *Doctor Who Magazine* poll—t's easy to hold the other nine to a standard that no other era of Doctor Who is really judged by. This is not entirely fair. The faults in *Planet of Evil* are genuine and obvious: Prentis Hancock is abominable as Salamar, spending so long to build the absolutely amazing jungle set for the first two episodes clearly left Roger Murray-Leach short-handed and short-funded when it came to the Morestran spaceship that's the major setting of the last two, and, most damningly, the script never quite works up the confidence to really sell its most interesting ideas for what they are.

But look, this is Doctor Who. One lousy actor and the fact that only one of the two major sets was an example of the absolute best work that the BBC can do simply does not constitute a meaningful critique of a story. By any reasonable set of expectations for Doctor Who, that constitutes praise. Which leaves us with the complaint that the script doesn't quite sell its best ideas. And it's true, it doesn't. But what all of this ignores is the fact that this story is failing to quite sell a concept that is jaw-dropping and unprecedented in its ambition.

As with much of Doctor Who from this point on, *Planet of Evil* is another story that goes beyond "we put the Doctor in genre X" into using the TARDIS as an excuse to mix genres that have no business going together. This is, as I said last time, a relatively new innovation in Doctor Who. While there are precursors throughout the Pertwee era, it's only in 1975 that the series gets to where its baseline approach is to have the TARDIS arrive in a scenario that's already fusing two genres before the Doctor's arrival as opposed to the TARDIS itself bringing one genre to meet another. In this case, the two genres are space adventure of the sort that, within Doctor Who, is most associated with Terry Nation and stark, quasi-Lovecraftian horror.

The contact point between these two genres is the antimatter planet/monster. And here we get to the first really fantastic thing this story does. The antimatter monster, and really all of the antimatter plotting, exists in a very strange space between the two genres. The story is full of technobabble explanations of what the antimatter elements do and how they work. This puts those elements firmly in the realm of science fiction. But in terms of what we see on screen, the antimatter monsters are straight out of ghost stories. They never explain themselves, they lurk silently and intangibly at the edges of the story, and in every practical regard they're indistinguishable from ghosts except in their color scheme.

That tension is a beautiful thing because it elevates the monster to a place that, in terms of monsters, only the Daleks (and briefly the Cybermen) have previously occupied: the realm of things that can actively manipulate and deform the narrative. The antimatter monster is wrong in a fundamental sense; it doesn't belong in the story it's in. Instead, it's part of another story that's butting up against the story we're seeing, and, more to the point, one that's terribly upset at the story we're seeing and wants that story to just go away and leave it alone. This isn't a story about a bunch of space men being attacked by an antimatter monster, it's a story about a space adventure story getting attacked by a horrifying monster from beyond the realm of what space adventures are supposed to encounter.

That's why so much is made of the idea that Zeta Minor is at the edge of two universes. This story explicitly takes place in a liminal space between two genres. Of course, that's where the TARDIS has always been. That's its basic concept: a portal that joins two mutually incompatible places together. So by positioning Zeta Minor as a liminal space in this regard, the story elevates it to something of comparable power in the narrative to the TARDIS itself. This is unsettling in a profound sense: no one-off monster or character has ever really managed that before. Which is probably about where a concept as ambitious as a planet that is apparently sentient and actively hostile should be.

So what we should really look at is how the Doctor's interactions with the antimatter and the Morestrans differ. The Morestrans are, simply put, meant to be bad at this. They're at the absolute edge of their genre, and aren't even particularly remarkable examples of their genre. We do not get the sense that this is one of the great military vessels of the Morestran fleet. These are mediocre space adventurers who have gone far past the point where mediocre space adventurers should be. And so they mostly blunder around and get slaughtered, because this story is fundamentally about the way in which their genre and narrative is overwhelmed by contact with the Other. The Doctor, as in *Terror of the Zygons*, treats people looking for energy sources as something that just tediously gets in his way, barely concealing his disdain for Sorenson's goals and clearly wishing the Morestrans would just get out of his way and let him deal with the real threat. This far from their narrative center, the Morestrans aren't adventurers at all but impediments to a greater adventure.

The Doctor, on the other hand, is altogether more capable when interacting with the antimatter creatures. That does not, however, mean that he does so lightly. Quite the contrary, the Doctor seems genuinely troubled and disturbed by the experience of entering and exiting the antimatter universe. Fear isn't quite the right word: what the Doctor demonstrates feels more like religious awe. He's not comfortable doing it but he's capable of doing it. This is a more remarkable thing than it appears. The story is clearly taking a hard turn into overtly Lovecraftian territory with its forbidden universe of unspeakable horrors lurking at the fringes of our experience. But the Doctor is, alone among the major characters, given leave to ferry back and forth between the two worlds. He's both a character who interacts with and is threatened by the Morestrans and one who can talk to the Lovecraftian horror. Not just face it down and win, but talk to it, reason with it, and negotiate with it. This suggests, in a real sense, that he resembles it somehow.

All of this means that there's a particularly big moment that gets swallowed at the end of the story. The Doctor, having brought Sorenson back to Zeta Minor and having caused him to fall into the antimatter universe, then proceeds to walk around Zeta Minor for a bit before using the TARDIS to get back to the Morestran ship. As he returns to the TARDIS, he discovers Sorenson, alive and well, lying by the pit and reacts with complete surprise. This raises the question, though: if he was not in fact waiting for Sorenson to get done in the antimatter universe and come back, why did the Doctor spend a bunch of time schlepping around Zeta Minor with no obvious goal?

The most obvious answer is that there was some communication he still wanted to engage in—that he was, in some sense, not done with the antimatter. This is interesting. Antimatter, after all, is treated as both alien and scary. And it's notable that when we first see the Doctor in the next story, he's standing morosely by the console acting more brooding and moody, even briefly mistaking Sarah for Victoria, a companion he's not travelled with in ages. The sense is that the events of *Planet of Evil* have genuinely disturbed him, exposing him to things starker and more alienating than he's used to. It's almost as if, in his final moments on Zeta Minor, he encounters something that shakes him in a very fundamental way.

So it's fairly easy to identify the biggest problem with the story The Morestrans are ultimately too undersold: they're made to seem so incapable of dealing with the actual threat in this story that they're ultimately pointless. If the Morestrans, and particularly Salamar, had been played as an at least above-average set of generic space adventurers, the sense that Zeta Minor is a place people are simply not meant to go would have come through more impressively. As the Morestrans instead seem pathetic, the audience is left never quite feeling the full effect of the concept. The story tries to collide two genres, but one genre so brutally eats the other that there's not quite a point to the exercise.

But let's stop here for a moment. We're talking about a story that confronts the Doctor with something that is terrifying and big in a way that his threats rarely are. This is a story that goes beyond just creating a monster and instead creates the idea of something utterly alien and foreign—a Lovecraftian horror that amounts to the very nature of the forbidden. Even if the collision doesn't quite work, the result is still by any measure intriguing and worth watching. In essence the critique of this story is that it could have been a classic, but instead is only very, very good.

This is the new baseline for the series: intelligent, challenging ideas executed such that multiple parts of the production are worthy of praise, and a sense of genuine and thoughtful horror perfectly suited for the time the story airs. That's way more than most shows, including Doctor Who for much of the preceding twelve years, offer at the best of times. To offer that at the middle of the road times is incredible.

Let it get dark, turn the lights out, and sit down with a cup of tea and *Planet of Evil*. It's not the best evening of Doctor Who you can have, but it's still something special.

Time Can Be Rewritten (*Managra*)

One of the points made throughout this volume is that Doctor Who under Philip Hinchcliffe was a postmodernist television show. But there is something at least slightly odd about that claim - postmodernism is typically treated as a fairly playful self-awareness, while the Hinchcliffe era is, while not devoid of humor (that would be difficult to accomplish with Tom Baker, after all), is largely a relatively serious affair. But as we also noted, the postmodernism of the Hinchcliffe era is largely proto-postmodernism, which in an odd sense makes it more powerful, as it's able to avoid the clichés of postmodernism.

Indeed, if you want "proper" postmodernist Doctor Who you need look no further than the next volume of *TARDIS Eruditorum*, which will spend quite a bit of time focusing on the more conventionally postmodern Graham Williams era, where comedy and pastiche were the standard tools. But the Hinchcliffe era was all Gothic revival and horror inspired, and is largely praised for its more serious elements. This is, admittedly, in part just an indicative revelation about Doctor Who fans and their belief, thoroughly unsupported by the evidence, that Doctor Who is at its best when it's serious and "epic." Nevertheless, there is a clear divide running through the Tom Baker era.

I say all of this because Stephen Marley's *Managra* is very much a story about flitting back and forth across the line between those two approaches. On the one hand it's an almost archetypal Hinchcliffe story: explicitly set in amongst the Gothic literature that the Hinchcliffe era pilfers, with a good old-fashioned possession for Sarah Jane and a nice threat from the ancient past. On the other, it's riotously funny, featuring as it does doubles of various literary characters, reports of Frankenstein's Monster haunting Mary Shelley, Mary Shelley struggling to write a sequel to *Frankenstein*, and a bunch of wonderfully wretched Shakespeare rip-offs written by who we are told is the worst playwright ever to live. Beyond that it seems almost a parody of the Hinchcliffe era's tropes, set as it is within a collage of elements from the period the Hinchcliffe era draws on and positioning itself as the sequel to an unseen story that the Doctor pointedly refuses to relate the details of because it's apparently too horrible to contemplate. In the Hinchcliffe era proper, of course, this is because stories about the chaining of a mad god or a massive war are rather difficult to do on a TV budget, whereas stories about a guy locked in a chair or a brain in a vat are fairly easy. But having no such excuses, *Managra* ends up poking gentle fun at these cost-saving measures by pointedly excluding details it would be trivial to portray.

And yet to treat the book just as a Hinchcliffe-era parody is blatantly unfair, in that it suggests *Managra* is somehow unserious. (This is also a problem we'll grapple with repeatedly next book.) What's perhaps most interesting is the way in which *Managra* provides for the odd relationship between Tom Baker and the Hinchcliffe era. Baker's status as the most iconic of the classic series Doctors rests on two basic facts: the fact that he held the role for longer than anybody else, and the fact that the Hinchcliffe era is, within fandom, the gold standard of the series.

The thing is, the Hinchcliffe era makes up only three years of Baker's seven on the series, three years being something of the "standard length" for Doctors. So it's the less-beloved Williams years and Baker's one year under John

Nathan-Turner that gave him his long-running distinction. As for the Hinchcliffe era's popularity among fans, the trouble with this is that it's not entirely clear that Baker was particularly pleased with the era. The Williams-era tendency towards humor is very much something Baker brought to the table, as is a solid dislike of violence and a preference for the Doctor mocking his enemies to defeat. Which is to say that the tension between humor and the Hinchcliffe era that underlies *Managra* is a real tension, and the tension existed within Tom Baker. His increasing clout after the Hinchcliffe era, as he'd now been around for longer than the producer, was a large part of the series' move towards humor under Graham Williams.

But it's too simple to say that Baker disliked the Hinchcliffe era and its violence. It was, after all, Baker's idea to play *The Seeds of Doom* as the Doctor being terrified of the Krynoids, thus justifying the violence. And while Baker may these days suggest a dislike for the violence of *The Deadly Assassin*, it's also worth remembering that the stories of Baker's poor behavior generally post-date the Hinchcliffe era. Some of that is no doubt just down to the fact that Baker, when faced with a new producer, pulled rank to an extent he hadn't with Hinchcliffe, who was functionally his first producer. But equally, it suggests that Baker was more settled in the Hinchcliffe era than one might expect.

From an external perspective, this is not difficult to understand. The tension between humor and Gothic horror within the Hinchcliffe era is very much its secret sauce, and drives the era's quality. As with many great creative partnerships, the particular balancing act among Hinchcliffe, Holmes, and Baker and the way in which they wanted different things proved electric. The show was good, in other words, precisely because nobody was quite getting what they wanted. Which is the point of collaboration.

But it's also worth noting that Tom Baker fits unusually well into this model. Jon Pertwee is no more obviously suited to Gothic horror than Tom Baker is, but it's nearly impossible to imagine many of the great Tom Baker stories working with Pertwee. Something about Baker's tendency towards humor enlivens the Hinchcliffe era's approach particularly. And *Managra* hits on it with particular aptness and confidence: Baker is good at self-aware humor.

Given that, in point of fact, the Hinchcliffe era is mostly made up of stitched-together bits from classic film and movies, the cheeky appeal of self-awareness is obvious. Especially when you have a character who is defined in part by fantastic intelligence and a clear appreciation of Earth's history and culture. There's simply no way that the Doctor isn't going to recognize when he's in a rip-off of *Frankenstein* or of an old mummy story. And so to have the Doctor realize this and poke fun at the genre conventions makes sense—it feels fundamentally Doctorish.

This is particularly apt for *Managra*, where the humor is extremely literary and self-aware. This is true not just in terms of the book being absolutely drenched with clever in-jokes and literary references, but in terms of structural jokes. The fact that the villain, the eponymous Managra, is an anagram of "anagram" is overtly acknowledged by the plot, for instance, and the forbidden Time Lord technology that causes all the problems is "mimesis," which is to say, basic literary principles. This isn't just a story in which the Doctor is aware of the genre tropes, but one where even within the story things proceed according to a narrative logic based on literary references. The Doctor doesn't have to "go meta" to mock the story's structure because the story has already gone meta. Noting that this is just a bunch of tropes out of a Gothic novel isn't canny self-awareness, it's the most banal observation possible about this story.

The result is unsurprisingly satisfying: a story that is self-evidently a Hinchcliffe-era Tom Baker story, but that also could not have been written in the mid-'70s. (Unless it was by Michael Moorcock, who'd been doing this sort of stuff for a decade by the time the Hinchcliffe era wound down.) It's a story that feels like a logical response to the Hinchcliffe era years after the fact—a fun experiment that extends its logic beyond what it could have imagined for itself at the time. More than that, one that sheds light on what it was that worked about the era, reminding us, helpfully, that it isn't the gothic darkness that appeals, but the way in which the Doctor flits brightly around within that darkness to illuminate and comment upon it.

Philip Sandifer

I Don't Exist in Your World (*Pyramids of Mars*)

It's October 25, 1975. Art Garfunkel, who only has eyes for you, is at number one. It lasts for two weeks at number one, and is improbably overtaken by David Bowie's "Space Oddity," rereleased six years after its original release and providing Bowie with his first number one single in the UK. "Space Oddity" plays out the story. ABBA, The Four Seasons, Roxy Music, and John Lennon also chart, the latter with "Imagine."

In real news, Peter Sutcliffe, the so-called Yorkshire Ripper, commits his first murder, killing Wilma McCann in Leeds. It is worth pausing here and commenting on the fundamental absurdity of the phrase "Yorkshire Ripper," combining as it does the macabre celebrity killer glory of Jack the Ripper with Yorkshire, a thoroughly working class region generally lacking in glitz and generally associated with the imagery of its mining regions, or with a more idyllic, pastoral imagery of agriculture, or, more broadly, with a wide variety of non-London cultural touchstones. Yorkshire, conceptually, is miles from the seedy glamor of Whitechapel and Jack the Ripper. "Yorkshire Ripper" is, in other words, a phrase that trades on the shocking contrast between the images evoked by each of its words. This is not to detract from the utter horror of Sutcliffe's crimes—he's one of the most brutal serial killers around—but rather to remark upon the sheer and callous skill with which he was transmuted into a media event, complete with a catchily incongruous brand-name that could be splashed across the red tops.

Franco steps down in Spain, beginning to bring that dictatorship to an end shockingly long after everyone assumes a country like Spain was democratic. (By "everyone" I mean "Americans" here and not "people like you, dear reader.") The first petroleum pipeline opens in Scotland, and the Green March—a mass coordinated demonstration to try to take over the Western Sahara—takes place in Morocco. And, for fans of truly great bad music, it's the wreck of the Edmund Fitzgerald. (For proper effect, read that sentence with a Gordon Lightfoot-esque inflection so that "-rald" is said about twice as loud and a solid octave higher than the prior syllable.)

While on television, we have a story that is, from a critical perspective, somewhat weirder than normal. Two of the sort of standard-issue angles to take on Doctor Who stories are, roughly speaking, "it's got some problems but it does some really extraordinary things" and "it's terribly unambitious, but it executes a standard type of story very well." It seems like these two things should be exact opposites, but somewhat incredibly, *Pyramids of Mars* manages to be a story that simultaneously does both.

In one very real sense, this is where the Hinchcliffe era comes together. It's not the best story to date, although it is very, very good. Rather, it's a story that finds something the Hinchcliffe era hadn't done yet, but which is so obviously something it should do that it feels completely natural. In this regard *Pyramids of Mars* is much like the era's debut: a story that feels like it's doing something that Doctor Who has always done while it's actually not something that's ever been done before.

Most of this hinges on a return to first principles. One of the most enduring observations we've made about Doctor Who is the one we made in our very first essay: Doctor Who is a show about people being where they shouldn't be. One of the earliest forms of doing that was the historical. Much is made of the supposed educational roots of the historical, and while those were clearly there, the historical also survived a good few years after the show had all but completely abandoned its educational mandate (which was never that clear itself anyway). Far less is made of the fact that the historical was just common sense for Doctor Who.

Remember, in the 1960s Doctor Who had to present over forty episodes a year that provided as many as ten different stories. Meanwhile, the BBC has always had incredible skill at period drama. If you need to get several distinctive and immediately recognizable settings on the cheap while working at the BBC and you don't go for period drama, you're not someone who is going to be working at the BBC for much longer. And because in the 1960s tropes of history were more familiar to audiences than those of science fiction, most of the recognizable genre pastiches were historicals: Shakespeare, the western, the espionage thriller, the pirate story, etc.

There's a point in the history of Greek drama where plays, which had just been a dialogue between a chorus and a single character, now have two characters on stage at the same time. And what's crucial about this moment of change is that it seems like an incredibly obvious development in hindsight but it's still absolutely transformative. And in a lot of ways, the fundamental change of the Hinchcliffe era is similar: exploiting the idea that you can lash different genres together to form new things. So you can do a werewolf Scottish moor UNIT story, for instance, or a Lovecraftian space adventure.

What's interesting about *Pyramids of Mars* is that there's not actually two genres here. Instead Hinchcliffe and Holmes abruptly go for the other obvious modification to the idea of genre collisions: instead of dropping the Doctor into a recognizable genre, they drop the Doctor into a recognizable story. This may seem like a subtle difference, but it's actually fairly large. In *The Gunfighters*, the Doctor showed up in a generic western. In *Pyramids of Mars*, however, the Doctor shows up in what is basically *Blood From The Mummy's Tomb*— a specific horror film. (*Blood From The Mummy's Tomb* is one of several horror films by Hammer Productions that feature mummies, actually, but its plot, which is lifted straight from Bram Stoker's *The Jewel of the Seven Stars*, is what's most similar to this story. As is widely cited all over the place, the Hammer Horror films are a major influence on a couple of stories in the Hinchcliffe era. The links have been discussed at sufficient length by other sources as to not need rehashing, but suffice it to say that the Hammer films managed a particularly attractive mix of sensationalism and quality, and that one of the Hinchcliffe era's standard tricks was to mimic their basic tone.) In this regard *Pyramids of Mars* is a different sort of historical—one in which instead of visiting a period, you visit a period piece.

Note that this is distinct from just doing a remake of an existing story. It's still doing a genre collision in which the Doctor is thrust into a story he doesn't belong in. Doctor Who, after all, is a science fiction show, while Sutekh, even if we're told he's actually an enormously powerful alien with robot mummy servants, is clearly supernatural. He works by magic. Eventually the show's repeated use of villains like Sutekh (or the anti-matter monster, for that matter) will firmly and permanently call into question whether it's best thought of as a science fiction show or a fantasy show, but in 1975, that's not quite where we are yet. Doctor Who is science fiction; ancient Egyptian curses are fantasy-horror. Putting them together is incongruous. And incongruous in a very strange way, because there's a perpetual tension over whose rules are actually in place. That gets at what's so interesting about this story.

For all that the Hinchcliffe era is the consensus highlight of the classic series, it does have its detractors. Among those, *Pyramids of Mars* is the usual story they single out as overrated. This is a bit of an odd claim. While it is difficult to argue that it's one of the absolute best Doctor Who stories ever, it's solid and easy to like. It's not like, say *Tomb of the Cybermen* or

The Celestial Toymaker where the people who praise it seem to be watching something very different from what's actually on screen. Watching *Pyramids of Mars*, you see exactly why it's beloved, even if you don't yourself drink the Kool-Aid.

Yes, it has problems. Miles and Wood are correct to point out that doing exteriors as a day shoot did massive harm to the story's ability to be scary. And as countless people have pointed out, the fourth episode is a train wreck of delay tactics that rehashes *Death to the Daleks*, of all stories. (Padding your story with material nicked from another one is bad enough, but *Death to the Daleks* wasn't even any good.) And, of course, it's irritatingly stereotypical in its portrayals of Arabs, though in a way that can be attributed to its thorough reconstruction of the Mummy genre. (This is not a good defense, but at least it's a revealing one. As is usually the case when Robert Holmes makes one of his occasional strays into being a bit of a bigot, he does so out of laziness. He can't be bothered to clean out existing bigotry, but at least he's not introducing new bigotry. There's a difference between leaving ethnic stereotypes in a period mummy story and leaving them in a futuristic mummy story, and a bigger one yet between that and inserting them wholesale into a story.)

But on the other hand, Sutekh is given an amazing voiceover by the fantastically named Gabriel Woolf, Baker and Sladen have finally evolved into iconic pair we remember them as being, and not for the first time in the Hinchcliffe era, almost everybody's A-game (and one guy's hand!) shows up at the same time. As Seventies Doctor Who goes, this is better made than most of the era, and a damn sight better than most of the competitors. (To jump ahead a couple of essays, the glossy American co-production of *Space: 1999* doesn't actually look that much better than this.)

No. The problem with this story is subtler one: it all seems a bit simple. Dropping the Doctor inside an existing story and watching him interact with and reshape it isn't quite as complex an idea as inserting the Doctor into an already fraught juxtaposition of two existing genres. This story thus feels like a bit of a step down in a somewhat ineffable sense—as though Doctor Who has given up on ambition and is just content to tell satisfying scary stories in different settings.

That's, frankly, a weak criticism. We've consistently held to the rule that criticizing Doctor Who for merely being an exceedingly entertaining piece of television is manifestly unfair. So obviously we're not going to start now. More importantly, all we're really doing is complaining that Hinchcliffe and Holmes had their second-best idea after their first. Yes, injecting the Doctor into a known text and watching what happens isn't quite as interesting as the postmodern genre-bending of the previous two stories. But that doesn't mean it's remotely uninteresting.

The thing about putting the Doctor inside another story is that the Doctor is so defined by the way in which he alters stories. So when you put him inside of a story not just a genre, but an already existent story—there's something truly unusual that happens. In one sense, this is the very definition of a fixed point in time. The Doctor can't change *Blood From The Mummy's Tomb* without making it no longer *Blood From The Mummy's Tomb*. He's more trapped and hemmed in here than he usually is, and it's reflected in the story. Part of what makes this such a satisfyingly taut story (at least for three episodes) is the way in which the Doctor seems genuinely afraid of Sutekh. Not for the last time, Holmes writes the Doctor as if he believes that he really isn't likely to make it out of this alive.

(Of course there's an alchemical element to this. Sutekh is specifically Set, the mythical figure who slew the risen god Osiris. Egyptian mythology is one of the mythologies most primarily drawn on by the major English occult traditions such as Aleister Crowley and, perhaps most significantly, Kenneth Grant. The conquering of Set by Horus is the fundamental event in Crowley's belief that he was to usher in a new Aeon of human civilization. In this sense, the Doctor dealing a final defeat to Set is readable either as the final confirmation of the transition to a new Aeon, albeit in a typically Robert Holmes sense of "well I guess that wasn't a utopia either.")

All of this culminates in the story's most remarkable scene, in which the Doctor takes Sarah forward to 1980 (UNIT dating sheds another tear) and shows her that if they fail to stop Sutekh, the world will be destroyed. This scene apparently requires a bit of care. Some people, by whom I mean Miles and Wood, make several paragraphs out of the supposed problems this scene causes before they finally conclude that maybe Sutekh is just special and... oh, what is it the Doctor says in the scene itself? "It takes a being of Sutekh's almost limitless power to destroy the future." Right. That. It takes them two paragraphs to conclude that.

Remembering that, the scene is fantastic—we're shown the future destroyed not, as some commenters seem to think, in order to make these historical stories have any weight— that's refrigerator logic at its worst. We're shown the future destroyed to make sure we understand how bad Sutekh in particular is. We're shown it in order to make it genuinely uncertain who is going to win. I don't mean who is going to win between the Doctor and Sutekh. That's not a real issue of suspense: we know that regardless of how despairing the Doctor gets, it's going to be OK. The Doctor's fear of Sutekh exists to make the story more epic, not more suspenseful.

No. The central debate of this story is whether or not this show is going to jump headlong into fantasy. It's what we initially talked about: putting the Doctor into a specific story constrains him more than putting him into a genre, and it creates a genuine tension. We can imagine circumstances in which the Doctor wins via magic: a psychic battle with Sutekh or tricking him into his own destruction. We can imagine ones where he wins via sci-fi techniques, as he ultimately does. And throughout the story, we don't actually know which one is going to win. This is interesting because we're in a run of stories where it's less and less certain what the rules that govern these stories are.

The problem, of course, is that Holmes doesn't come close to sticking the landing. The fourth episode is crap. Sutekh takes stupid villain pills and leaves the Doctor alive, the Doctor solves some logic puzzles, fails to stop the bad guys anyway, and then pushes some buttons to kill Sutekh. The fact that there are people alive in the world who sincerely believe this to be a pinnacle of storytelling while complaining about the plot logic of parts of the new series is, frankly, completely mind-wrenching. This story is less a stone cold classic than it's a good start. There are things to improve with the approach here. But the fundamentals are very, very sound. The basic idea of this sort of genre pastiche has legs, and it proves them admirably.

In the end, putting the Doctor in a setting defined by being a particular narrative rather than a place where a particular genre happens is an interesting way to ratchet up the tension, and something the Hinchcliffe era had to get to eventually. And, honestly, it also had to demonstrate that its approach could turn out a straightforward thrill of a Doctor Who story as opposed a deconstructive critique or a huge event. The Hinchcliffe era needed to do a story that just goes out and gets the business done. Doctor Who isn't high art or avant garde art, and if an approach to it doesn't lend itself to doing an exciting romp then it's worth asking what good the approach actually is.

Because the other thing about this story that's worth noting is that once you've taken the in-hindsight-obvious step of actually putting the Doctor inside a completely known story that isn't pure history, the next step is completely obvious: using a known story as one of the elements in a genre-bender. Which is where we're going to find ourselves in two stories' time, and it's going to be absolutely incredible. Unfortunately, there's just one thing standing in our way...

A Bit Dodgy, This Process (*The Android Invasion*)

It's November 22, 1975. Billy Connolly is at number one with "DIVORCE," a novelty parody about dogs and, well, divorce. The remaining three weeks of this story, on the other hand, belong to Queen's "Bohemian Rhapsody," one of the most epically successful singles ever. It is worth pausing and discussing what "Bohemian Rhapsody" does that's so significant. First, it's a high profile case of a band performing a successful end-run around their label: EMI had no faith in the single because of its length and lack of traditional song structure, so Queen just leaked it to some DJs. Second, it's aggressively not poppy. (It's telling that there's a lengthy period in 1975 where the number one song goes from a six year-old piece of protoglam to a novelty record to "Bohemian Rhapsody:" it provides a useful context for why postmodernist horror was proving to be adequate teatime entertainment.) Third, it marks some of the initial stirrings of New Romanticism, which will eventually be one of the dominant aesthetics of Doctor Who. Also charting are Bowie, The Bay City Rollers, Rod Stewart, and Steeleye Span.

Whereas in real news, Juan Carlos formally becomes King of Spain with the death of Franco, the IRA is officially outlawed, and *The Rocky Horror Picture Show* is released. Plus, New York City receives a massive bailout to handle its massive cash-flow problems.

While on television, we run into one of the fundamental weaknesses of the Hinchcliffe era, especially compared to the Letts era. I've discussed the idea that there are two approaches to take when trying to improve a television show: increasing peak quality and reducing badness. This may sound like an obvious point but it's significant, in part because it gets to the heart of an art vs. entertainment debate that nothing on the BBC can ever truly escape. Barry Letts improved Doctor Who by targeting weak episodes and trying to eliminate them. Hinchcliffe did it by targeting strong episodes and trying to make them masterpieces. So just as the Letts era was never so frustrating as in its Sloman/Letts 'Curate's Egg' scripts (see *The Time Monster* in Volume Three) that could have been great and weren't, the Hinchcliffe era is never more frustrating than when Hinchcliffe and Holmes obviously have decided to allow a story to be crap.

So, for instance, when they decide to hire a writer with a massive list of television credits and pair him with the show's previous producer as director, it's pretty clear that they're just going to pay attention to other stories and let this one be whatever it's going to be. As it happens, what it's going to be is absolutely horrible. *The Android Invasion* is boring, unambitious, and terribly plotted. It is, in every regard, the story *Terror of the Zygons* was making fun of. Well after the need to bring UNIT back is over and done with, it brings back UNIT characters, and not even with any particular reason. It's not even bad in interesting ways. It's merely bad in boring ways. There is very, very little interesting to say about this episode. Barry Letts—always a pretty good director—has some nice visual moments, but they're few and far between.

Let's talk about Terry Nation instead. I, like virtually everyone who has engaged in extended critique of Doctor Who, am really hard on Terry Nation. That said, while I'm not going to back down and become an unabashed Terry Nation fanboy, I think Nation deserves the sort of extended analysis offered to many other creators. This isn't his last story but it's the last in a run of consecutive seasons that he contributes to. Obviously, you don't create two successful television series, the Daleks and have a writing career on Doctor Who that spans seventeen seasons, by being an incompetent hack. On the other hand, you *can* do it by being an extremely competent hack. Which is to say that while Nation was deeply flawed as a television writer, there are things he's extraordinarily good at.

The heart of it is something that we've talked about before, way back in *The Keys of Marinus* when we observed that Nation had more or less hit on the correct plot structure for a video game, only he did it in 1964. Nation is as good as writers get at crafting action and events. Even when Nation's scripts are, as here, stultifyingly dull, they're not dull because nothing happens in them. A Nation script is a constant blur of people doing things. And there's often a charm to the things he manages to come up with. For all that they're irritating because of how badly they line up with other conceptions of the TARDIS, his scenes in which the TARDIS develops technical faults in his two Pertwee stories are quite pacy little numbers that involve people solving problems in ways that the viewer understands but that still look clever. Likewise, in *Android Invasion* the Doctor noticing that all of the coins in the village have the same date is exactly the sort of thing Nation does well. It's a detail that the audience recognizes as anomalous but which they wouldn't have noticed themselves, and thus one that gives the Doctor a useful and interesting role mediating between the audience and the narrative.

Being able to pack in a lot of events into serialized television is certainly useful, but it's not as though Nation is the first person to crack that nut. Terrance Dicks and Robert Holmes are both at least as good as Nation at that, and it's a stretch to say that either learned from Nation. No. What makes Nation so fascinatingly important is that for all the skill he displays at making things happen, he has zero sense whatsoever of structure or of watching television as an event.

The Android Invasion is a prime example. Everything that anyone would enjoy about this premise—namely watching everyone get into spats with their doppelgängers—takes place in the fourth episode. Other than a brief bit of having a fake Sarah in episode two, the actual part of the story where androids invade Earth is put off until episode four. This isn't just bad plotting in the "Oh bugger, we don't have an ending, let's have the Doctor play logic games and then throw the 'Kill Sutekh' lever" sense of that phrase. This is bad plotting in the sense that every single aspect of the plot structure of *The Android Invasion* is comprehensively misconceived. The twist of "They're not on Earth after all! We're just sitting around waiting for the plot to start" has to go down as a jaw-droppingly terrible idea—one that's not only uninteresting on its own merits but one that actively tells us we've been wasting our time during the preceding weeks, as nothing that happened actually mattered.

In essence the problem is that Nation has very little sense of what an event is. He can do action well enough, but only in the sense of keeping things constantly moving. What he can't do—what, in fact, every single Terry Nation story has massively lacked– is getting the story to move in anything other than circles. The archetypal Terry Nation moment is something like the appearance of, say, giant clams or the Slyther or the Mire Beast: a monster that adds nothing to the overall impact of the story and instead fills some time with monster-avoiding shenanigans. The problem is that these situations virtually never build up to a satisfying climax. In fact, *The Android Invasion*, much like *Death to the Daleks* and *Planet of the Daleks* before it, ends with the same slow-decline ending in which the Doctor, in basically sequential scenes, takes care of his various opponents, generally moving from the most immediately threatening to the least. Nation isn't alone in favoring this sort of anticlimax—Robert Banks Stewart did a similar thing with *Terror of the Zygons*, for instance—but it's still a desperately weak ending for the

Doctor to stop all the androids before polishing off the one not-very-interesting alien baddy.)

On top of that, Nation has an idiosyncratic sense of the visual, which is obvious from his very first appearance in Doctor Who. Remember that while Nation invented the Daleks, he actually invented some shrieking robots in an abandoned city. Almost everything that made the Daleks brilliant was due to Raymond Cusick's visual design. There's nothing about the original idea of the Daleks that's any better than the original idea of the Voord or, for that matter, the Kraals. But the Daleks ended up in the hands of one of the BBC's best designers, and he in turn did his career-best work on them. That doesn't mean Nation just got lucky—the Daleks are also an enormously successful execution of a basic malevolent alien race. But he didn't invent a massive pop culture success. He invented something that Cusick could design into a massive pop culture success.

Once you realize that, the flaws throughout Nation's Doctor Who work become clear. He has no sense of what's going to work on the screen. Whether he badly misestimates what BBC budgets can do (*The Keys of Marinus, The Chase, Death to the Daleks*) or if he just never quite grasps what's going to be exciting on television, Nation does a poor job of coming up with action sequences that are going to work well once they're filmed. For all that I quite like the landmine scene in *Genesis of the Daleks*, Nation's belief that men fiddling with machines is gripping TV viewing is badly misguided—a problem that afflicts the climax of this story as well.

But there's another way to look at all of this. Let's start with Nation's extreme pacing issues. There's a phrase used by comics fans: "writing for the trade." What this means is that a given story is written with very little consideration for readers who are waiting a month between instalments but is instead being written for people who will read the whole run in one shot when they buy the book version. Nation, in a real sense, writes for the novelization, and did so long before novelizations were a thing. Look, for instance, at the ginger

pop sequence in *The Android Invasion*. He introduces a detail—
that Sarah hates ginger pop—in the first episode. In the
second, he used this to explain why the Doctor knows that
the Sarah he's talking to is a duplicate. It's a nice deduction.
Except that with a week between episodes, basically nobody
is going to pay enough attention to Sarah's preferences in
fizzy beverages for the setup to work. The fact that there's a
week gap between those two scenes is something that Nation
seemingly doesn't even care about. He's writing as though the
episodes will be watched in one stretch (while simultaneously
not putting in nearly enough of an overall structure to make
them fun that way either).

This also gets at the problem with Nation's sense of the
visual. Ultimately, it's a mistake to think of Nation as a
screenwriter. I mean, sure, most of what he wrote was for the
screen, but he didn't actually write like a screenwriter. He's a
pulp sci-fi writer who belonged writing for Hugo Gernsback
or William Clayton magazines. Or, better yet, he's meant to
be churning out cheap novels in an H. Rider Haggard style.
Almost all of the foibles of his writing—his obliviousness to
episodic structure or to how things will play out visually, but
instead just writing fast-moving sci-fi adventure stories—
wouldn't be foibles in the least if only he were writing in that
medium. And almost all of the things that he's good at owe a
clear inheritance to that medium.

This is why, for all the flaws evident in that approach (and
there are many), Nation is so important to the development
of the program. Because Doctor Who has always been TV
for people who read. I don't mean this in a pompous or elitist
fashion either: it's not TV for people who only read the finest
literature or anything like that. No, it's TV for people who
read just about anything. That's why the Target novelizations
happened, frankly. It's a fair part of why the series was, unlike
any comparable cancelled TV series, able to sustain itself for
over a decade as a series of novels. A real part of that is that
Terry Nation embedded a strangely textual sensibility into the
program from almost the start. Just by writing stories that

appeal so heavily to readers of science fiction instead of viewers, he played a large part in instilling an aesthetic of literacy into the program.

And the Hinchcliffe era, even if it quotes film as much if not more than it quotes literature, is one of the biggest beneficiaries of that. The fact that Doctor Who has always been for bookish people is a large part of why, in 1975, when "postmodern" was a term still associated entirely with the avant garde, Doctor Who was able to quietly appropriate the logic of postmodernism and use it to tell thrilling adventure stories.

Yes, *The Android Invasion*, which I've managed quite satisfyingly to avoid saying much about (although I would argue that I've said everything worth saying about it) is a disaster. And by 1975—heck, by 1973—Nation was sufficiently far behind the standards of modern television that he couldn't supply good material without an excellent collaborator to help him. (Ideally, it turns out, David Maloney) But for all the vast and cratering flaws of this story and of Nation's writing in general, let's instead just say this: there was a reason Nation seemed like a safe pair of hands for Hinchcliffe and Holmes to put this story in and leave be. They shot for reliable mediocrity, and he hit it with depressing accuracy.

Pop Between Realities, Home in Time for Tea (*Space: 1999*, *I Clavdivs*)

Yes, we really are tackling *Space: 1999* and *I, Clavdivs* (or, as it's apparently "supposed" to be known, *I, Claudius*) in one entry. It even makes sense to do so. Because one thing that we're going to have to deal with over the remainder of the series is the fact that the nature of television shifts rapidly starting in the mid-1970s. The beginnings of that shift are starting to happen around what we're watching now. One of the easiest lenses to look at that through, at least for our purposes, is the way in which British television is made for the export market. In other words, shows designed to make money by being sold to other countries.

The BBC, of course, had done this to some extent for years. In terms of Doctor Who, these sales were mostly to Commonwealth countries, with Hartnell and Troughton stories often airing well into the 1970s. Despite Innes Lloyd eying the possibility in the 1960s (hence the conscious reintroduction to the premise of the show at the start of *Tomb of the Cybermen)*, no successful effort to show Doctor Who in the US happened until 1972, when Time-Life, who bought the distribution rights, sold a package of Pertwee episodes to a PBS station in Philadelphia. (To explain things to a different side of the Atlantic than usual, PBS is basically what the BBC would be if Rupert Murdoch got his way: an underfunded and stitched-together coalition of local stations with an extreme lack of money for producing new content outside of the children's market. They market to the sorts of people who in the UK watch a lot of BBC4 and read *The Guardian*. But more on them in a few paragraphs.) But it's not really until the late 1970s/early 1980s when Doctor Who manages to take off in a meaningful sense in the US, so we'll mostly drop that strand until two books from now.

The logic behind cross-Atlantic sales is fairly straightforward: there are a whole lot of English speakers in the US, so it's a really obvious market. But right around now there's an odd transition going on in the nature of what a typical UK to US export looks like. In the 1960s, had we done a piece on exports, we'd have talked mostly about ITC: Lew Grade's production company that made, of the things we've talked about so far, *The Prisoner,* and which designed them for sale in both markets simultaneously. In the UK, Grade's shows went to ITV, whereas in the US they usually ended up in CBS.

Several things characterize the ITC approach. First of all, they were budgeted with the export market in mind, which gave them the budgets to do glitzy action set pieces that BBC productions couldn't touch. Second, they were generally put together so that episode order didn't matter that much. Even a limited run show such as *The Prisoner* really only needs its first and last two episodes aired in the correct positions in the run. Third, the shows were often made by Gerry Anderson.

We should pause here and talk a little bit about Gerry Anderson, just because I've kind of ruthlessly and inexcusably skipped him. Anderson, basically, is one of the great masters of schlock action stories. He's Terry Nation with a flair for the visual. His initial success was in children's television in the 1960s with a technique he cleverly branded "Supermarionation," in which marionettes were controlled by extremely thin metal wires that also transmitted electricity to handle facial movements and things. The result was an iconic visual style that could be used for quality action pieces, just so long as nobody actually had to walk.

In the 1970s, however, Anderson reinvented himself as a live action producer with some significant successes. Then there was *Space: 1999*—his Waterloo, if you will. For a variety of reasons, *Space: 1999* is something of a punchline in science fiction fandom. The most obvious reason is that, along with *2001: A Space Odyssey* and *1984*, it is one of the great examples of a title that took a gamble on a date and got it completely wrong. Tragically, our nuclear waste dumps on the moon did not explode in 1999 and didn't send the moon hurtling out of orbit onto an interstellar voyage.

But there are subtler reasons. *Space: 1999* is one of the archetypal examples of the fringe cult show. By this I mean that it has enough fans that if you go to a sci-fi con, or at least an American one, you will see several, often very, very dedicated *Space: 1999* fans (though this is less true now due to generational shifts in fandom). However, and this is equally if not more important, you will never find enough *Space: 1999* fans to make doing anything that caters to them financially sensible. (Other examples of the fringe cult show include *Buck Rogers*, classic *Battlestar Galactica*, and until recently, erm... Doctor Who, actually. At least in the US.)

There are many things that characterize this sort of show, and a much larger discussion to be had about science fiction post-*Star Trek* and, in turn, post-*Star Wars* and the demise of the golden age aesthetic, but let's save that for the *Star Wars* essay next volume. Instead, let's just sum up the basic logic of *Space: 1999*. It's this: "let's do a really big budget sci-fi show." This is, you will note, not the subtlest of goals. This is not necessarily a deal-breaker, but it's one that doesn't leave a lot of margin for error.

The problem is that the show was basically a complete disaster. Within the UK it failed for straightforward reasons—the fragmented nature of the ITV system meant that it didn't have a consistent airtime, which meant that ITV's fabled Doctor Who killer actually failed to air opposite Doctor Who consistently. This led to extended and focused efforts to revamp ITV, generally with the tried and true method of hiring BBC talent and paying them about four times as much to do shows that weren't as good as what they'd been doing on the BBC. (See also Forsyth, Bruce and, more recently Ross, Jonathan.)

Its failure in America was more subtle. The show was, after all, carefully tuned to the US market, grabbing Barbara Bain and Martin Landau from the recently-finished *Mission: Impossible* as stars so that the show felt American. But US networks were getting increasingly good at making homegrown shows in a more or less ITC style—things like *Land of the Lost*, or, for that matter, *Mission: Impossible*—and so they were increasingly less interested in just buying a huge chunk of British episodes. As a result, US distribution of *Space: 1999* was often outside of prime time and on local unaffiliated channels, only some of which were major powerhouses.

Of course, there was perhaps the larger issue: *Space: 1999* sucked. Barbara Bain, in particular, was godawful in it. The plots were wretched. The dialogue was often more wretched. The show even hired Pip and Jane Baker. The effects were quite good, but that's about the only remotely positive thing that can be said about the series. The result basically ended Anderson's career until a 1990s nostalgia revival in his old Supermarionated material allowed him a late career comeback. But if *Space: 1999* marked more or less the end of the era where the UK exported glossy and cinematic action serials to the US, there was at the same time a rise of a very different sort of UK-to-US export with a considerably more enduring legacy. And for that we turn to *I, Clavdivs*.

It is not that *I, Clavdivs* is the first BBC series of its kind. It's not. But it is without a doubt one of the most important and acclaimed. It didn't actually make it out to the US until 1977 as part of *Masterpiece Theatre*, a PBS series devoted substantively to airing British (usually BBC) dramas, focusing largely but not exclusively on period drama. *Masterpiece Theatre* has in fact been around since 1971, but the gist of it is straightforward: PBS realized that their upmarket viewers would probably enjoy British programming that felt British, and that nobody else in the US would air most of these programs, which meant they were relatively cheap to acquire as such things went.

I, Clavdivs is the archetypal example of this. I'm actually not going to go too into detail on the specifics of *I, Clavdivs* (although rewatching a few episodes, I admit that I was vaguely scandalized that my Latin teacher in high school showed us the series senior year; Jesus that's a lot of sex) mainly because for our purposes here the specifics of the show are far less interesting than its basic approach. The heart of *I, Clavdivs*—and really of the classic BBC period drama in general—comes from the fact that it developed not out of the cinematic tradition that *Space: 1999* (and the ITC genre in general) aspired to, but out of a theatrical tradition.

The BBC, at least in its earliest conception, was in part a sort of national theater. We haven't talked about this tradition in a long time but it has come up before. On the most basic level, BBC drama worked like theater. On one level, this is just a nice way of saying that BBC drama looks cheap. I mean, the BBC has some fantastic costume designers and can knock together a period set like nobody's business, but the fact of the matter is that *Space: 1999* is a glitzy action series with explosions and space adventures, and *I, Clavdivs* is a bunch of middle aged men talking to each other at great length. (Perhaps more tellingly, *Space: 1999* is a glitzy action series with explosions and space adventures and Doctor Who is a bunch of middle-aged men talking to each other at great length, but with some of them in rubber suits.) Another way of looking at it, however, is as a facet of a fundamental division between American and English styles of drama. And the easiest way of doing that is probably to look at actors.

It would be too much of a generalization to say that British and American actors have completely different approaches, but there is a real difference in what you might call the default technique of each. American acting, since the mid-20th century, has been dominated by various forms of the Method. Although it's much more common now to see actors reject that label, Method acting is usually defined by a heavy focus on the actor's psychological state and on matching it to the state of the character (though this is often accomplished by finding experiences in the actor's own past or aspects of the actor's own personality to draw on).

The British tradition, on the other hand, tends to be based more on the actor making conscious decisions about the character and following through on them. In this approach, the actor focuses less on the authenticity of the character and more on acting as a communicative practice: on how the acting conveys information about the character. This school tends to be based heavily on gesture and facial expression.

These days the dividing line is pretty lax. Matt Smith, for instance, is British, but uses lots of Method techniques in his acting. But he modeled his portrayal of the Doctor on Troughton, who is just about the least Method actor ever. This still captures a basic division in aesthetics that is close to that of the cinematic/theatrical distinction between *Space: 1999* and *I, Clavdivs*. *Space: 1999*, like the Method, is about creating things to be looked at. The Method tries to create a seamlessly realistic character that is observed voyeuristically through the fourth wall. *I, Clavdivs*, on the other hand, is about displaying the complex machinations of people and about communicating the various depths and contradictions of them. In other words, we're not supposed to look at characters in *I, Clavdivs*. Instead we're supposed to study them and try to understand them. In fact, if we don't pay attention and think carefully about what actors are trying to communicate in *I, Clavdivs*, we'll miss information. Whereas with the Method, the actors are supposed to disappear.

So it's worth noting that at almost the same time the cinematic ITC style was flickering out as a viable form of export, the BBC was busily nailing down a new style of export in which the old television play dynamic is used and a bunch of the really excellent actors that the UK is practically

infested with will sit down on a BBC set and talk to each
other a bunch. This proves a reliable success for the BBC that
continues to the present day; indeed, not just for the BBC, as
ITV are busily proving these days with *Downton Abbey*.

This is a thread that will develop a lot more in future
volumes, as these two approaches begin to intermingle more
and more. But for now let's simply observe that, for all of its
love of the occasional action set piece, one of the absolute
most interesting things about Doctor Who right now is that
it's a science fiction show—a genre usually associated with
the cinematic approach—that nevertheless acts like a
television play in most regards. (Even today this is the case:
for all of its special effects shots, consider that the climax of
The Name of the Doctor consisted of Matt Smith and Richard E.
Grant arguing on a standing studio set.) That distinction, in
both the extended and immediate future (and for that matter
in the past), will prove enormously significant for the series in
both good and bad ways.

Sheer Poetry (The Brain of Morbius)

It's January 3, 1976. Despite the fact that we have jumped three weeks into the future, Queen remain undisturbed at #1. "Bohemian Rhapsody" doesn't move from number one during the next four weeks. Also charting are David Bowie, ABBA, Michael Oldfield, Barry White, and Greg Lake, the latter with "I Believe in Father Christmas," which I would like to point out is easily one of the five best Christmas songs written by a popular musician in the latter half of the 20th century. Seriously not a bad four weeks for music there.

During the few weeks in which Philip Hinchcliffe's bold new idea of a midseason break for Doctor Who (also known as Christmas) have played out, Carlos the Jackal and others kidnap delegates at an OPEC meeting in Vienna, and a bomb at LaGuardia Airport in New York kills eleven but doesn't lead to a decade of pointless war for the United States. While during this story's transmission, the trial of members of the Red Army Faction begins in Germany, the first commercial Concorde flight takes off, and the Scottish Labour Party is formed.

While on television, we get a classic. I mean, a bona fide, proper one—another one of the stories that people rave about as one of the best Doctor Who stories (the Hinchcliffe era has a lot of these, as we've said). But here, I've got to admit, I was definitely under the spell. I had the irritating cut-down hour-long version of this story that came out on VHS;

on the one hand I could tell it was great, but on the other I could tell that something was missing. And I remember being absolutely thrilled when the full version came out, and devouring it. I must have watched this one a good half-dozen times over the course of two years. (This would have been... ooh, 1993-94.) So this is another one, like *Genesis of the Daleks* and *The Ark in Space*, that's a tentpole of both Doctor Who and my childhood.

In many ways, this story is the high point of what we might think of as the Hinchcliffe era's first act. Everything we've praised in the era so far comes together in a story which has as much density and power as *Genesis of the Daleks*, only it's better written and not reliant on nostalgia for its evocative power. It is another story that raises the bar for what the show is capable of; it's utterly and completely fantastic. So let's just talk about why. And then maybe towards the end we'll try something ambitious, like declaring what the entire point of Doctor Who is.

First of all, there's the writing. This story benefits from extraordinary fortune at the scriptwriting stage. Terrance Dicks pitched a script based on the idea of doing a reverse Frankenstein story in which the scientist was a hideous monster who creates a perfectly normal-looking human. Then, after delivering the scripts, he went on vacation. Reading them, Robert Holmes observed the same problem with this concept that any script editor worth his salt (Dicks, no doubt, included) would have noticed: a story in which the impressive monster appears at the start and the big reveal is an ordinary person has some serious structure problems. And unlike *The Android Invasion*, he stepped in and fixed the problems this time, doing a massive rewrite on the script to flip it back to a more traditional Frankenstein setup. The result is a script with the structural zip of Terrance Dicks and the delightful characterization of Robert Holmes.

Then there's the acting, in which three things stand out. Baker, as always, is marvelous. Over the past chunk of stories he's been increasingly developing ways to simultaneously show that the Doctor is genuinely scared by the things he's fighting while also showing the Doctor's steadfast refusal to take the villains seriously. Here he has something of a breakthrough, figuring out how to play the Doctor as someone who clearly believes these villains might kill him, but who is more annoyed at the prospect of losing to them than he is scared of them.

Sladen finds new highs for her character. The scene in which she engages in hysteria-laden banter with the Doctor after she is blinded is absolutely jaw-dropping, providing a better depiction of someone's terror at hostile circumstances than anything seen in a "serious" drama like *Survivors*. What's particularly great is the way in which Sladen manages to simultaneously convey anger at the Doctor for dragging her into this situation and awareness that she's always known that this sort of thing could happen. It is, simply put, one of the greatest acting performances the series has ever seen: not just up to this point, but ever.

And then there's Philip Madoc as the main villain of the piece. This is just a sensible thing to do. In general, the answer to "should I hire Philip Madoc" is "Yes." Here he does a phenomenal job of turning a generic mad scientist into an interesting character, managing to nail the megalomaniacal speechmaking ("You chicken-brained biological disaster!") while still giving his character a wealth of subtle inflections and turns of phrase that keep him unpredictable and charming. He manages to swing gamely from raving lunacy to genuine menace and is utterly compelling the whole time. The scene in which he apologizes to the eponymous brain of Morbius for making a bad pun is, in particular a highlight of the season.

All of this, of course, is just surface matter—it's another case of Hinchcliffe starting from the raised baseline of quality that he inherited from Barry Letts, successfully pushing one or two elements to the point of being fantastic, all the while matching Letts's skill at avoiding major screw-ups. All we've noted so far is no more than what we got in *Pyramids of Mars*:

a story whose classic status amounts to doing nothing terribly wrong and several things very right. *The Brain of Morbius,* however, is miles ahead of *Pyramids of Mars. The Brain of Morbius* is much closer to what we'd have gotten if everything in *Planet of Evil* had actually worked right.

Back in the *Pyramids of Mars* essay I talked about how that story opened a door that would be taken advantage of later. Now it's later. *Pyramids of Mars* came up with the idea of injecting the Doctor into an existing story. The next obvious step is to merge this with the genre collisions the show experimented with in *Terror of the Zygons* and *Planet of Evil*— that is, inject the Doctor into an existing story that's already framed as a genre collision of its own. Here we accomplish that with no fewer than four distinct and coherent narrative logics in play.

Anchoring it, of course, is *Frankenstein*: the fixed and known story that the Doctor must find a place in. *The Brain of Morbius* is a straight homage to that story, and, as ever, to its Hammer adaptations. But already there's a marked difference to *Pyramids of Mars.* The mummy stories that *Pyramids of Mars* retold were simply standard-issue horror movies deep into their respective franchises. *Frankenstein,* on the other hand, is both a classic of British literature and arguably the first real work of science fiction. This is territory with a deep and mythic resonance for Doctor Who. Miles and Wood suggest that this story has the tone of Lord Byron showing up and checking on how everyone has been doing since he died, and that's not entirely inaccurate, even if it does reiterate an unfortunate sexism of Byron's era, given who it was who actually came up with *Frankenstein.*

The effect of this is to heighten the inevitability that comes from juxtaposing the Doctor with an existing story. Putting the Doctor in a mummy story is an exercise in contrast. But in a real, albeit mildly ineffable sense, *The Brain of Morbius* puts the Doctor in a situation he is oddly suited to. This may be a story that is fundamentally about magic but it's rooted in one of the earliest modern explorations of the implications of technology. *Frankenstein* is, in many ways, the original "blur the lines of science fiction and fantasy" story: a science-fiction story written as a ghost story. As such it's perfect for the Doctor. This means that the danger of the story is enhanced, especially because of a deft sense of what to use as cliffhangers. The story's three cliffhangers are, in order, Sarah Jane being menaced by Morbius's body, Sarah Jane being menaced by Morbius's brain, and Sarah Jane being menaced by Morbius in *toto*. By opening with Morbius's body, there becomes a Chekhovian tension to the whole thing: a continual knowledge that there's nothing the Doctor can possibly do to prevent Morbius's return as such. And this is fitting. This is a story that the Doctor actually fits into perfectly—one that makes a credible case for being able to impose its narrative logic on him, instead of, as we are used to, the other way around.

Let's move on to the second narrative logic: the beautiful cynicism of Robert Holmes. It has been some time since we have really seen this Robert Holmes. The irony of his tenure as script editor is that the bulk of the scripts he wrote while in charge were the least like what he's most remembered as being. But here we are given the delightful spectacle of a struggle to stop the most feared war criminal in all of history from rising from the dead in which the main characters besides the regulars are: 1) an old woman who's literally dying of dullness (for the record, you will never convince me that the Sisterhood's tendency to, at seemingly random moments, begin hissing "Sacred fire! Sacred flame!" isn't intended to be as hilarious as it is); 2) a mad scientist who seems continually uncertain whether he cares more about raising his war criminal master or just doing terrible things with bodies (let's face it, the only reason the line "to know death, Condo, you must fuck life in the gallbladder!" doesn't appear is because it was BBC1 at teatime, not because it wouldn't have fit. If you have no idea why this parenthetical comment exists, go track down the film *Flesh for Frankenstein*. We'll wait here); 3) his idiot assistant who's mostly obsessed with pretty girls and getting his hand back; and 4) his war criminal master's disembodied brain, which is suicidal and envies vegetables, and which gets dropped on the floor.

So it's classic Robert Holmes: a set of characters, none of whom are, on their own merits, even remotely a problem for the Doctor but who happen to align just right to pose a massive threat. And against this bunch of ludicrous characters is our hero, a madman with a box who is simultaneously capable of making the audience believe he faces a terrible threat to the entire universe and making them aware that he thinks he's surrounded by idiots. This is one of Holmes's biggest skills as a writer: he is extremely good at making a world that feels authentically absurd. It's a strange sort of realism, one that manages to be as screwed up as reality. But it's also by far the most compelling sort of realism. Far too often being "realistic" means that the writer avoids the odd and the fanciful, resulting in an account of reality that is irreconcilable with actual human experience, which is, let's face it, absolutely mental.

On to the third narrative logic. In which we're going to have to return to an aspect of production design again. Because *The Brain of Morbius* is a masterpiece of how to do design and effects work on a BBC budget. The decision here is clearly to make a couple of things—Solon's castle, the inner sanctum of the Sisterhood, and the Morbius outfit—look very good. The rest of the story looks like cheap BBC studio sets. And why not? *I, Clavdivs* looked like cheap BBC studio sets. Cheap BBC studio sets are a valid genre trope unto themselves. This story is a textbook example of taking your bubble wrap seriously, and doing so with beautiful bravado. It is unapologetically an epic science fiction story done as a BBC television play at Saturday teatime. It makes no apologies for this; it just gets on with it.

There's a fire to this. When I talked about *Terror of the Zygons* it was possible, if I'd wanted, to suggest that we were in "so bad it's good" territory (indeed, William Whyte suggested just that commenting on the original blog post).

There it was a risk. Here there's something else going on. There's no shortage of science fiction series that have fallen down badly attempting to stretch low budgets to cover epic stories. But that's not quite the sort of science fiction series that Doctor Who is, and here's the story in which we can really see that clearly. The story isn't "so bad it's good." Rather, it's at peace with the fact that it will continually juxtapose the ridiculous and the sublime. We can see here how these narrative logics start to piece together, in fact. The dodgy low-rent universe of Robert Holmes, in which epic threats to the universe are suicidal vegetable enviers, is one that lends itself to the slightly low-grade approach of the cheap BBC studio. At its core, what Doctor Who is doing here is not the cult aesthetic of "so bad it's good" but rather forming of a new aesthetic that merges the epic grandeur of *Space: 1999* with the affordable maturity of *I, Clavdivs*. This is the story to use to refute every claim that doing sci-fi epics on a BBC budget is embarrassing or a bad idea. The answer is this: Doctor Who doesn't do epic sci-fi on a BBC budget. It does BBC television theater on an epic sci-fi scale. And it's bloody brilliant, both as an idea and in execution.

Finally, then, we come around to the fourth narrative logic. Much is made (and I'll make even more) of Robert Holmes's dramatic reinvention of the Time Lords in *The Deadly Assassin*. And while *The Deadly Assassin* is indeed radical, it's far too easy to overstate the degree to which it marks a reinvention of the Time Lords. Quite frankly, much of the reinvention happens here, in this story. Consider the significance of finding out, for instance, that there exists a matriarchal sect of immortal psychics who the Time Lords consider equals and with whom they have a peace treaty. For that matter, it's easy to understate the significance of finding out that somebody like Morbius exists.

Miles and Wood observe that a large number of the Hinchcliffe stories deal with the return of an enemy long thought dead. In *Revenge of the Cybermen*, the undead threat was one drawn from the show's own history and legend. In

Pyramids of Mars, the undead thing is a powerful being from another story who offers a real threat to the Doctor's story. Now we have a third variation. Morbius is a threat from within the series: the most feared renegade Time Lord ever. He is presented, in other words, as a dark and twisted template for the Doctor.

The most obvious comparison is the Master. But the Master was always neutered by being a recurring villain. Closer, perhaps, is Omega, but Omega was presented to us as legend, as something out of stories. Morbius is stranger; he's presented to us as the ancient history of the Time Lords. We have never really been asked to think of the Time Lords as having a history, as opposed to merely having a legend. Previously our image of them has been as the sentinels of history. Now they seem subject to something over which they previously ruled. Or, rather, over which they previously guarded. (It is perhaps here worth thinking of nothing so much as the oddly powerful impotence of the House of Lords. But more on that in *The Deadly Assassin*.) This is the fate that the Doctor brought down upon the Daleks, and now we see that it has, in turn, come down upon the Time Lords.

Yet even as the Time Lords are bound into history and regional politics here, they are also given a new sort of power. It's easy to make far too little of the moment in which the Doctor suggests that the Sisterhood of Karn's use of psychic powers to transport matter is a sort of primitive system that the Time Lords have outgrown—a moment that seems to suggest what the Time Lords do not isn't advanced science (as it at least pretended to be in The Three Doctors) as much as it's advanced magic. This may seem a small change, especially given that these books have tracked occult and magical elements in Doctor Who since day one. But it's usually been a persistent subtext. Here it begins to break decisively into the realm of the explicit.

So even as the Time Lords become subject to history, they acquire a magical power. But we also see this magical power condemned. The Doctor eviscerates the Sisters of

Karn for being unchanging, and thus for never progressing. He implies that in some fundamental sense this is why their precious Elixir of Life is drying up: that they do not progress. And we're told that death is the price of progress, death being a concept that has always been associated with the Doctor, both in its positive magical connotations and in the terrible ruin he leaves in his wake.

So those are the four narrative logics: *Frankenstein*, Holmes's cynicism, the theatrical tradition of the BBC, and this mythic rewriting of the Time Lords. Past stories that have juxtaposed a laundry list like this have done it through rapid shifts—changing tones constantly, whether deliberately or through sheer incompetence. Here, however, all four narrative logics are braided tightly to one another, and the result is stunning.

There's a line of history that leads to this episode. Starting from *Frankenstein* in 1818 and the Gothic romanticism that gave birth to science fiction, through the Victorian science magic that Doctor Who descends from. And it's all presented in a slightly theatrical way that recalls the original idea of "televisual theatre" that led to BBC television and, not too long after, Doctor Who. There's a real and meaty strand of history that is carefully woven through this story. All of the component parts are explicitly laid out in a way that's both epic and firmly grounded in a sense of reality, of the mundane viscera of history. The story shows all of this. It goes out of its way to point it out, and to stress the importance of social progress, of moving forward.

And through all of this, we know, because the story is rooted in *Frankenstein*, and so a story that's conspicuously well known, that Morbius is going to return. The one thing that is guaranteed, which not even the Doctor can possibly stop, is that this terrible threat from ancient history that the Doctor is terrified of (and rightly so, because Morbius is the original renegade Time Lord, and thus the template for all that the Doctor is) and the most monstrous criminal in history will rise again. In the end, the Doctor is going to have to face Morbius and defeat him.

The Doctor even knows this. Watch how he leaves Solon, who's obsessed with raising Morbius, unattended with the instruction to kill Morbius. This is either the single most stupid thing that Dicks and Holmes have ever had the Doctor do, or it's the moment where the Doctor accepts that he will have to face Morbius. Certainly when the Doctor does face him, the Doctor seems ready for him, already having figured out how he will fight him. The Doctor is in full-on Troughton mode here, goading and manipulating Morbius, bullying and hectoring him into a trap he has already planned..

Then the Doctor and Morbius lock minds and the story makes a staggering retcon, a retcon that has, by general consensus, been retconned out itself. Morbius regresses the Doctor through his previous incarnations. We see Pertwee, Troughton, and Hartnell. And we get a cascade of other faces. Modern convention has it that these faces are Morbius's past incarnations, but that's clearly not the story's intent. Morbius shouts about taking the Doctor "back to the very beginning" just as these faces appear, which clearly establishes that they are meant to be pre-Hartnell versions of the Doctor.

In other words, *Frankenstein*, positioned as the story from which all of Doctor Who has flowed, gets into a fight with Doctor Who and successfully deals a mortal wound to it. In its own way, this is a version of Steven Moffat's oldest question in the universe being "Doctor Who?" Morbius breaches the boundary of the Doctor's story; he breaks free from Doctor Who. In a truly staggering comment on the nature of history and narrative, he does it by kicking in the back door, pushing past the beginning of the story into the unknowable fathoms beyond it. (The faces, incidentally, are various production crew. One is Graham Harper, then a production assistant, who will go on to direct two stories in the 1980s, and then be brought back again by Russell T.

Davies to direct multiple stories from Seasons Two through Four of the new series. Consider this moment to be the equal of Peter Davison's daughter, who played the Tenth Doctor's daughter, having a daughter with David Tennant, whose childhood Doctor was Peter Davison, as the single most inadvertently meta moment in Doctor Who history.)

At the end of the confrontation, both the Doctor and Morbius seem to be killed. This makes sense for the Doctor, given that his own story has been attacked and punctured. But Morbius? Clearly it's also essentially fatal for him. When he breaks Doctor Who's continuity, there's an explosion around his head, and smoke pours out. He runs away, screaming madly, and gets driven off a cliff by the Sisterhood of Karn. This is a wonderfully bold statement. Doctor Who and *Frankenstein*, when they try to destroy each other's fundamental narrative structures, fight to a draw of mutually assured destruction.

Only they don't. The Doctor faces *Frankenstein*, dies, and then... sneaks away. He survives. He has one more trick up his sleeve. The Elixir of Life. Here we come to the one last detail that makes everything fit together. The Elixir of Life. Which for once I don't even have to stretch for. I mean, it's obvious what's going on there. A bunch of chemical reactions that create an elixir that grants immortality. Or, as the Doctor describes it, "The impossible dream of a thousand alchemists dripping like tea from an urn."

Which brings us to the moment where I make a definitive statement of what it is that this series argues, in which I finally lay my cards down and make my thesis statement. In which I stick my neck out and say "This is, in the end, what Doctor Who is about." (And good, it's only been four books, right?)

We have already been told, after all, that the Sisterhood's flame is drying up because of a lack of progress and change. Which means that the goal of alchemy—a concept that we have discussed before and found lies at the very roots of the show—can only be achieved via the progression of history, which the show has taught us to consider as a social phenomenon? We are told that the actual chemical synthesis is easy, that getting the Elixir under a spectrograph would be sufficient to crack its secrets. That, it seems, is the easy part. The tricky business is this stuff about death and progress. The show has never actually said this before. It feels in every sense like the culmination of everything that the show has been doing for twelve years now. Of course this is the real answer to alchemy. What else could it be?

This is not just trotted out as a moral: it's distilled out of ninety minutes (or three weeks) of television. No. More than that. This is squeezed out of over a hundred and fifty years of literary progress. This is a statement not simply made as a moral, but as something positioned to be the inevitable teleological consequence of the arc of history itself. It's also a literary claim; Doctor Who is being presented as the most powerful evolution of a hermetic spirit intrinsic to storytelling, and particularly prominent within British literature. But no. It is even bolder than that. This is being presented as part of the BBC tradition of television theater—one of its oldest traditions. The BBC is a public institution, something that was conceived to perform a service for the country on the grounds that it is a just and moral thing to do. So it's with all of that laid on the table, all of that acknowledged and accepted as a necessary part of what it is the show does, that it delivers the secret to alchemy.

And it doesn't deliver the secret merely as a part of that duty, as if to say "Oh, yes, if a BBC producer happens to understand alchemy they should really put that on the air." It is far more than that. The secret of alchemy is shown to spring inevitably from the entire cultural and intellectual logic that underlies that duty. Out of the very moral and intellectual forces that turn the BBC from some broad philosophical statements into a living, breathing entity with a moral duty. From those centuries of intellectual, moral, and cultural heritage comes at last this message:

The solution to alchemy is material social progress.

An Unintelligent Enemy (*The Seeds of Doom*)

It's January 31, 1976. Queen is dead, but it's not particularly lonely on the living because ABBA are at number one with "Mamma Mia," a song that performs that classic pop trick of setting itself a low bar to clear and sailing miles over it. It lasts for two weeks, and is unseated by Silk's "Forever and Ever," which lasts one week before falling to The Four Seasons' "December '63," better known by its not-actual-title of "Oh What a Night," a song that is frankly alarmingly easy to argue is about someone watching Barbara Wright be menaced by a Dalek so long as one ignores the detail that it's an American song. It lasts two weeks before Tina Charles takes over with "I Love to Love." Donna Summer, ELO, Manuel and the Music of the Mountains, and The Who also chart.

While in real news, Cuba adopts its present constitution, an earthquake in Guatemala and Honduras kills over 22,000, and the Sahrawi Arab Democratic Republic, the disputed government of Western Sahara, is formed. For our purposes, however, most interesting is the revocation of Special Category Status for people arrested as part of the Troubles. (Special Category Status was a system whereby IRA members who were arrested for bombings and other crimes were treated as political prisoners and given certain privileges, most famously not having to wear a uniform. Its revocation was unpopular among IRA members, and many when arrested refused a uniform, engaging in protest by wrapping themselves only in their prison blankets. This became a powerful symbol for the Irish republican movement.)

Speaking of blowing things up, then, we have *The Seeds of Doom*. Which is apparently the sixteenth greatest Doctor Who story ever, at least if the readers of *Doctor Who Magazine* are to be believed. Which, given that it thinks that *The Brain of Morbius* is only 40th, they probably aren't. But despite the popularity of *The Seeds of Doom* , there's a significant minority that dislikes this story. Since we don't get to agree with *About Time* much, let's look at it here, since Tat Wood declares it his least favorite story of Tom Baker's first six years. So let's use this as our contrarian perspective on the Hinchcliffe era, since as it happens Tat Wood is largely correct and this is one of the most overrated Doctor Who stories ever.

There are three things that everybody (by everybody, of course, I mean pathetic fans like me. Sane people, on the other hand, wonder why the same show has unrelated stories called *The Seeds of Doom* and *The Seeds of Death*—though a more striking example of the sort of weird confusion that happens along this line is my wife, who confused *The Mind Robber* with *The Brain of Morbius*) knows about *The Seeds of Doom*. First, *The Seeds of Doom* is structured as a two-parter set in Antarctica that leads into a four-parter set in England. Second, *The Seeds of Doom* is the last gasp of the UNIT era. Third, *The Seeds of Doom* is staggeringly violent. This third of these is, unsurprisingly, the one where the problem comes in.

First, let's acknowledge that the basic observation is accurate. The Doctor engages in an unusual amount of fighting here, and the fighting is quite visceral, including an extremely violent? bit of combat with Scorby, the story's henchman villain. The Doctor whips up Molotov cocktails and packs a gun. And, of course, there's the conceit of grinding people into plant fertilizer, a fate that happens to two characters over the course of the story. It's a genuinely shocking level of brutality – one that creates a real sense of unease in the viewer.

It's worth noting that this should be seen in a larger context within the series. The Hinchcliffe era has been consistently more violent than the Letts era. For the most part, this hasn't been that big of a problem. To argue that the Doctor embraces nonviolence as such requires, after all, a tremendously blinkered view of the character. The Doctor is not a pacifist. It's important to note that he not only doesn't relish violence, he dislikes it and wants to avoid it; he just fails sometimes. The Hinchcliffe era captures this very well: violence is shown to be horrifying, even when the Doctor is the one engaging in it.

Baker, however, was never that comfortable with violence, and in this story it seems to have bothered him more than usual, and with good reason. This led to extended conversations between him and Douglas Camfield in which they decided that Baker would play it as if he was genuinely afraid of the Krynoids. The problem is that this trick has already been used for much better villains. It bolsters Sutekh as a threat to show the Doctor afraid and out of his depth because Sutekh is supposed to be a god. Even the Doctor should be scared of a god. But the Krynoids are just Axon costumes repainted green. And frankly, the most interesting thing about the Axons was that they were bright orange.

I mean, yes. Baker is in fine form here. He finds new ways to merge his continual undercutting and mockery of villains with a real sense of fear and danger. This time he does it with anger, several times going from mockery to either actual shouting fury (generally at Scorby) or to an ice cold rage (with Chase). But it's not enough. Nothing in the story gives the audience the sense that the situation is so bad that the Doctor thinks he needs to pack heat. When the rest of the story has turned up the volume on its violence just as much, the Doctor's violence doesn't look like a reaction to the magnitude of the threat. It just looks violent, like the sort of thing you'd expect from a story that has a man-sized meat grinder.

The entire story seems spectacularly mis-toned. Right from the start, in which the Doctor is apparently on Earth and at the beck and call of government agencies, there's a sense that this story just doesn't belong in Doctor Who as it exists at the start of 1976. This brings us to the second thing that everybody knows about this story: it's the last story of the UNIT era. In practice, it's not. Yes, some troops show up who are apparently from UNIT, but there's no serious effort to make this feel like a UNIT story—not even the token "fake Brigadier" we got for *The Android Invasion*.

Ever since *The Sea Devils* we've had the distinct sense that the actual UNIT cast might have been getting in the way of the UNIT era at times. Even if this story wholly rejects the standard UNIT paradigm, it's clear that, as with Robert Banks Stewart's last story, this story is engaged with the basic ideas of the UNIT era. (That *The Android Invasion* also featured the standard UNIT paradigm is largely irrelevant to this point.) And it even has something distinct to say about the UNIT era. But to understand that, we're going to have to go back to violence in the Hinchcliffe era.

We addressed this question when we observed the way in which Robert Holmes adds a level of realism to *The Brain of Morbius*, albeit not the sort of realism people usually talk about when they use that word, by making the characters all low-rent and absurd in a way that felt more honest than broad and straightforward "seriousness" ever could. This visceral feeling provided an interesting contrast to the increasingly magical tone of the series. Broadly speaking, violence in the Hinchcliffe era accomplishes the same thing. Because the stories trend more towards the cerebral and the fantastic, making the physical action more violent helps compliment that, making the fantastic seem real. And not real in the sense of seeming as though it could actually happen, but rather real in the sense of feeling intimate and physical. At its best (and picking up from the last essay's themes) violence even makes stories feel more material.

It's not just that lots of people die in Hinchcliffe-era stories. It's that they die bleeding or actually being strangled by people. They don't just say "argh" and fall over as a zap gun goes off; it's not glamorous action movie violence or Jon Pertwee shouting "Hai!" and people flipping over. It's ugly, painful looking violence. It's messy and, the word I keep coming back to, visceral. It feels like this is a world in which actions have consequences.

Once you take the violence in that context—and I think given the Hinchcliffe era at large, that context is very clear—it becomes possible to see what this story is doing, or, at least, trying to do. Unfortunately, as we said, it's January of 1976 and the end of Season Thirteen. If you flipped the first and last stories so that *The Seeds of Doom* opened the season and *Terror of the Zygons* closed it, the season would have, on the whole, been much stronger. Or, better still, *Seeds of Doom* this had been at the end of last season (where *Terror of the Zygons* was supposed to be).

Placing the story in this order would have let it exist in the gruesome context of *Genesis of the Daleks*, and let it be an edgy pushing of the limits. It could have been what I suggested *The Wheel in Space* might have been: an aggressive challenging of the audience's pleasures. This would have made perfect sense with its two episode base-under-siege opener, which would have dovetailed off of the Troughton-critique of *Revenge of the Cybermen*. And *Terror of the Zygons'* critique of UNIT and its last hurrah for the Brigadier would have slotted in just fine at the end of Season Thirteen?

Considered this way, the story begins to seem much more appealing. The UNIT era, after all, always depended on a vision of the show as an action thriller, so here the show gives us an action thriller in which the action is so brutal and horrifying that it critiques the superficial pleasure of the genre. It's a straightforward and time-honored technique—the sort of thing that, in later decades, Frank Miller or Zack Snyder made careers out of. This could be an absolute triumph, quite frankly.

Unfortunately, that's not when the story aired. Instead it aired long after Doctor Who was working on a level far more complex than just taking one of its own past genres and subverting it, and long after Doctor Who had done a far more complex and devastating critique on UNIT (and from the same author). And after hitting those heights, offering a story that has nothing more to say than "man, action movies are pretty violent" just doesn't quite cut it.

Still, we should be fair to the story. After all, watching Doctor Who in the order of transmission was not something that was easily possible for most of fandom's existence. Most of us got this story as a bespoke video release, not as something that follows from *The Brain of Morbius* and precedes a spring/summer break before *The Masque of Mandragora*. If you watch it outside the context of its season, as a six-episode serial that stands on its own, it's a taut, visceral action thriller with some very, very good Tom Baker bits. And while I'll admit that I'm baffled why it's apparently the sixteenth-best Doctor Who story of all time, when you remember that fandom formed its canonical opinions based on stories in the video era, and thus experienced them as stand-alones instead of as a season, you can at least see why this story is beloved.

But there's more to it than that. Not to skip to the end of the book, but eventually Hinchcliffe, despite his talent, is sacked as producer of Doctor Who because of complaints from a woman named Mary Whitehouse that the series was too violent. Given these facts, this story is unfortunate. No. It's worse than unfortunate. It's irresponsible. The Hinchcliffe era works because it pushes the envelope and intends to be complex, challenging, and genuinely frightening. It's excellent children's television because it treats children like adults. And that, in the end, is what gives it a moral authority to shout down the voices of idiots who complain that it's too dark and scary for children and inappropriate.

Given all of that, it's infuriating to see the show faffing about with gruesome violence in pursuit of such a slender and overly simplistic goal when, just last story, it proved that it could be so much more. Worse than that, its cynical. Especially as a season finale. Say what you like about the curate's eggs of Robert Sloman, but one had the sense that the show was trying to go out on a high note and that it cared about making its viewer happy. *The Seeds of Doom* is a season finale that has nothing to say and doesn't even try to top the bulk of its predecessors.

This is a story that assumes that children just want to see over-the-top sensationalism. This is Doctor Who as Rupert Murdoch would design it: the sensationalist, sick and nasty show that Mary Whitehouse believed it was??. And even though for most of the Hinchcliffe era she was spectacularly and horrifyingly wrong, it's honestly hard to say she is in this case. Right now, Hinchcliffe is blowing the license payers' money on a kiddie lit crossover of *Saw* and *The Quatermass Experiment*. Yes, it's entertaining. And I've in the past been willing to give Doctor Who stories a pass just as long as they're entertaining. So in that regard, calling this a worse story than *The Android Invasion* is unfair.

But as entertaining as it is, it's also irresponsible. And coming after a story that demanded material social progress, it's materially regressive. It's bad alchemy. Because here's the thing: Mary Whitehouse was, as we'll see, a terrible human being. She was quite literally evil, and directly embodied everything that Doctor Who fights against when it's at its best. And the show, with this story, plays right into her hands by being exactly the piece of cheap sensationalist trash she declared the whole show to be.

So yeah. Tat Wood is right. At least *The Android Invasion* didn't make Mary Whitehouse look good.

You Were Expecting Someone Else (*Doctor Who and the Pescatons*)

There is a thread in the preceding essay that we should follow up on. *The Seeds of Doom* is quite entertaining but there's a serious ethical critique to be raised against it. More to the point, you'd kind of hope more people would prioritize the ethical critique over the entertainment defence. There's something terribly unfortunate about the fact that fans genuinely believe the sixteenth greatest Doctor Who story ever is a story that is at best wholly amoral and at worst outright ethically bankrupt. It says something very unsettling about Doctor Who fandom.

Which brings us to *Doctor Who and the Pescatons*, about which it's far more easy to find things to criticize than it is to find things to praise. This in and of itself is hardly an unusual position for Doctor Who to be in. Nobody gets to active Doctor Who fandom without going through a few paragraphs that begin: "In spite of..." There's even a complex if unofficial set of rules to this sort of thing. It makes sense— loving Doctor Who necessarily means taking an awful lot of bubble wrap seriously. But there are also pathological elements to it.

Sometimes the pathology is harmless and, if you look at it the right way, even kind of endearing. There are people who factionalize hilariously within fandom, and love or hate a particular era with a verve that pushes them to absurdly indefensible positions. Let's go back to an example I mentioned in an earlier entry. Say what one likes about the plotting of the Moffat or Davies eras, but to complain that their season finales are letdowns in terms of their resolutions while still praising *Pyramids of Mars* is to be just completely disconnected from reality. *Pyramids of Mars* isn't even broadcastable in 2013: absolutely no responsible television executive would allow a script with that broken an ending to go out.

But there are cases that go further than this. Fans want desperately to love Doctor Who, and sometimes are far too willing to excuse real problems in order to do so. This is not unique to Doctor Who fandom, nor even, really, unique to fans. People are defensive of the things they love. A normal person would look at *The Celestial Toymaker* and say "well that's racist crap." But a Doctor Who fan, if they can bring themselves to admit that it is racist, is going to be actively depressed by that fact. And so many opt not to admit it, pretending that it or *Tomb of the Cybermen* or, for that matter, *The Talons of Weng-Chiang* are just fine. This is a more pathological and upsetting aspect of fandom, one we see pretty clearly with *The Seeds of Doom*.

This brings us back to *Doctor Who and the Pescatons*. Because while fans are willing to blind themselves to the faults of television episodes, it's rare to see them so willing to protect spin-off material. Few people are moved to defend the New Adventures or Big Finish Audios with the same passionate fervor as they'll have to explain why, despite the overwhelming pile of evidence (and let's just use the example that's going to eventually wrap up this book) *The Talons of Weng-Chiang* is not simply indefensibly and unwatchably racist.

I say all of this to set up the feeling of frank bewilderment that listening to *Doctor Who and the Pescatons* inspired. There's not a lot out there in the world of Doctor Who that surprises me. Even if I'm watching a story I've never seen before, I've read too many guidebooks recreationally to be surprised. When there are surprises, they tend to come in the form of

"Huh, none of the guidebooks ever mentioned that" as opposed to genuine surprise. But with *Doctor Who and the Pescatons*, I knew absolutely nothing about it except that it was an audio drama, that it was released in the break between Seasons Thirteen and Fourteen, that it was written by Victor Pemberton, and that I was going to have to cover it. This last point is more important than it sounds. When I originated the *You Were Expecting Someone Else* features in the Hartnell era to cover things like the Peter Cushing films and the World Distributors annuals, it was already self-evident that there would be an entry covering this story. Because it's a landmark—a piece of Doctor Who lore that, were I to skip it, I'd have to spend more words defending my decision than I'll use just write the entry.

I had, as a result, made the understandable assumption that it was good. And so you can imagine my surprise upon listening to it. To some extent I shouldn't have been surprised. Victor Pemberton has come up three times before in the project: as script editor of *Tomb of the Cybermen*, writer of *Fury From the Deep*, and writer of the *Ace of Wands* episode I covered in the Pertwee book. In none of these cases did he make a particularly compelling case for his talents. So it's not a particular surprise that *Doctor Who and the Pescatons* is a barely-connected series of action sequences in which every concept is either a giant fish or lifted directly from *Fury From the Deep*. (Hostile seaweed, monsters with menacing heartbeats, mind controlling aquatic life, and a susceptibility to high pitched noise. And the Doctor acquiring a sudden piccolo obsession. You can almost hear Victor Pemberton saying, "What do you mean he doesn't play the recorder anymore? How am I supposed to do monsters are destroyed by sound with no recorder? I can't work like this!")

It wasn't offensively bad. Nor, however, was it particularly good. Mostly it was exactly the sort of thing most of the contemporaneous spinoffs are—generic tosh that happens to feature the Doctor, or, at least, a character called the Doctor who's often visually represented similarly to the actor playing him on television. This brings us around to where we started: why is this particular spin-off so beloved, given its lack of apparent virtues? I'm forced to speculate here, but I think this gets to the heart of the less-pathological aspects of why we forgive Doctor Who its faults. And this is important to look at, because this book marks a dividing line in Doctor Who. These first four volumes have had the luxury of covering eras of Doctor Who that the general critical consensus favours. The next four will be devoted largely to eras that aren't nearly so beloved, even though they have individual stories that are. So it is worth looking at what is and isn't beloved by fandom, and what makes the difference.

The first thing we should observe about *Doctor Who and the Pescatons* is that, as it came out in 1976, it's among the first wave of permanent Tom Baker stories. We've talked repeatedly about the way in which being among the early Target novelizations is clearly directly related to being considered a classic story. And at this point in 1976, there were only twenty-three novelizations, consisting of four Hartnell stories, three Troughton stories, eleven Pertwee stories, *The Three Doctors*, and four Baker stories, two of which came out the same summer as this audio. So the then-current era of the show – an extremely popular one – was at the time one of the least represented in the medium through which stories were permanently preserved.

That's the context in which *Doctor Who and the Pescatons* was released. It's a classic for, ultimately, the same reasons that *The Web Planet* or *The Moonbase* are—they're all stories that it was possible to own a copy of, and thus stories that are remembered. Except add to that the fact that this is the first time the Doctor has appeared in a story outside of television. I mean the real Doctor: not a drawing of him, or some words about him, or Peter Cushing, but Tom Baker himself, playing the Doctor, somewhere other than television. This is common enough now, in an era where Big Finish releases multiple audios with classic series actors every month and Matt Smith's first CD release dropping the same week as *The*

Time of Angels, but in 1976, it was extraordinary. Add to that the cachet of being the only proper, numbered, classic-era Target novelization to be based on something other than a television story and it's not at all hard to see why this story evokes nostalgia.

And this brings us to why we excuse Doctor Who. More than that, it's ultimately the reason that I try to engage in what I call redemptive readings of stories. Because yes, *Doctor Who and the Pescatons* is rubbish. It's dull. All of its ideas are pilfered from *Fury From the Deep*, and it's not like *Fury From the Deep* was a pinnacle of innovation in 1968, little yet eight years later. But goddammit, who cares? It was Doctor Who that people could own. It has Tom Baker with at least some good lines, and a good delivery even of his crappy lines. It has some decently exciting bits in which monsters rampage through London. It even has Tom Baker fighting monsters by singing "Hello Dolly." If you're ten, what the else do you want out of life?

So we forgive Doctor Who. Because it is a part of our childhood and a part of who we are. I could have been harsher on the Pertwee era than I was last volume. This volume, I could take seriously the critique that the Hinchcliffe era has a few too many Hammer Horror tributes. I could have gotten really upset that the Troughton era has too many bases under siege, or that the Hartnell era... well, I mean, take your pick of the Hartnell era. But... I didn't want to. Any more than I want to go up to a family member or loved one and just list off all of their flaws. It's not that they don't have them: it's that I just don't want to do that. This is another reason that I insist this project isn't about reviewing stories. If I were reviewing Doctor Who I'd have some sort of obligation to be objective. No. Objectivity is for things I love less than this.

That doesn't mean ignoring the flaws or pretending they don't exist. It just means forgiving them. And, more broadly, it means forgiving our own childhoods, and even to some extent forgiving ourselves. Doctor Who is rarely perfect. But it's frequently good enough to be enthralling, and it enthralled an awful lot of people over the years. It was precious to many of us. And so when we come upon something like *Doctor Who and the Pescatons*...is being a rehash of a story that aired when much of the record's buyers were around two or three years old really something worth condemning?

Especially because, while it's easier to identify its flaws, it's not as though this story doesn't have merits. Say what you like about Pemberton, and obviously I'm far from a fan, but he's put some real thought into how to make Doctor Who work as a three-character audio. The decision to trim the plot down to the major set pieces, thought of this way, is a clever concession to the fact that the record is going to be played multiple times. In essence, every part of the story that might be less exciting to kids (which just so happens to be a subset of "scenes not requiring anyone but Baker, Sladen, or the monster") is removed so that the story is always heading into another "good part." It's not a hugely brilliant technique, and it certainly pales in comparison with the narrative techniques that will become standard issue in the Big Finish era, but for 1976 and for a writer who is a bit of a hack, it's surprisingly well thought through. Pemberton understands his medium. The worst thing one can say about the audio is probably that the focus on the exciting bits makes it in some ways as violent as *The Seeds of Doom*. Here, it's played very differently, however. For one thing, the audio medium takes the edge off any critique of violence in that it is only as violent as the listener's imagination. More importantly, the story plays everything for laughs. This isn't a big exciting adventure—it's larking about with giant fish monsters smashing up London. The Doctor distracts them by singing "Hello Dolly," for God's sake. If *The Seeds of Doom* had treated its violence with such charming whimsy it would have actually deserved its reputation for quality.

The biggest reason this works is that Baker, instead of playing everything seriously like he does in *The Seeds of Doom*, here he plays it like he's having a blast. Baker is, frankly, imperious here. Pemberton, if we're going to be charitable, wrote a script that would work well for any incarnation of the Doctor. (If we're being less charitable, he wrote a script that gives little evidence he has ever actually seen a Tom Baker episode.) The Troughton-esque characteristics are clear enough, though they perhaps stand out more because we know Pemberton's only television credits came in the Troughton era than because Pemberton is overtly writing for Troughton. But also present at points is the cantankerously alien tone of Hartnell (in particular when the Doctor irritatedly points out that Earth isn't his planet), and the dashing defender of Earth that Pertwee gave us.

All of this, though, is held down by Baker, who puts in a performance that really helps identify how he completely redefined the role—which, of course, he did. Every actor until at least David Tennant has stepped into the role being compared primarily to Baker. And once we see—or rather, hear—Baker with a script that isn't written particularly for him we can see what it is about his performance that made him so definitive.

His central trick in *Doctor Who and the Pescatons* is one that will, with admittedly somewhat mixed results, migrate into his television performance before too long: his asides to the audience. Baker serves double duty here as both the main character and the narrator, and he frequently cracks jokes about the proceedings he's relating. Crucially, these jokes tend to be at his own expense as often as they are at the expense of the plot, which prevents them from purely being means by which Baker asserts power over the narrative. Instead, they serve to establish the Doctor as part of the audience of his own story. This inverts the normal (that is, clichéd) order of things. Normally people talk about the audience being invited into the world of Doctor Who, but this goes exactly in the opposite direction. The Doctor, by making jokes about the narrative, exits the narrative and becomes part of the audience's world.

The result is a combination of the defining aspects of his two predecessors. To an extent every Doctor's character is a reaction against the previous one, but Baker's relationship with his predecessors is remarkably deft. The joking asides only work because the Doctor is the star of the story, and Baker's use of his magnetic charisma to position himself as the focus of the narrative evokes Pertwee's tenure. Yet what he does with this charisma is firmly in the Troughton tradition of becoming a narrative force unto himself. And when you see Baker acting with a script that is so evocative of his predecessors and so unevocative of his own tenure (both he and Sarah Jane have several lines that are deeply inscrutable given the context of the series), these aspects of the role become clear.

Which isn't a lot. But it's something. Certainly it's enough to make *Doctor Who and the Pescatons* an entertaining way to spend forty-five minutes as an adult Doctor Who fan in 2013. Yet perhaps than any other story we've covered in the blog, that's really not the way to approach this story in the first place. This is for the ten-year-olds of 1976, and through them it's more than earned its classic status.

Pop Between Realities, Home in Time for Tea
(*Shadows*)

A commissioned essay for Ken Finlayson.

Much of the discussion of the Hinchcliffe era of Doctor Who focuses on the question of horror. In hindsight, of course, this is what the era is praised for—the "Gothic horror" era of Doctor Who. At the time, equally, it was a source of considerable controversy, or, at least, of considerable kvetching from Mary Whitehouse—most notably the famed description of the show as "teatime brutality for tots"—that eventually got taken seriously by the BBC brass. But it is not as though Doctor Who was the only scary British television show for children at the time. To wit, *Shadows* was a children's horror anthology series produced by Thames Television in the mid-1970s.

While it's important not to equate the shows too much,, there are numerous similarities. Both Doctor Who and *Shadows* were anthology shows doing six stories a year, though Doctor Who did its as multipart serials, whereas *Shadows* did half-hour stories. Doctor Who also had a small regular cast, whereas *Shadows* was a true anthology, changing cast and premise entirely every episode. Perhaps most importantly, though, *Shadows* visibly takes from a more literary tradition than Doctor Who did, with relatively serious children's writers like Joan Aiken, Penelope Lively, and Susan Cooper all contributing episodes.

But the real difference is that the shows have fundamentally different views of horror. *Shadows* tends towards an almost lyrical mode of storytelling. The standard plot of an episode is "mysterious things go on, and the episode ends with a character realizing the nature of these things." Typically this realization comes a ways after the audience has sorted things out for themselves. Rarely does the realization come along with any sort of decisive action or consequences—it tends to simply be a moment where a character figures things out.

If this sounds clumsy, it's because it often is. The pattern is set up in the first episode, Roger Marshall's "The Future Ghost," which features a Victorian woman in a guest house encountering a young woman suffering from the flu in a 1970s hospital. The episode is all reasonably sharp, with a nice extended comedy bit of the Victorian woman being puzzled by all the things in the hospital room, but it comes to nothing like a resolution. The Victorian woman realizes that she's encountered a ghost from the future. The credits roll. It feels for all the world like setup for an extended serial about the time leakage between these two places or whatever, but instead it's just a sketch—all setup and premise with no payoff.

Later writers manage to make something out of this. P.J. Hammond, later of *Sapphire and Steel* fame and writer of two episodes of *Torchwood,* does a lovely bit with a magician who's tempted by an unexplained power, ignoring the way in which the new trick he's discovered is slowly making his possessions disappear into thin air until it's too late and he also vanishes without a trace, which manages to have the "what's happening here" explanation coincide with an actual plot resolution, though the connection remains, perhaps, somewhat oblique. Susan Cooper, meanwhile, just puts an actual, proper climax slightly earlier in the episode, allowing the end to be a sort of slow fizzing out of characters reacting to and recovering from the actual climax.

But in every case there's still a tendency to treat the supernatural at a remove, as something to look at without quite engaging with. *Shadows* trades in concepts, casting, if you'll forgive the overly literal metaphor, shadows of them and looking at those, but leaving the actual concept—the future haunting the present, or a cyclic battle between light and darkness—there to be thought about separately from the episode itself.

Doctor Who, on the other hand, has always grounded its sense of horror in the idea of monsters. And monsters require being seen and witnessed. Monstrosity is not mere fear but an a visual property. Which means that Doctor Who cannot exist at a remove from its objects of horror. This also extends from its premise; Doctor Who is about entering into other worlds. You can't do that while remaining at a remove from those worlds. From day one, the show has been about dumping its regulars in terrifying places and watching them get out of them. That kind of approach simply doesn't allow for the lyrical structure and contemplative distance of *Shadows*.

Which form of horror is more successful? It's telling, perhaps, that *Shadows* does not usually come up in surveys of the careers of Susan Cooper or Fay Weldon, nor is it one of the go-to examples of scary children's television in the 1970s. This is not exactly surprising: its plot structure really doesn't work. It has literary ambitions but ends up feeling muddled. It's certainly going to avoid a major backlash from Mary Whitehouse, but that's probably not a good thing. By any empirical standard it's pretty clear that Hinchcliffe-era Doctor Who was far more successful than *Shadows* in terms of terrorizing a generation of children forever.

On the other hand, for all that *Shadows* is at times a bit detached, it at least avoids the crass excesses of *The Seeds of Doom*. The pressure that monsters exert on Doctor Who can make it as difficult for it to be effective horror as *Shadows*'s sense of detachment does for it. Proper fear seems to happen on the line between what is shown and what is hidden, and it's telling that many of the scariest elements of the Hinchcliffe era are, in the end, conceptual horror: watching the Doctor be forced to kneel before Sutekh, for instance, is scary because of the sense of the order of things being disturbed. While there are probably a few people who had nightmares about Sutekh controlling them, one does not have the sense that this was the normal order of things.

Even when the Hinchcliffe era dabbles in outright visual horror—something *Shadows* basically never did—it tended to have a conceptual bent. Consider the scene of robot-Sarah's face coming off in *The Android Invasion*. Here the scary thing is definitely what's being shown, but the scene's basic horror is still the wrongness of doing that to Sarah Jane. This is a technique that *Shadows*, with its completely rotating cast, never really has access to. For all its focus on conceptual horror, *Shadows* can't tie that into its plot structure in a meaningful way, which is a big weakness.

Equally, for all that the Hinchcliffe era was pilloried by Mary Whitehouse, it is not as though it was doing proto-splattercore or anything. Yes, the Hinchcliffe era got violent, but it was still basically playing with conceptual horror, existing at something of a happy and terribly effective midpoint between *Saw* and *Shadows*, finding ways of fusing the spectacle of visual horror with a strong conceptual element. That, it seems, is the secret to really terrorizing a generation.

On the other hand, this is not to dismiss *Shadows*, which is appealing in spite of its flaws. No, actually, because of them; because there's something intriguing about seeing the ghost story run as an exercise in form instead of terror. It's not a surprise that the series was able to attract such a high caliber of writers, because what it offered was, from a writerly and readerly perspective, interesting. And it gives *Shadows* something Doctor Who has never really had: a veneer of literary respectability and seriousness. This is children's television made to the old "uplifting and edifying" mandate, only with ghost stories. That it's not something that dements and warps children forever does not mean that it doesn't accomplish interesting things. It's only when you try to compare it to Doctor Who that it appears at all inadequate.

Which is to say something that perhaps we don't acknowledge enough in the course of this project; there are actually ways to grow up besides as a Doctor Who fan. There aren't just other rabbit holes, there are entire other kinds of rabbit holes. This literary, theatrical, structure-centric approach to storytelling works, albeit in a very different way from Doctor Who, and one can imagine an entire other history of television and the world that looks at this aspect of it. It's just that this approach isn't Doctor Who's, no matter how many similarities there may be.

Also, the second season opening credits of *Shadows* are divinely creepy.

Time Can Be Rewritten (*System Shock*)

When I covered this book on the blog it surprised some people, several of whom thought I would go for Stephen Marley's *Managra*, a metafictional romp through the history of British culture in the far future that even features Aleister Crowley. And that's fair, and notably, I've added *Managra* in this book, but my decision led to some questioning at the time as to why I picked this, of all things.

The answer, to be perfectly honest, is that I am a sucker for nineties techno-thrillers about computers, and that I am completely powerless to resist any book that is set, quite literally, "when the information superhighway comes online" in 1998. So crack open a bottle of Zima and put on some Jewel. Because it's 1995, and people are about to make some very, very embarrassing predictions.

That is of course, terribly unfair of me. But it's very difficult to read Justin Richards's *System Shock* in 2013 without laughing at its naiveté. The most obvious example is the one we've already alluded to— the charmingly dated phrase "information superhighway." This phrase rightly serves as a sort of memetic tombstone for a particular historical moment in digital technology: the last point where it was possible to talk about it without actually knowing a single thing about it.

While the phrase doesn't have a clear inventor, its prominence is due largely to Al Gore. Gore, who had been closely following digital issues as a Senator for decades, used the term with reasonable frequency, and so upon becoming Vice President, his newfound profile catapulted the term into the mainstream. Equally crucially, Al Gore was a politician who liked giving money to the geeks, but he was not actually a geek himself. And so his favored term had absolutely no currency whatsoever among the online community that already existed.

And notably, an online community definitely existed in 1995. Doctor Who fandom, by this point, was already dominated heavily by what went on on rec.arts.doctorwho. In 1995 Doctor Who was firmly in the "cult sci-fi" era of its history, and so there was a large overlap between Doctor Who fans and early adopters. (This is still the case, albeit to a smaller degree - observe how Doctor Who's gets a larger ratings boost from time-shifting and higher iPlayer numbers than comparable dramas.) So what's so interesting about the phrase "information superhighway" isn't interesting in the same way as, say, *The War Machines*, which is the classic series story most similar to *System Shock*.

The War Machines, after all, is nonsense on a stick. But being completely wrong about the nature of computers in 1966 is fundamentally different from being wrong about them in 1995, and that's what "information superhighway" ends up signifying. It's not that it's a spectacularly wrong term: it's just one that nobody who actually used the Internet took seriously. Those who used it were clearly not talking about the actual technology, but an abstract idea of it that was based on a fuzzy understanding of what it did.

(While this fuzziness can and did spring from genuine ignorance, it was more often a point of marketing. There's a fascinating moment in Bill Gates's basically terrible book *The Road Ahead* where he imagines how using the Internet for video would allow customers to monitor and comment on how bouquets of flowers were being arranged at the florist. Gates, however, is far too savvy a businessman to miss the fact that this was a terrible idea that would serve no purpose other than slowing down florists as they deal with neurotic customers who don't know what they want while virtually hovering over their shoulders. Gates included the example in his book not because it's a good idea or will ever happen, but because he likes the image and bets that his readers will like it too and thus decide that the technology he's talking about sounds wonderful.)

Which brings us back to *System Shock*, which definitely displays a...fuzzy understanding of digital technology. It's a host of little things: references to the compact disc revolution as a big historical moment, for instance. (Which, yes, the CD was important, but in hindsight its moment as the dominant storage medium for digital technology was no longer or more significant than the floppy disk. There was nothing particularly good about the CD except its higher storage capacity, and in fact, it was a pain to write to. It was always certain to give way to a high-storage capacity medium with better read/write capacity, and, perhaps more significantly, to cloud-based distribution where storage stops being an issue in the first place.)

Likewise the idea that I2 would rise above other tech companies because it offered a standard that it had no stake in, as opposed to, say, the cold-blooded way Microsoft operated is noble. And, given the failure of the open source movement to completely take over the world of digital technology, hopelessly naive. Or, for that matter, the biggest issue: the idea of a single type of chip that somehow unifies toasters, computers, train schedules, airports, and everything else into a single network, an idea that completely disregards the fact that toasters and airports have very little to talk about.

Which gets at the heart of why this fuzzy understanding is for our purposes interesting: because it lets us make a distinction between two kinds of science fiction. The first is, as I understand it at least, what's usually called by its adherents SF, and which was previously called hard science fiction. It describes stories in which the specific material conditions of technology are what matter. This is what I'm basically making fun of *System Shock* for failing at being. Basically, the problem here is that imagining the "information superhighway" as a single entity that just connects everything is hopelessly misguided.

And it's misguided in a way that really matters in terms of how the technology works and affects people. The nature of the Internet, as the sixteen years since Richards wrote *System Shock* have largely shown, is that it works on a logic of hodgepodge and jerry-rigging. The Internet is manifestly not a single unified structure, but a massive din of independently developed technologies, data structures and purposes that are lashed together by a bunch of (at least initially) half-assed technologies that are only upgraded when they stop working. And it's glorious. This is, in fact, exactly what makes the Internet as transformative a technology as it is.

But Richards gives no sense of that. By failing to display any fealty to the actual technology he's writing about, he ends up talking about something that doesn't quite connect to any actual reality. Richards falls into what was a standard trap of Nineties fiction about the Internet by viewing digital technology primarily as a mechanism of control and homogeny. This badly misjudges what actually happened in two regards. It badly underestimates how hard it is to sort through the masses of information moving around online. Second, it fails to appreciate how transformative self-publishing would be—both on the large scale of things like (ahem) blogs and on the smaller scale of social media. The result was a future that's less Skynet and more LOLcats. And, crucially, the reasons for this are exactly the things Richards gets wrong about the technology.

That said, this is exactly the sort of science fiction Doctor Who generally isn't. For the most part, it belongs to a different tradition—one in which instead of focusing on tracing the probable consequences of scientific development we focus on broader ideas. For the most part, *System Shock* isn't really about how digital technology works. It's about its monsters, the Voracians, which are a sentient network of office machinery that decide to destroy all organic life, and so invade planets by masquerading as corporations.

This is responsible for most of the really clever bits of the book, including the revelation that the Voracians' speech patterns are modeled on the language of board meetings. If you view this, as opposed to the bits about digital technology, as the heart and soul of the book, the whole thing makes a lot more sense. The digital stuff is really just window dressing, put there because that's the sort of stuff that goes in a story about offices written in the mid-to-late nineties.

So the book isn't really about technology. It's about cultural norms and values, and it uses the freedom that science fiction offers to radically reconfigure the structures of society in order to explore what a society with a particular set of values would look like. In its purest form, this gives the opportunity to explore genuinely alien values—values that are not human. In practice, this never happens and alien cultures are all, as the great Ted Sturgeon points out, just Meiji Japan with scales. (And, of course, the idea of the purely alien is meaningless anyway.) Instead, the values tend to be distorted or extend versions of existing human values. So, for instance, the existing culture of a 1990s corporate office gets extended to an entire civilization and we get the Voracians. Here the technology used to explain how the society is set up is just a plot device to get to the main point: social transformations.

The problem, though, is that the book is trying to have it both ways. It wants to be a techno-thriller and the Doctor Who version of *Dilbert*, despite the fact that those are irreconcilable goals. The techno-thriller, after all, depends on the power of the technology, whereas *Dilbert* depends on the absurdist combination of power and impotence. The former depends on understanding the implications of the technology, the latter depends on sending it up.

And the really unfortunate thing for this book is that, in 2013, it's actually so close to being right, since everything it got wrong now looks absolutely typical for corporate blather about the Internet circa 1995. Because if you were writing a

Doctor Who version of Dilbert, particularly one set in the 1990s, you'd pack it full of mentions of the information superhighway. But you'd do it because you were highlighting how silly the Voracians are and how little they understand human culture. The absolute last thing you'd do is have the Doctor take any of it seriously. Instead, here Doctor delivers a line like "we're dicing with death on the information superhighway to hell," a line that apparently should in some way be taken seriously. (This is a narrow point—the book indicates that the Doctor meant the line as a joke, but that it came off as very serious. But frankly, the idea of Tom Baker delivering that line should not even have a vague hint of seriousness.) Instead, the book tries to both be a pastiche of the absurdity of corporate culture and a serious-minded thriller about the future of digital technology. As Doctor Who is only good at one of those, doing them both at once is a bad idea anyway.

In this regard the TV episode to compare it to is *The Bells of Saint Johns*, a ludicrous attempt at a techno-thriller based around the prospect of "the wi-fi" stealing people's souls. Being as it's done in 2013, it seems almost unforgivable in terms of actually reflecting how computers work. (As, actually, do several other Steven Moffat plot elements, perhaps most notably his virus that affects every counter and clock in the world in *The Eleventh Hour*.) This again highlights the way in which *System Shock*, for all its rough edges, actually comes terribly close to fitting into a perfectly sensible genre. Because, in fact, the wilfully sloppy techno-thriller has, by this time, become a coherent genre unto itself. Neither *The Bells of Saint Johns* nor *The Eleventh Hour* rankle because they're obviously depicting the sort of fictional computers that we recognize from decades of stories like, well, *System Shock*. And so what makes *System Shock* such a delightfully strange artifact is precisely that it exists at the point where "sloppy techno-thriller" and "legitimate exploration of technology' were diverging, and thus ends up caught oddly between them.

There's one aspect of all of this that's worth remarking upon. If, as I have proclaimed, the end message of Doctor Who is that the solution to alchemy is material social progress, what do we make of the fact that Doctor Who is, generally speaking, at best merely apathetic about the actual material details of science and technology, and at worst (as this story ends up somewhat demonstrating) actively hostile to it? (Especially since "evil alien office machinery" is a far more Doctor Who idea than "generic techno-thriller" is.) It would, after all, seem as though in order to effectively achieve the goal the series has set out for itself, it would have to take technology seriously. And yet it doesn't—even in the modern series, as we've seen, there's a persistent tendency to not take technology entirely seriously.

This is what we're going to work towards over the next stretch of essays. Until then, I leave you with the two greatest sentences ever written about computers. For context, Voractyll is a sentient computer virus. The Doctor has created a deviant strain of the virus, and has unleashed it onto the network:

"With a digital hiss, the original Voractyll creature pulled back on its coils, then sprang at its opponent. It wrapped the Doctor's copy in a tight loop and hurled subroutines at it."

God I love trashy Nineties cyberspace writing.

How Easy it is to Be a Magician (*The Masque of Mandragora*)

It's September 4, 1976. ABBA are at number one with "Dancing Queen," a fact that says more about the zeitgeist than anything else I can hope to say. But for the sake of completism, it stays at #1 for all four weeks of this story. Wings, Bryan Ferry, Rod Stewart, The Bee Gees, and Elton John and Kiki Dee also chart. And The Ramones release their first album, which is the sort of thing that means we can start talking about punk when the mood strikes us.

Since *The Seeds of Doom*, the most obvious thing to say happened is that Harold Wilson unexpectedly resigned as Prime Minister on March 16th, and the Labour Party voted James Callaghan in as his successor. This is, as it happens, not going to end well. In other news, Apple Computer was formed, the UK actually won Eurovision (with Brotherhood of Man's "Save Your Kisses for Me"), the Soweto riots began in South Africa, Viking 1 landed on Mars, the Son of Sam killings began, and Big Ben broke down for nine months.

While during this story, Mao Zedong dies, which is a kind of definitive end to an era. A fatal air collision occurs in what is now Croatia between a British Airways flight and a Yugoslavian flight, killing 176. The 100 Club "Punk Special," an iconic and formative punk concert that put The Damned, The Clash, The Buzzcocks, The Sex Pistols, and Siouxsie and the Banshees all on a two-day-long bill, takes place, which means, again, that we can really talk about punk just as soon as Doctor Who bothers to make that option relevant. In a less fortunate rejoinder to this, U2 forms.

While on television, we have the start of a new season of Doctor Who, and a return to the wide world of human history. *The Masque of Mandragora* fits into the increasingly classic genre of shoving the Doctor into a historical period for a runaround with evil space aliens. But its real focus, very much the product of its writer, Louis Marks (who was a Renaissance scholar when not writing sci-fi) is on the conflict between magic and science. Which gets us to a fairly large and fundamental philosophical point about Doctor Who: to what extent is it a science fiction show, and what are the implications of that?

There is, you see, an unfortunate tendency towards scientism within science-fiction fandom in general. I mean, I'm obviously a fairly pro-science kind of guy, and I salute the people who devote time to taking down "alternative medicine" cranks that, in a real and literal sense, kill people. But there's a second flavor of skepticism that amounts to an effort to eradicate non-scientific thinking and proposing that science is the only meaningful form of truth. This is the sort of skepticism favored by the so-called new atheists, anti-postmodernists of the Alan Sokal school, and other groups of people I am less than fond of. In fact, in extreme cases— people who take Alan Sokal seriously, most noticeably—I kind of loathe them with every fiber of my being.

So needless to say, I am disinclined to see Doctor Who dragged in as a supporter of rigorous and absolute skepticism—the belief, if you will, that science constitutes an overarching ideology that ought reign supreme over all others. Plenty of others, however, want exactly that. To some extent this desire is understandable—the series, after all, comes out of a postwar investment in science as a sort of saviour of mankind. As we've noted several times, including in *Genesis of the Daleks*, there's a tendency to equate "is a scientist" with "is a rational and reasonable human being" within early Doctor Who (and even more recent Doctor Who: *Utopia*, for instance). But Doctor Who's relationship with that perspective has always been tense—it's just as likely to look at the dangers of science as to praise it. More interesting is its relationship with science's supposed opposite, magic. And in this regard *The Masque of Mandragora* is exhibit A for those who suggest that Doctor Who sides unambiguously with scientific rationalism.

It's easy to make this mistake. A quick glance at the story finds the Doctor talking about how the Renaissance is the midpoint "between the dark ages of superstition and the dawn of a new reason." One of the two main human villains is an astrologer, characters can be more or less defined by whether they are scientific or superstitious, and the Doctor's end advice is basically "keep developing science." This looks like more of a defence of hardline skepticism than almost any other Doctor Who story. Which is why I'll make my stand here for why, whatever Doctor Who is, it's not a defence of hardline skepticism. Because one of the basic rules of criticism like this is that you take on your opponents' best argument, not their worst. I can point out how *The Mind Robber* gestures at mystical thinking until the cows come home, but that's easy. No, if there's a story to have the fight with hardline skepticism on, it's the one that, at least initially, looks like it's on their side. But it's not. You can tell, for one very simple reason: Louis Marks isn't an idiot.

One of the most important things that rarely comes up when talking about the Tom Baker era is that Baker is the last Doctor to have stories written by writers who also wrote for the Hartnell era. Marks is one of three Hartnell-era writers to write for Baker, having gotten his start with *Planet of Giants*. In one sense, this is actually the story's biggest weakness. Marks's sense of pacing and timing—which we should note was wonky even in 1964, when his story required Verity Lambert to hastily edit the last two episodes into one after the episodes were shot—is strangely out of step with almost everyone else writing Doctor Who in the 1970s. Even the scripts of Terry Nation, with his skill at keeping a story moving (albeit often without going anywhere), don't feel as stilted as Marks's.

But underneath the pacing we have a writer who cut his teeth on Doctor Who under David Whitaker, and who is still in a fundamental sense writing for that show. This is not entirely a bad thing. Yes, Marks's scripts are a bit pokey and don't quite hold together into the climaxes, but both this and *Planet of Evil* are extremely intelligent scripts with lots of good ideas in them. In fact, that's the basic difference between Hartnell scripts and Baker scripts. While both are intelligent scripts that play with the world of ideas, in the Hartnell era, Doctor Who was simply a vehicle to explore a lengthy series of interesting ideas. By the Baker era, it's more than just that. And unlike the exploding spectacles of Baker and Martin-style "idea" scripts, Marks's ideas are as intelligent and complex as you'd expect from someone with a PhD in Renaissance studies.

Which is the other thing about Marks and this script: there's just no way that Marks is so ignorant of the Renaissance as to suggest that the period was meaningfully a transition between superstition and reason. I mean, yes, obviously the Renaissance was a major step forward in numerous intellectual and artistic fields. But the idea that it was based on throwing off the superstition of the past is, as a matter of historical fact, farcical. This should be evident to anyone who even thinks about the Renaissance, an era most defined by the return of classical Greco-Roman thought into mainstream European culture.

The thing is, the Greeks and Romans, brilliant as they were, were not arch-rationalists. There is no sane way to argue that Aristotle or Plato were empiricists. Nor is there a good way to argue that the political institution of the Catholic Church, which dominated the Renaissance, was opposed to mysticism. (Indeed, given that one of the major groups of hardline skeptics are the new atheists, it's more or less impossible to ally this viewpoint with religion at all.) To say that the Renaissance, which was about adding one set of non-rationalist thinkers into the worldview of another, is the dawn of scientism is sloppy in a way that no actual expert in the Renaissance would be.

And all of this is compounded by the fact that, other than some speechmaking about rationality and how the Mandragora Helix is just advanced science, everything about this story looks like magic. Much like *The Daemons*, we're in that territory where a scientific explanation ends up being little more than a wordy confirmation of an underlying mysticism. The Mandragora Helix works according to a logic of astrology—it moves in to influence the Earth, then moves out again. Its goals are not scientific but alchemical—it wants to eat human nature, not some definable energy source. And in the end, the Cult of Demnos and the astrologers are, broadly speaking, right.

But perhaps most problematically for the arch-rationalist crowd is the fact that the supposed scientific explanation is not so much nonsense as it's absent. This begins to relate back to what we were talking about last time. Quite frankly, a show that is aspiring to support hardline rationalism needs to be proper SF: invested in the material realities of science and technology. That is to say, it needs to not just hand-wave about "a case of energy squared," but to have some actual relation, if not to a real scientific concept, at least to some sort of coherent worldview. (For all of its faults, *Star Trek* does relatively well with this. None of its technology makes a damn bit of sense, but its writers do an excellent job of having a coherent set of technobabble explanations that at least look like they come from a defined scientific worldview, even if that worldview is inexplicable to the audience.)

Doctor Who, in other words, betrays the hardline position on a very fundamental level here. It flagrantly fails to actually support science or rationalism. Sure, it opposes evil astrologers, which is certainly a worthwhile pursuit, but in the end, Hieronymus isn't evil because he's an astrologer but because he's an authoritarian dick of the sort who are always evil in Doctor Who. Indeed, Hieronymous continues to have power in the narrative, largely because, as Miles and Wood point out, the basic structure of the medium is on his side. When he predicts the Count's death, he audience knows then that the Count is toast. Yes, he's wrong on the method of the Count's demise, but the very fact of Hieronymous prophesizing it still foreshadows it and conveys information to the audience. This gives Hieronymous an irreducible power within the narrative that no amount of rhetoric about rationalism and science can defuse.

This raises the very sensible question of why Marks makes such a big deal of the rationalism/superstition debate. As it turns out, we've already answered this question: Marks is writing a script that in many ways resembles the Hartnell era, and the point of historicals in the Hartnell era was always to be educational. The lines about rationalism and superstition aren't declarations of the theme of the story. They're little educational nuggets—the Renaissance simplified for eight-year-olds. And it's not, taken that way, a terrible explanation—the Renaissance was a major moment in the history of science, and its non-rational ideas did give birth to the scientific method in the end. Yes, it's overly simplified, but a lengthy explanation about the evolution of science as a methodology and the reconstituting of classical ideas into a Christian society isn't really pre-teen material. But, crucially, since we are not eight years old, we should not be using the kiddie history lesson for our sense of what is going on in the story.

So if the story isn't a rousing defense of arch-rationalism, what is it? It's certainly not a defence of arch-mysticism. Rather, it's a proper dialectical moment. Magic and science are presented as opposites, and the Doctor crafts a position that's a synthesis of them, not a midpoint between them. Let's look to the end. We are told that the Doctor has not permanently stopped the Mandragora Helix, but has rather delayed it by five hundred years so that it will arrive more or less in the present day of the viewer. In other words, the story is overtly eschatological, suggesting that humanity is again at a point where it risks losing its very identity and drive. But, equally significantly, it suggests that humanity is at the point of some sort of major intellectual/cultural leap forward that's akin to the Renaissance.

We're left with, in essence, another variation of the stock Hinchcliffe scenario of an ancient threat long-considered defeated that's coming back for one last round. Except we're coming at it from the other end: we're seeing its presumptive defeat but being told it has one last round, as opposed to seeing its last stand, as we typically do. But, crucially, there's a big piece of symmetry in place here. The idea of the past returning is, after all, the heart of the Renaissance itself.

In other words, the structure of this story is almost fractal. At multiple points and levels, we are faced with the idea of the past returning and affecting the present. Which makes sense—the idea of the past returning is fundamentally recursive. But more importantly, even though this story doesn't feature the Time Lords in any active capacity, it gives us a sense of another step in the evolution of what the Time Lords are.

The last definitive statement we came to (in Volume Three) was that the Time Lords were protectors of history in a Marxist/dialectical sense—that they safeguarded the tendency of history to lead towards certain ends. Now, under Marks, we see an acknowledgment of the logical consequence of that. If history tends towards certain ends, this suggests that there are also common sorts of historical events: that the past does, in fact, recur. This offers an interesting situation in which the Time Lords would simultaneously have to be seen as a progressive force pushing the universe towards some sense of destiny and also as an atavistic force that continually bends the arc of history backwards towards recapitulating past events.

And furthermore, we should look at the particulars of how the Doctor defeats Mandragora. Here I must give particular thanks to one of my readers (which leaves me in the slightly unusual position of thanking someone named Dr. Happypants), who observed that the Doctor's defeat of Mandragora is based on clever use of schoolboy science. This gives a particular sense of the Doctor's synthesis—he commits to the pragmatic and the clever in a way that reflects a specifically British form of patriotic self-identity. He does not endorse either ideological position. Instead he commits himself to the material act of advancing history through its messy reality instead of through the sort of grand manipulative design of Mandragora (who actually is a representative of hardline mysticism).

The Masque of Mandragora, of course, doesn't completely go through the door that it opens. It doesn't connect the materialism of history with its circularity. But it does introduce some key concepts. First, it helps us start to understand another way in which the show can be materialist without committing to hard SF. If we accept this atavistic tendency of history then we find a new sort of materialism that can be captured: accurate depictions of recurring social forces. And so Marks is, here, paying attention to material social progress by paying attention to the nature of the Renaissance, at least once you get past the didacticism for children.

The result is, as with *Planet of Evil*, not one of the classics of its era. But it's also not a massively flawed number. This is in some ways helpful, at least for critical purposes. We can see what the Hinchcliffe era is doing more clearly in a script like this than by looking at a massive classic like *Brain of Morbius* or *Genesis of the Daleks*. Much like *Pyramids of Mars*, this is not a great story. But in all likelihood, the next one to walk through this door will be.

And also like *Pyramids of Mars*, however, there's one annoying bit of business to get through before that story comes.

Havirefny Genafyngvba: Ubj Qbrf Vg Jbex?

Thanks to Bennett for the essay idea.

In *The Masque of Mandragora*, the Doctor finally gets around to settling a decade-plus continuity debate by explaining that the reason everybody has been able to talk to each other over the past thirteen seasons is "a Time Lord gift" that he's sharing with Sarah Jane. As with most attempts to explain the basic premises of the series, this makes no sense whatsoever and opens up far more questions than it answers.

These days the explanation has been fleshed out from the Virgin Books explanation: the translation is because of the TARDIS's telepathic circuits, although the particulars of this remain hazy. It's not clear if the TARDIS reads the minds of the people around it and then deposits the intended meaning of a statement inside people's minds, or whether the TARDIS simply has an exhaustive knowledge of languages that it checks. The implication is usually the latter: the TARDIS generally translates written language as well these days, which suggests it doesn't need the mind crafting the speech to be present for translation to occur. Instances like the untranslatable language in *The Impossible Planet* suggest that there are just some languages that aren't in the database, although why Gallifreyan can't be translated in *A Good Man Goes to War* is obscure, to say the least. Even if we use the database explanation, there are problems, however, as the TARDIS also translates the Doctor and his companions' speech, presumably by altering what Sarah Jane is saying so that it comes out in Italian (since the Doctor specifically shares the gift with Sarah, not generally), and thus has to read her intended speech in her mind and translate it.

But all of this is terribly inconsistent. The TARDIS can't translate written language in several instances, and there are cases where it can't translate spoken language (*The Leisure Hive*) or a language that takes more idiosyncratic forms (*The Ambassadors of Death*). Case-by-case explanations might be made: the non-functionality of the TARDIS in *Ambassadors of Death*, for instance, could in theory have impacted its translation abilities. But at the end of the day the basic fact remains that TARDIS translation is idiosyncratic at best.

This is almost a relief. The implications of universal translation are, after all, absolutely nightmarish. The discussion of whether translation is accomplished via mind-reading or a language database, for instance, quietly elides a huge philosophical point about what the meaning of language is. How, for instance, would a mind-reading TARDIS handle sarcasm, or outright lying? If Hieronymous were to write a sign saying "there's a big pile of gold this way" that in fact led to a death trap, would the TARDIS translate the sign to suggest that there's a pile of gold, or would it reflect Hieronymous's intention and say "this sign is trying to trick you into walking into a death trap?" What of actually ambiguous sentences? How does the TARDIS successfully adjudicate a sentence like "he gave her cat food," which could suggest a woman receiving cat food, or a woman's cat receiving food?

Answering these questions requires us to decide what language and speech actually mean—whether a sentence that's poorly phrased means what its speaker intended, or what the actual words mean. If the former, lies and sarcasm become a problem. If the latter, ambiguity does. More broadly, the existence of universal translators suggests that language is actually universally translatable. This is not straightforwardly the case: idioms, figures of speech, and particularly jokes are notoriously impossible to translate. And yet the TARDIS can handle all of them with aplomb, calmly retaining the idiomatic expressions of the Optera and Menoptra in *The Web Planet*, and casually maintaining the rhyme scheme of the "above between below" rhyme in *The Five Doctors*.

Again, this is not merely a matter of quaintly advanced technology. The issue isn't merely that it's hard to phrase things in a different language, but that different languages allow you to express entirely different sets of thoughts. Translation isn't just a matter of literal meaning. And yet it's phenomenally rare for anything to be lost in translation in Doctor Who; it's not just that everyone appears to speak English, it's that everyone appears to think in mid-20th Century English with an RP accent or a language that can be translated to English readily. Of the long list of unnervingly imperialist tendencies in Doctor Who, this may actually be the most unnervingly imperialist of all.

Tellingly, when TARDIS translation fails in some way, it's almost always in a way that interestingly advances the plot. It is not a new observation that the TARDIS takes an almost authorial role in the Doctor's adventures, taking him, as declared in *The Doctor's Wife*, where he needs to go as opposed to where he wants to go. This suggests a TARDIS committed to the Doctor's personal growth, but it could equally well imply that the TARDIS has some sort of larger plan and is translating speech in accordance with this plan, allowing gaps in meaning only when strategically useful to it. How mad one wants to allow this theory to become is largely a personal matter, although there are certainly some plum opportunities.

A final and more sinister option comes from the fact that the Doctor describes translation as a "Time Lord gift" and not in terms of the TARDIS. The TARDIS may be the material technology used to accomplish the gift, but that doesn't mean it's the TARDIS doing the translating. The idea of the Time Lords as observers of history is well-established throughout Doctor Who, but the consequences of this are not necessarily thought through. In a later essay I suggest that the nature of the Time Lords is that their memory and individual perspective defines time and history for them. If we take them also to be powerful forces in the universe, it follows that their interpretation of history would be equivalent with the writing of history—that is, by observing history, they fix the ambiguity of events into particular narrative structures such that history is not so much written by the winners as by the observers. In other words, the Time Lord gift might be taken as a means of interpreting history so as to fix it into a particular form. Taken to its full extent, this might even suggest that it fixes conversation and speech according to a particular ideology or logic—one of Aristotelian narrative logic, specifically. The Moffat-era declaration that "we're all stories in the end," in this light, seems less a philosophical comment than a declaration of intent: the TARDIS isn't only a machine to take the Doctor where he needs to go, it's a machine to ensure that there's a story once he gets there, even going so far as to reshape language itself to be more dramatic.

I Don't Look Back; I Can't (*The Hand of Fear*)

It's October 2nd, 1976. ABBA remains at number one with "Dancing Queen." After two weeks, Pussycat unseat them with "Mississippi," which sounds innocuous until you realize that Pussycat is a Dutch country music band, and that this is one of those moments where the British charts do what sane and rational people never would. Rod Stewart, Manfred Mann, and Chicago also chart.

In other news, the InterCity 125, a high speed train, begins service in the west of Britain. The Cultural Revolution formally ends in China. Cearbhall Ó Dálaigh resigns as President of Ireland after being loudly denounced by the Minister of Defense. As for Fords, Motors begins production of the Fiesta, and Gerald flubs badly in a debate against Jimmy Carter.

While on television, it is the end of an era. And not the obvious one. Yes, this is the story where Lis Sladen departs the series. But in terms of screen time, she's only actually two-thirds of the way done with her tenure in Doctor Who and related shows. This is, for her, a sort of midpoint pause in her Doctor Who career. It's the end of an era, but it's not "Goodbye Sarah Jane."

That is not, of course, to say that the apparent end to her involvement with the show is anything less than vital to this story. But in this case, we shouldn't focus on the sentiment of Sladen's departure, because doing so loses sight of a far bigger fact: this story marks a fundamental shift in the relationship between Doctor Who and contemporary Britain. More specifically, this is the story where Doctor Who gives up on the idea that it is by default grounded in the real world of the viewer.

The easiest way to show this is with some raw facts. So here they are. *The Hand of Fear* is the last story until *Terror of the Vervoids* to feature a companion from contemporary Britain—a run of over a decade. The last story prior to this not to feature one was *The War Games*. And even the Troughton era never lacked at least one companion from Britain, albeit from its history. The last time there were no regulars who were overtly from Britain—the only time, in fact, in the series' history before this point—was *The Daleks' Masterplan*, which fell between stories featuring Vicki (from Britain's future) and Dodo (from its present). After this story it will be more than four seasons—until *Logopolis*—before the Doctor travels with anyone who is from Earth at all.

More telling, however, is this: from *The War Machines* (the first story in which the TARDIS straightforwardly arrives in contemporary Britain) to *The Hand of Fear*, twenty-eight of the sixty stories depict contemporary Britain under threat: a rate of about 47%. From *The Deadly Assassin* through *Survival* only eleven of seventy-two do: a mere 15%[1].

---

[1] For pedants, the twenty-eight stories from *The War Machines* to this are: *The War Machines, The Underwater Menace, The Faceless Ones, The Evil of the Daleks, The Web of Fear, Fury from the Deep, The Invasion, Spearhead from Space, The Silurians, The Ambassadors of Death, Inferno, Terror of the Autons, The Mind of Evil, The Claws of Axos, The Daemons, Day of the Daleks, The Sea Devils, The Time Monster, The Three Doctors, The Green Death, The Time Warrior, Invasion of the Dinosaurs, Planet of the Spiders, Robot, Terror of the Zygons, The Android Invasion, The Seeds of Doom,* and, of course, *The Hand of Fear.* The eleven after this are *Image of the Fendahl, The Stones of Blood, Shada, Logopolis, Time-Flight, Mawdryn Undead, The Awakening, Resurrection of the Daleks, Attack of the Cybermen, Silver Nemesis,* and *Survival.*

This, more even than the departure of Sladen, is the major legacy of this story. *The Hand of Fear* is where that line of thought essentially gives out and Doctor Who, basically until 2005, abandons contemporary Britain as a primary setting. It doesn't abandon contemporary Britain entirely, but the intrinsic connection the series had to it up to this point goes away. And here I'll adopt something of a heretical position regarding Doctor Who—albeit one that Miles and Wood sketch out as well when they suggest that the whole Yeti-in-the-Loo idea was a disaster: the abandonment of contemporary Britain was a good thing.

First, let me add the corollary that the return of it in 2005 was also a good thing. The problem, much like the temporary waning of the influence of social realism on Doctor Who, is not that Doctor Who set in contemporary Britain is a bad idea, but rather that the next major insight into how to do Doctor Who set in contemporary Britain wasn't ready to emerge out of the culture in 1976. The idea needed to be rested for a bit. I'm not going to go into considerable detail on how Davies solved the problems, but they were most certainly solvable in the general case. (Inconsiderable detail: a combination of successfully merging soap opera narrative techniques with Doctor Who [which both Letts and Nathan-Turner had done at earlier stages, but soap operas evolve too, so you can do that trick more than once in the history of the show] and enmeshing Doctor Who into the overall television landscape so that it existed as a cultural event, thus giving it a metafictional tie to contemporary Britain instead of just a literal one. *Bad Wolf* is, after all, the most contemporary-Britain focused story of the first season.)

But in terms of 1976, contemporary Britain wasn't working. I mean, to some extent we can just say this aesthetically: if we look at the Tom Baker years, the contemporary Britain stories have had a visibly lower average quality than the others. This isn't an issue specific to *The Hand of Fear* at all. It's not as though one mediocre earthbound story invalidates the genre. But a lengthy string in which the stories focusing primarily on contemporary Britain are mediocre is a bigger problem. And that's much closer to the situation at hand.

The Hand of Fear happens to also double as a story that clearly illustrates the problems. But to some extent, those problems are best illustrated in terms of a different issue: the evolving career of the Bristol Boys, Bob Baker and David Martin. The thing about Baker and Martin is that the level of quality of their writing coincides almost exactly with what era they're writing for. Under Barry Letts, they were one of the best writing teams, penning three very solid stories that are among the most interesting things the Pertwee era has to offer. Under the show's upcoming producer, Graham Williams, they're going to bring up the rear, with all of their stories fairly widely reviled and not even particularly praised by the proponents of the era. And under Hinchcliffe, they're... decidedly mediocre. Not particularly offensive in either of their stories, nor particularly exciting. In other words, we have here two writers whose Doctor Who careers have a fairly straightforward downward arc.

I don't mean this as an insult to Baker and Martin at all. Almost every writer who has an extended engagement with Doctor Who over multiple producers and Doctors has a downward trend in quality at some point. Some have an upward trend first (Robert Holmes), but eventually, pretty much every writer who sticks around on the series for a long time enters a period of terminal decline. Even David Whitaker, who I consider one of the three great writers of the classic series, had trouble in the end, though he lucked out and had a good rewriter to cover his inability to get scripts for *The Ambassadors of Death* to work under the Letts/Dicks regime.

That shouldn't surprise anyone. As we talked about with *The Sontaran Experiment* (the previous Baker and Martin story), and have talked about in general throughout the blog, television evolves. A writer who is good at 1971 television is genuinely unlikely to be as good at 1976 television, because being good at 1971 television means you are good at a different set of visual and storytelling conventions than works in 1976. This is why most of the claims that the new series should hire writers from the old series are misguided— because as good as many of those writers were, they're not 2011-style television writers. For a sense of how problematic this can be, one need only look at the later scripts of Terry Nation, Brian Hayles, Gerry Davis, or, yes, Bob Baker and David Martin. (Actually, given the series' adamance on only commissioning established writers, and given that he's co-written an Academy Award-winning film, Bob Baker is by miles the classic series writer who has the best chance of writing for the new series.)

And what's particularly interesting is that it is the very things that made, say, *The Claws of Axos* very good that makes *The Hand of Fear* so lackluster. *The Claws of Axos* worked because it treated every aspect of the show as a performative spectacle instead of messing around with "realism." And *The Hand of Fear* doesn't work because it makes zero effort towards any engagement with the real world.

The thing about *The Claws of Axos* is that it was a UNIT story. I have documented my mixed feelings on UNIT at length, and have even suggested that the earthbound format might have worked better without them. But that's too simple. The more accurate way to phrase it is that, when adopting the earthbound format in 1970, the show could have gone in either of two directions: the glam performativity it actually went for, or the more ripped-from-the-headlines approach of, say, *Doomwatch*. Or, to put it in the terms we framed in the *System Shock* entry, whether it wanted to be a sci-fi show in the cultural commentary tradition, or whether it wanted to be an SF show.

It picked cultural commentary. Decisively. In fact, and this is something for which Letts will never get the recognition he deserves, the refusal to go for SF in 1970 did more to ensure the preservation of the Whitaker/alchemical tradition in Doctor Who even more than Whitaker's fundamental role in the show's development did. By refusing to go SF in 1970, when going SF was by far the easiest thing for Doctor Who to do, Letts ensured that Doctor Who was never really going to be an SF show.

And UNIT was a big part of that. As we saw last volume, UNIT is in effect a cast of exaggerated caricatures. By centering itself on that concept, Doctor Who made a fundamental commitment to being a show that wasn't about material realism. UNIT was consciously designed to look like a television army as opposed to a real one, which set the tone for the entire show. Yes, this had its own attendant weaknesses, including making it far too easy for the show to spin its wheels in the latter days of the Letts era. But in terms of the overall direction of the show in the period where Baker and Martin got their starts, UNIT was essential. And Baker and Martin were very, very good at the spectacle of the UNIT approach.

Now Baker and Martin are stuck writing a contemporary Earth setting without UNIT to serve as an interface between the Doctor and contemporary Earth. And without UNIT, Baker and Martin are left with a story that isn't about anything. It's a story in which a nuclear reactor is threatened and risks exploding, and in which military airstrikes are called in, but in which there's no connection to the world. The nuclear reactor could be out in a quarry for all we care, and for all practical purposes it basically is. There's a profound emptiness to this story.

In some ways, the airstrike sequence characterizes this perfectly. Airstrikes have been a common enough trope of earthbound stories in Doctor Who, such that there's nothing inherently odd when they get called in. But there's always the lurking refrigerator logic of how it is in seventies Doctor Who that nobody has noticed all the domestic military actions in the UK and the alien invasions. In the UNIT days, UNIT serves as an interface for these situations. Because the UNIT era was really the Doctor juxtaposed with the UNIT show, not the Doctor juxtaposed with our world, it was OK when things occurred that made it very clear that Doctor Who wasn't in our world. (And remember, up until *The War Machines*, nothing in Doctor Who ever really made it impossible to say that the world of Doctor Who is just like ours except that the Doctor is in it. The only exception is the cricket game in *Daleks' Masterplan*, and that was a joke. It's not until the show ostensibly becomes part of our world that it becomes impossible to reconcile within it: a problem that occurred for Russell T. Davies as well.)

But now the show runs in our imaginations, and that makes it more real. When Moffat says that Doctor Who takes place under your bed, this is the exact era of the show he's talking about. Not the UNIT era, but this era where the monsters are ideas and the adventures happen not on made-up worlds but in stories the audience knows. Far, far more of the audience has some sort of instinctive familiarity with *Frankenstein* than they do with Welsh mining towns. So when we talk about which story is more "realistic," we should remember that there is a sort of reality that the obviously fictional has that the "real world" never can. Ideas are, in their own way, as material as anything.

So in that case, the airstrikes, absent UNIT, are a problem. Because at that point, everything that makes it sensible to set Doctor Who in contemporary Britain is gone. The show is still not an SF show, but it's also not commenting on anything. With UNIT, it was a commentary on a cultural image of the military. Here is a world that doesn't have any new and interesting ideas that make it different from ours, but which is still a place where the military randomly calls in airstrikes on domestic targets and that doesn't affect anyone's life. It might as well be Zog.

And at that point, you may as well just give up on the approach. There is no point to doing contemporary Britain if you're going to do it like this. So, for very sound reasons, the show stops. For the most part, from now on, when the Doctor intersects contemporary Britain, he does so at its margins, far from the eyes of authority. He doesn't engage in the whole world, but in particular corners of it that lend itself to particular stories. He still might have a skulk around a country manor now and again, but nobody from the outside world is likely to come rescue him, and whatever the threat is will actually be in the manor instead of off through a time portal.

In fact, the show does more than stop. It disappears completely into the realm of ideas, and stays there for the next four stories, after which the show goes through what is, to date, its most decisive shift not to involve a major cast change. It all begins by jettisoning Sarah Jane. Actually, in some ways it is more accurate to say that it's initiated by the decision not to immediately replace her, and then to replace her with Leela, the first outright unearthly child we've had since Susan. Companions have left before, after all. Jo Grant was at least as landmark a companion as Sarah Jane, but her departure wasn't nearly as much of a watershed moment because she was replaced with a similar sort of character. But the transition from Doctor Who being this sort of show and Doctor Who being the sort of show that does *The Face of Evil* is profound.

And another part of it is, of course, Lis Sladen. This isn't the end for her, but nobody knew it at the time. This was the apparent end of the single best actress to tackle a companion to date. To be fair, Sladen benefitted enormously from having Katy Manning before her. Manning made colossal strides with the role of companion, and was the first person to really do so since Deborah Watling. Sladen was thus in the enviable position of inheriting a role that, under Manning, had just undergone a dramatic improvement. Unless she bombed it, all she had to do was stick around for a few years and she was basically guaranteed to look like one of the two best actresses ever to play the role. Even if she was only pretty good, she could probably fine-tune it and do quite well for herself.

Lis Sladen, of course, was far more than "pretty good." She took the role up after the most transformative actress ever to have played it and then transformed it just as decisively. With Manning, the companion had a role in the narrative beyond being a plot device/exposition tool. Now Sladen changed the role so that instead of being a supporting character, the companion could, done right, be a co-lead. And, of course, her final scene with Baker is amazing. It's the best TARDIS scene of the classic series, bar none, and is one of only a handful of sequences in the classic series that can stand up to the new series. Both Baker and Sladen are amazing in it, and it really is all them, as the scene was apparently largely improvised.

Equally significant, though, is the tone of the departure. For the first time since Susan left, there's a sense that neither the companion nor the Doctor want to go. The love between the Doctor and Sarah is obvious, and it hurts to see them forced apart. There's a reason that, for years afterward, there was the constant sense that Sarah should come back, and it lies here in her ending—in the fact that the Doctor could come back for her, and that she clearly wants him to.

This means that The Problem of Susan here recurs in its most intense sense to date. The Doctor doesn't return for her. This says bad things about him. In a strange sense, this parallels Baker's own problems with the role that begin to arise after this story. Perhaps the highest praise that can be given to Sladen as an actress is that she was the only co-star Baker was unfailing in his respect for. After she was gone, Baker was actively resistant to the idea that there should be another companion at all; he wanted to be the show's sole star.

But an ugliness creeps in here that I would be remiss not to mention. Not just for Baker, though. The Doctor himself is sullied here. The audience is made to want him to return for Sarah, and he never does. The audience may have been perplexed why he never returned for Susan, but if we're being honest, Susan is nobody's favorite companion. Sarah is many, many people's favorite companion. It's terribly brave scriptwriting to do this: it's the first real jump towards making the Doctor less trustworthy instead of more since *The Power of the Daleks*, and the first really, shatteringly decisive one since *The Massacre*. This scene fundamentally changes who we think the Doctor is.

And that parallels the real ugliness in Sarah Jane's departure. But, of course, this ugliness is also what Sladen plays so jaw-droppingly well when she returns in *School Reunion*. Because, as I said, this isn't actually the end for her. She gets to come back.

No. It's the end for the Doctor. Not just in the Problem of Susan sense where he is, in a real sense, sullied by this. There's something more fundamental happening here. Because we're also given an event that can force the Doctor to abandon Sarah. He hasn't kicked a companion out since Susan, and that decision was at least fundamentally about Susan. Now he kicks Sarah out, not because he wants to, but because he has to. Because he has been summoned to Gallifrey. Even Sarah is awed by that, saying, "I can't miss Gallifrey." But she has to. The Doctor has to face this alone. The last time the Doctor went to Gallifrey, it was to be condemned to die. Whatever he's been called back for this time, it must be something absolutely massive.

Far More Than Just (*The Deadly Assassin*)

It's tough to pin down, but it's probably somewhere in 1994—I've got myself around 6th grade for this one. I've still got the VHS tape on my shelf. Well, by my hand now. Because my shelves are cluttered, I had to move two objects to get to it. The first of these was a DAPOL action figure of K-9—the inexplicable green one. The second was a bottle of Yankee Candle-branded Balsam and Cedar oil for use in an oil diffuser. I went on a cedar kick a few years back in my ritual and meditative use, for reasons too arcane to go into. It was in my bedroom, near the table where I put candles and incense. I wrote this in an armchair maybe two yards from it, which is also where I watched these episodes, and, indeed, most of the episodes discussed thus far in the project.

The cover is exactly what I remember - Tom Baker in Prydonian robes staring straight out of the tape. He's looking straight at me, right now: an eerie reconstitution of Patrick Troughton's screen-peering for a no-longer new media age. The tape was on the third shelf of books. This is a fact that will be lost on anyone who does not know me well; in the first year of my PhD program, I had started class before I had finished unpacking. Or, rather, I had done a very hurried unpacking in which I shoved books on shelves from out of boxes, however they were packed, vowing to organize my library later.

In one of my classes, we were reading Henry Petroski's *The Book on the Bookshelf*—a history of the bookshelf. Which is to say, it's a history of how we store and organize our knowledge. It ends with an amusing essay proposing various ways in which one could organize one's books in the modern world, ways beyond the obvious ones like alphabetically or by subject. Petroski shares amusing anecdotes or comments on the pros and cons of various methods. He talks of one friend who had a room that was, among everyone he knew, considered a marvel of interior design because she had orchestrated a complex scheme for her library whereby various regions of the room, from paint to decor to the books themselves, were organized by color: reds fading through oranges to yellows across a wall of the room.

One method he proposes is by strict order of acquisition. That is to say, he proposes that whenever you get a new book, you shelve it immediately to the right of the previous newest. And I realized that, for reasons relating purely to my own idiosyncrasies, I could actually remember to a usable degree of detail the order in which I had gotten my books back to about 5th grade. Since then I've stretched it back further, though only with about five or six books from childhood. Currently my library runs from *Matilda* by Roald Dahl to Lance Parkin's biography of Alan Moore.

I like this system of organization for several reasons. First, I find it convenient. It is easy to maintain, and does not require me to ever commit periods of time to full-scale library reorganizations unless for some reason I reintegrate books obtained from my parents' storage, and even then I have to do a hefty chunk, as I leave small gaps for that purpose. I just put the newest book on the rightmost position on the newest shelf, and buy new bookcases as needed.

More importantly, I find it easy to use. I value my media collection. It is very large—I believe it required over 40 boxes the last time I moved. It spans a very long period of my life, and I have strong associations with almost every part of it. I remember very well the circumstances I obtain and read books in. It borders on synesthesia. As a result, I can find things this way - by going "Ah, yes, I'm going to need Constance Penley's *Nasa/Trek*, which I bought on Amazon in Chicago along with two other books on slash fiction for my Master's thesis." This highlights a second organizational benefit. There tends to be logic in what books I get at what time—I will get a number of books on one topic or by one author—so the shelving doubles as an approximate subject ordering. There are a few glitches I allow myself to facilitate this—sometimes I will move a newer edition of something back to where I acquired the original edition because the associations are stronger for me there. Other moves happen for similar idiosyncrasies: if there is a series of books in which I got one volume at a different time from the rest, I might still shelf this volume with the others for convenience.

I say all of this to explain how a given point of shelving in my library represents a moment in my history. When I pulled this video off of my shelf, I didn't pull it from the Doctor Who videos section, but from the space that, to the best of my knowledge and recollection, is immediately between the book or video that I experienced before *The Deadly Assassin* and the ones I absorbed after (*Pyramids of Mars* and *Shada*, as it happens). The fact that the video came from the third shelf indicates further that it is one of the oldest media objects I still own, from one of the earliest points of my life in which I had anything that could be called a media collection. And that period of my life is, in a literal sense, looking at me right now, middle school oculus glaring at me from a grotesque perch on the opposite end of my life.

The VHS is the movie version of *The Deadly Assassin*, with an 85 minute runtime and no cliffhangers. This is how the early video releases (and often US reruns) of Doctor Who pacakaged stories, and it's why I continually stress that Doctor Who stories should be understood episodically instead of in this format. The movie versions do real violence to the sense of pacing in the stories, eliminating the logic of cliffhanger and discrete episode that, in the best-written stories, governs what happens when. The result is often awkward, with odd delays in what happens that serve no obvious narrative function when the episodes are recompiled as cinema.

The back of the box is a monument of VHS blurb writing:

DOCTOR WHO ON TRIAL FOR MURDER! The President of the Time Lords is dead. Only Doctor Who predicted the assassination. Only Doctor Who was seen firing the rifle. And at his trial, with quite probably three hours to live, who else but Doctor Who would announce that he now wants to run for President!

THE DEADLY ASSASSIN is a Masterpiece of special effects and pure spectacle. It's the ultimate showdown between Doctor Who and his arch enemy, The Master—now more deadly than ever in his twelfth, and final, regeneration!

And, yes! This is the program with the now-legendary hallucinatory battle to the death between The Master's relentless, mysterious champion and the wildly wily Doctor!

I remember this one vividly. Everybody does. It's one of the big classics: the story where we properly encounter Gallifrey for the first time. It's a self-consciously epic story. And yet watching it this time, I noticed for the first time the chalk outline of the Time Lord President, complete with the tracing of the elaborate Time Lord robes, and I burst out laughing. It isn't just an epic, in other words, but one with a wealth of odd details and incongruities.

This essay is, accordingly, a bit of a beast—a massive chunk of verbiage. In four distinct episodes, although also quite viewable in movie form. Ladies and gentlemen, *The Deadly Assassin.*

Part One

(This section was written prior to *The Day of the Doctor*, and has not been revised to reflect that story.)

It's XXXXXXX. XXXXXX are at number one with XXXXXXX . XXXXX, XXXXXXX, XXXXXXXX, and XXXX also chart. In other news, XXXXXXX in XXXXXXX on the XXXXXXXXX, and XXXXXXX took place. While on television, XXXXXXXXX's time playing the Thirteenth Doctor comes to an end in a stunning sequence in which XXXXXXXXXX. She does not regenerate. The series ends.

We are told, at least, that's what will happen. Because *The Deadly Assassin* says so. You get twelve regenerations, and then you're dead. And this is, for some reason, taken enormously seriously. Russell T. Davies tried to retcon it with a line in *The Sarah Jane Adventures* and... failed. It didn't stick, and he quickly admitted it was just a throwaway line.

What's bewildering, of course, is that it's a throwaway line in *The Deadly Assassin* too. And yet for some reason, that line is taken as gospel by a significant number of people, as some rule that demands that Doctor Who is, with Peter Capaldi, coming perilously close to its end. *The Deadly Assassin* is, in this regard, accurately named. There remains a bizarre faction of Doctor Who fans—a death cult of sorts—who view this story as something that provides a necessary reason why Doctor Who as it exists must someday die completely. This is the story, it seems, that assassinates Doctor Who itself.

However, if we're being remotely sane, of course we know the show will survive. Writing your way around the twelve regeneration limit is as trivial as Holmes dropping it in is. The bewildering thing, though, is that when the time comes and XXXXXXXX regenerates into the Fourteenth Doctor there are going to be fans who are upset. Somehow, this story has created the phenomenon of fans who want the show dead, and who will be terribly upset if it doesn't end forever.

Certainly, in a narrative sense, this story feels like an attack on the show. *The Deadly Assassin* willfully cuts a transgressive path across what Doctor Who is. Its most basic heresy is its concept: the decision to set a story in the midst of the Time Lords themselves. Not merely to have them as supporting characters facing the same crisis as UNIT, as they were in *The Three Doctors*, but to set a story in their culture and, more to the point, to do a story that depends on the details of that culture.

Conventional wisdom would have it that the content of this transgression is simple Holmesian mockery. The Time Lords are shown to be stodgy old men in funny robes. Holmes's stated inspiration is the structure of British universities, but let's face it—this is an overly mild version. Holmes is, in essence, making Gallifrey into the House of (Time) Lords: an aristocratic edifice that's fundamentally detached from real events and is at best able to ineffectually nudge events around. But even this is too simple.

Consider one of the more interesting supporting details of *The Deadly Assassin*: the fact that the centerpiece of Time Lord society is the Panopticon. The term is borrowed from a prison design created by Jeremy Bentham (himself the namesake ancestor of the Jeremy Bentham well known within Doctor Who fandom for somehow convincing the bulk of it that *The Gunfighters* was the worst Doctor Who story ever).

Bentham's Panopticon is a prison designed around the idea of surveillance. The cells themselves are arranged in a ring around a central tower. This central tower—the Panopticon itself—can thus observe any cell at any time. Thus the people in the cells can never know whether they are being observed or not, and so will operate on the principle that they are always being observed. The Panopticon, in 1976, was in a strange vogue. It was also one of the major examples in Michel Foucault's landmark study *Discipline and Punish*, which saw its first English translation in 1977. Here Doctor Who, seemingly independently, crosses that path as well. Again, history repeats itself across structural levels.

The Deadly Assassin, however, subjects the Panopticon to observation. The logic of the Panopticon is indistinguishable, after all, from that of the camera within a piece of visual narrative. The camera can observe any portion of the diegetic world, but is itself unobserved within this world. Until this story, at least, where Tom Baker, bereft of companion, begins to function by conducting a running dialogue with the camera. But this is just a reiteration of a larger point: that the Doctor has always been unobservable by the Panopticon. Even as they send him on occasional missions, he possesses a larger freedom to work outside of their sight. Not even the viewer has this power – they cannot observe the Panopticon, because they're a part of it. But the Doctor occupies a space beyond both the narrative and the viewer – the sole figure in the system who can both observe the Panopticon and avoid being seen by it.

Equally unseen, however, is the Master. Like the Doctor, he is capable of moving unseen by the Panopticon. In fact, the bulk of Time Lords have never even heard of him. Here, more than ever, he forms the Doctor's exact opposite. It is implied that the conflict between them is a more fundamental ordering principle of the universe than anything the Time Lords involve themselves in—a more ancient conflict than Gallifrey is set to handle. Outside the gaze of the Panopticon—the all-seeing ordering principle—they fight. This is inevitable—primal, even. A prophecy. An impossible alchemist will rise from the deep and strike the Time Lord dead.

It is, after all, alchemy. In several regards. We have always defined alchemy—and magic itself here—as a practice based on the belief that manipulating a symbol is in some sense equivalent to manipulating the thing it represents. In a spectacular world in which mere images are real beings, alchemy is by necessity the prevailing logic. And alchemy is embedded deep within Doctor Who's DNA. This is our first conspiracy theory: that David Whitaker, at once the most important figure in Doctor Who's development and the least understood, created a show that is genuinely magical—that is, in a sense, alive and thinking for itself. And more to the point, that Whitaker's influence cannot be erased from within the show.

I say our first conspiracy theory because the origin of Doctor Who is, of course, inseparable from the greatest conspiracy theory of the 20th century, the Kennedy Assassination. The two events are in fact the same event. And *The Deadly Assassin* invokes that event directly. The entire thing is a Kennedy Assassination joke: hence the infamous and overly influential mention of the CIA. The Doctor is the (wrongly framed) Lee Harvey Oswald, left to frantically search for the shooter on the grassy knoll. The giveaway clue, of course, is that the Time Lords, otherwise modeled from British aristocratic institutions, have a President as their head of state. This sets up a strange parallel—another repetition of history. As the story creates the moment of the show's death it invokes the moment of its birth.

But wait. The Master is the one who plots the assassination of the President of the Time Lords. Thus the Master is the one who kills Kennedy. Following this logic, the Master is the creator of Doctor Who. By reconstituting both the beginning and the end of Doctor Who within the Panopticon, the Master seizes a fundamental and total control of the narrative, becoming its writer, performing his own dark mirror of the Doctor's alchemy in *Genesis of the Daleks*.

This brings us to another case of history repeating itself: the Master alchemically seizes control of the narrative of Doctor Who. This is reflected within the narrative by the Matrix sections, in which the Master forms a world in which he has absolute power. Within Doctor Who, the Master creates a new show—a nightmarish parody of the show itself.

It is worth stressing early on how disturbing these sequences are. Because episode three—the one that takes place primarily within the Matrix—is unlike anything we have seen in Doctor Who before. We've spoken before of how the show grapples with violence. Here we see that pushed to its limits: an entire episode of gripping, well-shot action sequences comprised of nothing but fear and brutality. The Doctor spends the entirety of the episode wounded, dirty, and struggling not to save the universe but only to survive for a few more minutes.

Even his visual iconography is taken from him. He trades much of it in as soon as he arrives on Gallifrey, having to give up his coat and scarf for robes in order to sneak around. But in a particularly ingenious and subtle moment, when he first ventures into the Matrix he regains his most iconic prop—his scarf. Nothing else of his outfit makes it, just the scarf. And within minutes, that's destroyed. The message is clear—the Doctor loses the very things that make him who he is here.

The nature of what is done to the Doctor here is sheer violence to the concept of the show. The Doctor is shot. Twice. Consider that, at the end of *Interference*, the notion of Pertwee's Doctor dying of a gunshot wound in the dirt is transgressive brutality for that era. Here, less than three seasons past that point, the Doctor takes two gunshot wounds, albeit non-fatally. Then, for good measure, he is drowned, in a sequence of utter viscerality: his head is shown bobbing underwater. It's a shocking sequence. But unlike the violence of *The Seeds of Doom*, here it feels earned. The Doctor is in a TV show created by the Master, being hunted like an animal. That should feel scary. And it does.

Perhaps, in fact, too scary. The Doctor is, ultimately, able to worm his way out of the Master's narrative. But the brutality of it, in a literal sense, fatally wounds him. This is the story where Mary Whitehouse's constant refrain of "teatime brutality for tots" finally drew blood, resulting in Philip Hinchcliffe being swapped out for Graham Williams.

This is, in other words, narrative collapse in the extreme. The subversion of the Time Lords is one detail in a far bigger and more terrifying picture that reaches across vast swaths of the series' psychochronographic terrain. Crucially, it is not mere happenstance that has left this story with the narrative gravity necessary to doom the show in the future. There is a reason for it.

Part Two

It's November 5, 2011. (At least, it was when I first wrote this.) Tomorrow will be thirty-five years to the day since Part Two of this aired. Rihanna is at number one with "We Found Love." Also in the top ten are Maroon 5, LFMAO, and Kelly Clarkson.

An account of the news. Top headlines on CNN are an army staff sergeant testifying in a trial who is charged with murdering civilians in Afghanistan, and a story on a Mississippi ballot referendum to outright criminalize abortion by declaring a fetus to be a person. The *New York Times*'s website leads with Greek Prime Minister Papandreou surviving a confidence vote and the death of Colombian guerrilla leader Alfonso Cano. While the *Guardian*'s top headlines are lawyers warning Downing Street that interns should be paid, and the declaration that a global recession is closer because the G20 summit has failed.

Out of the headlines but very much in my mind are the Occupy movements: a growing swirl of global leftist activism. These movements are interesting, attracting more sympathy on the right than any leftist movement I have seen in some time, while deeply unnerving chunks of the establishment left, who predict their inevitable failure with inexplicable glee given how sympathetic their stated aims are. As is surely unsurprising given my inclinations, I am tremendously fond of them and think objections to their tactics are ludicrous. Their tactics are visibly adapted from those of the Situationist International, who, we should note, ran the most successful leftist uprising of the 1960s. Yes, it failed, but it failed spectacularly and having come impressively close to success. There's not a better playbook to pull from.

The general spirit of the times is uneasy, as though things are on the brink of some collapse. The Occupy protests are not in the headlines today, as I said, but have been a mainstay for weeks now. Before them were the London riots: *The Guardian* has several stories on the results of government inquiries into them today. It's a slow, ratcheting up of tension—a growing sense that some historical shift is beginning. One reaches around, trying to find some larger narrative to fit into. Conspiracy theories appeal.

I've already published many of my thoughts on the conspiracy theory as a genre in my defunct blog *The Nintendo Project*. The conspiracy theory is the flash of ordering insight behind the chaos of a world that defies explanation. Alan Moore, one of this project's major intellectual influences, observes that there is obviously a conspiracy. There are, in fact, hundreds of them, all running around. But the truth of the matter is that the conspiracies just crash into each other. No conspiracy actually runs the world, in no small part because conspiracies, like everything else in the world, are run by power-mad incompetents. The horrifying truth is that there is nobody driving this thing. The world is, as he puts it, completely rudderless.

But the conspiracy theory gives the illusion that it is otherwise. That there is some sort of master signifier that orders creation. Understood this way, we realize that the paranoid logic of the conspiracy theory is more prevalent than we give it credit for. Hardline rationalism is, in the end, as much a conspiracy theory as any other—an adamant belief that there exists one explanation that accounts for everything that there is. In this case, that only in mathematics will we find truth.

The conspiracy theory is a defect of reasoning given animus. The compelling nature of an explanation metastasizes from solving a material problem to an ordering principle of the universe. History repeats itself. These data points form into patterns, patterns form into narratives, and we find ourselves with a story that explains everything.

These narratives are not false. This is the true appeal of the conspiracy theory. Even the most vile and baseless contain somewhere within them a germ of truth. A conspiracy theory is not nonsense, but a kind of parasense. Birtherism is a pathological form of the observation that the election of a biracial and cosmopolitan intellectual marks a tipping point in the cultural balance of power in the United States. 9/11 Truthers are an insane form of legitimate observations about how the underlying geopolitical narrative that led causally to 9/11 has been erased in favor of 9/11 as an origin point for a new geopolitical configuration. The conspiracy theory is never quite wrong even as it is never usefully right.

Clearly a new approach is necessary: a new heuristic for a world with a surplus of conspiracies and a deficit of ordering principles. A new kind of paranoia. A new kind of conspiracy theory. Let us further refine the rules here. We will define this type of conspiracy theory through its construction; bootstrapping it, to borrow from the language of computer science. We will create a new form of conspiracy theory by writing a conspiracy theory about it. And by dint of the larger rules of this book as a structure, we will form it in relation to the Doctor Who story entitled *The Deadly Assassin*.

This is not, of course, by accident. *The Deadly Assassin* is, after all, the point of death for Doctor Who as a concept. We know from *The Brain of Morbius* that death is the engine that drives alchemy itself—a thesis reiterated in softer forms through previous stories. If *The Deadly Assassin* is the point of death for Doctor Who—and at the very least it is a point of death for Doctor Who—then it is the perfect place to locate this effort. This is a story that can, at least for a moment, be located at the absolute center of Doctor Who—in the Panopticon, if you will. A conspiracy theory about it gets at the heart of Doctor Who.

The logic of the conspiracy theory is the opposite of falsifiability. For some, this is prima facie evidence of their inadequacy. The criterion of falsifiability, however, was never designed for this sort of situation. Its originator, Karl Popper, set out not to define truth but science, distinguishing it from metaphysics. Science is, under Popper, defined by falsifiability. A claim is scientific if it is possible to disprove it. Science, under Popper, proves no affirmative truths; it merely provides statements that can in theory be disproven, but that in practice have resisted all attempts to do so. Those theories that have resisted the most are considered the most important and fundamental; those that have resisted fewer attempts are emerging and interesting theories.

You can read as much Popper as you wish and you will never find a line that dismisses the importance of metaphysics. This is largely because Popper does not dismiss them, but merely treats them as a separate category from science. But if you think about the structure of Popperian science—a wealth of contingent truths, any of which could shift out from under the very foundations of knowledge with a single experiment—this is hardly a surprise. Popper, by coming up with a clear and simple rule that drives science, renders it more postmodern than any attempt at deconstruction ever has. (There is a reason that the hardest of hardline rationalists—the likes of Alan Sokal—despise Popper as well.)

The conspiracy theory, like Wikipedia and occultism, functions on a logic of verifiability. This is a profoundly different logic than falsifiability, requiring the demonstration of affirmative evidence as opposed to the repeated demonstration of failed counter-evidence. Superficially this may seem more straightforward and sensible, but consider the fact that the lengthening autumnal nights are just as much solid evidence that the sun god Orb is dying as they are that the earth's angle of rotation with regard to the sun has changed due to its position within its orbit. Verifiability is nice, but there's a limit to its ability to sort amongst plausible explanations, whereas two falsifiable explanations are more likely to be subject to an either/or experiment.

We cannot possibly function without the logic of verifiability, but it has its limits. Or perhaps its potentials. Within the logic of verifiability, multiple contradictory perspectives become true. The Situationists, to whom this book is as indebted as much as it is to Alan Moore, build from this logic their idea of the spectacle: the contradictory nexus of representations that, through material systems of power, is actualized, not just in spite of its contradictions, but because of them, becoming the dominant paradigm of the social order.

The spectacle is the apotheosis of the conspiracy theory: the fusion of all conspiracy theories into a worldview so totalizing that it has become material. As Guy Debord puts it, "When the real world is transformed into mere images, mere images become real beings." Thus the spectacle rejects attempts to deny its reality as a mere computational matrix.

If we cannot deny this reality, what other options are available to us? Continuing within the theory of the Situationists, we have two major artistic concepts: détournement and the derivé. Détournement is defined by the Situationist International simply as "the reuse of preexisting artistic elements in a new ensemble." That is, taking established portions of culture and transplanting them into new contexts, or severing them from existing ones. To take an example at random, mashing up the iconography of the House of Lords with an ancient alien civilization of "Time Lords" and the Kennedy assassination. Or putting a starchild, two schoolteachers, and a grumpy old man into an alien city inhabited by Nazi salt shakers. The derivé, on the other hand, is "a technique of rapid passage through varied ambiences." Designed originally for use on physical geography, "in a derivé one or more persons during a certain period drop their relations, their work and leisure activities, and all their other usual motives for movement and action, and let themselves be drawn by the attractions of the terrain and the encounters they find there." So, for instance, an extended and aimless journey through the whole of space and time. For instance.

Subsequent development, particularly Alan Moore's suggestion of "Ideaspace," a realm in which ideas arrange spatially into a landscape of associations, suggest that the Situationists have in fact identified two instances of the same tactic. The derivé détournes the city, and détournement is simply a derivé through psychic spaces.

For this to work, we must find a psychic equivalent of the attractions of physical terrain. This is inherent in the concept of Ideaspace. Moore's standard example for how Ideaspace works is that in Ideaspace, Land's End and John o' Groats are adjacent to one another despite being defined as being opposite ends of Britain. If we take a broader view, we can see clearly how Ideaspace works. History repeats itself. These repetitions form leylines and paths through psychic spaces—patterns that can be walked, albeit not in a physical sense but a mental sense. To follow from our earlier examples, instead of literally traveling through the whole of space and time we can imaginatively do so, creating, perhaps, a narrative contrivance that allows for rapid passage through varied conceptual ambiences. So that we can go from Renaissance Italy to a contemporary thriller to a surrealist battle in a computer for the fate of the House of (Time) Lords.

The derivé is used to produce psychogeography: an account of the subjective experience of physical space and its influence on life. Here we create instead, long after we've developed the technique in practice, its obverse: psychochronography: an extended perambulation through imaginary places. The lines we walk are, of course, conspiracy theories. But here they are conspiracy theories with their usual motives for movement and action stripped out. We do not seek a totalizing explanation, but seek instead to slide out from one conspiracy theory into the next—to fall out of the world, if you will. A conspiracy theory is not a path out of the labyrinth of the spectacle, but merely one of a multitude of roads and paths within it. We will reconfigure the psychic space to our liking. We will tear out its logic and replace it with our own.

In contemporary media terms, we call this the retcon: the retelling of a story along an aggressively different logic that is alien to the original telling. Which means that *The Deadly Assassin* is itself a psychochronography of Doctor Who. Its technique and the technique of this project are indistinguishable.

But this has always been true of this project; history repeats itself. However, a reiteration is distinct from the initial event. This is what historical progress is: the sum total of deviations from progressive iterations of events. It is necessary to repeat ourselves. It is necessary to revise. We can see these repetitions across this story. *The Deadly Assassin* assassinates Doctor Who. It also, however, features a literal assassination—the striking down of the President of the Time Lords at the end of its first episode. This is itself a recurrence of the more famous assassination of a President, JFK. This event is itself indistinguishable from the start of Doctor Who. These events are iterations of a larger whole. There are big things afoot. As we said, this is a narrative collapse story.

We have already developed a basic principle of narrative collapse in the first volume. To reiterate, a narrative collapse is a story in which the threat is not merely to the lives of the characters but to the basic ability to tell further stories. It's not just the characters who might die; the ability to do any sort of story at all with these tropes and concepts again is in danger. Doctor Who does these types of stories periodically: they're the standard operating procedure for new series finales where, for instance, the Daleks threaten to destroy reality itself or the Doctor finds himself retconned out of his own history. Obviously the Doctor generally escapes the narrative collapse, finding some way to reconstitute the narrative after its complete collapse. But there are rules: there is always some sort of great cost paid for the aversion of a narrative collapse. Most often it's a regeneration or the loss of a companion. What is the cost in *The Deadly Assassin*? After all, the Doctor has no companion in this story and does not regenerate.

As it happens, there are three costs, all among the most severe the series will ever pay. The first, as we have discussed, is the setting of an endpoint for the show. The second is one we've also mentioned, and will deal with primarily in a few more entries' time: the sacking of Philip Hinchcliffe at the hands of Mary Whitehouse. You can trace a line of causality from this action to the cancellation of the show a decade later. It is not the strongest argument that can be made, requiring as it does the almost total condemnation of both Graham Williams and John Nathan-Turner, neither of whom are all bad, but as with any conspiracy theory, it is not quite wrong either. The fallout from Hinchcliffe's sacking results in a neutered show less equipped to handle shifts in the television landscape than it has been before; a show that begins to die by a thousand cuts. It is the third consequence, however, that is potentially the most damning: fandom.

I have, throughout this project, and, for that matter, throughout my life, maintained a love-hate relationship with fandom. As is obvious by the fact that this project exists, I am as much a ridiculous fanboy as they come. But my issues with fandom as a gestalt entity are numerous—throughout the first two volumes I complain bitterly about the inaccurate received wisdom of fandom and how it obscures the reality of early stories. In later volumes fandom will be blamed for imposing a frankly dull order of continuity and demand for the "epic" that strangles the wonder of Doctor Who. In any era, fandom is a problem. Indeed, the case that fandom led to the demise of Doctor Who is far stronger than the case that Hinchcliffe's sacking did. And this story has one of the strangest roles in fandom imaginable.

On the one hand, *The Deadly Assassin* is as much a cornerstone of the series' continuity *as The War Games*, if not moreso. Its reconception of Gallifrey becomes the canonical one. This is in and of itself a bewildering phrase: "canonical." This is perhaps the most chilling legacy of the story—it creates an idea that there is some sort of unifying explanation of Doctor Who. This is the most bizarre conspiracy theory of all: that Doctor Who forms a single coherent story that is resolvable and understandable. That there is such a thing as "canon."

But what is strangest about this is that, at the time of transmission, Doctor Who fans flipped out at the story because of its capricious disregard for past canon. The story that went on to become the cornerstone of Doctor Who's canon was, initially, hated for its violation of that same supposed canon. The cornerstone of this is Jan Vincent-Rudzki's review of the story, in the first issue of the second volume of the fanzine *TARDIS* (1977). The review floats around a fair amount: a simple Google search will find it.

There are many things that are very strange about this situation. First of all, canon is based on a sort of extreme exegesis of the text itself, but that exegesis still isn't even possible at this point in the series. There are no VHS tapes or copies of past episodes. At best you have novelizations, and at this point only 26 of the preceding 87 Doctor Who stories even have those. The series has not obtained repeatability in a meaningful sense. Accordingly, the very evidence required to build a canon doesn't exist yet. Any attempt at canon in late 1976 is wholly archeological, stitched together from memories and the distorted recollections of paratexts. At this point, Countdown to TV Action contributes more directly to the sharable evidence of what Doctor Who is than the actual series does. Among the sixty-one un-novelized stories are such tentpoles of the eventual "canon" as *The War Games*, *The Time Monster*, *Power of the Daleks*, and *Evil of the Daleks*.

Second, and perhaps more importantly, only the fans believe in canon. The production office doesn't give a damn. In all likelihood, the problems Vincent-Rudzki identifies all come down to one very simple thing: Robert Holmes in no way cared enough about consistency with past stories to check them. Because let's be clear about how Robert Holmes works and why he creates iconic bits of Doctor Who "canon." Take an example from *Spearhead from Space*—the establishment of the Doctor's two hearts. If you look at *Spearhead from Space* it's clear why this got established: Robert Holmes needed some reason why, upon discovering the Doctor's unconscious body, the hospital would call the

Brigadier. So he gave the Doctor two hearts so that there would be something weird they'd notice. Never mind that several stories had previously established the Doctor's single heart. Holmes needed him to have a weird physical feature, and so he acquired a second heart. This is the exact opposite, in other words, of a serious attempt to build mythology. This is a harried hack coming up with narrative expedience with no regard for the long-term except perhaps what he's going to spend his paycheck on.

Any notion of canon is, in other words, being imposed entirely from outside the show. Nothing in the show itself is attempting to be anything other than an ongoing TV show working roughly along Terrance Dicks's old rule that anything from within the last year can be reintroduced without explanation, while anything older than that should be assumed to have been forgotten by the audience. Canon is something that a particular weird set of fans do; if anything, it's a complete misreading of how the show works.

So the cornerstone of Doctor Who canon—the story that envelops both the beginning and end of Doctor Who—has several problems. The show cannot possibly have a canon, it is not intended to have a canon, and the most prominent person at the time to argue for its canon, Vincent-Rudzki, lacks the ability to review the text in sufficient detail to construct a canon.

Here, then, we make our stand. Here is where we build our new conspiracy theory. In the most obvious gap available. *The Deadly Assassin* is the centerpiece of Doctor Who's canon, and yet nobody has made a sincere effort to build a canon out of it. Let us, then, break the rules productively. One of the primary tricks that this book series has used since its first page is that it has been willing to treat any given moment of Doctor Who as the Panopticon that fixes the actions of all other moments. This is one of the basic derivés we've developed. We let ourselves drift along the logic of each story on its own, instead of in accordance with the supposed master map of Doctor Who. Let us, then, take that to its most radical level. Let us ask precisely what is going on in *The Deadly Assassin* and allow, for a moment, at least, that to be the primary lens through which we view the series.

Our methodology will be straightforward: we will assume that whatever we see in *The Deadly Assassin* is correct, and that all other stories must be understood in terms of it. Beyond that, we will apply a sort of Occam's Razor to the matter—we will attempt to alter readings of past stories as little as possible, but will always opt to retcon them instead of rejecting the apparent implications of this one. What we won't do is care at all about what comes after this story: we are going to limit ourselves entirely to what could have been observed or remembered in 1976.

Our technique will be equally straightforward. We will play the same game that Vincent-Rudzki is trying to play, albeit with a significant advantage: we have reference books and video recordings of episodes that Vincent-Rudzki necessarily lacked. The form will be, then, a mad folly—an extended fanzine rant written 35 years too late. A systematic debunking of Vincent-Rudzki's points long after they stopped being immediately relevant. Or, to put it another way, an attempt to see what other default positions were available to fandom.

A thought experiment. A alternate reality. Or perhaps just a computational matrix.

Part Three

It's...

Vincent-Rudzki starts with what seems the most obvious point to raise: the fact that we are told that this is the greatest crisis ever to face the Time Lords. He raises the obvious point in response to this: "I suppose Omega was only a minor nuisance!" This is actually a subset of a larger problem, one Miles and Wood deal with at length in their side essay "Did Rassilon know Omega." Essentially the problem is this: *The Three Doctors* and *The Deadly Assassin* give us two very similar stories about the early history of the Time Lords, but in one Omega has the starring role, and in the other Rassilon does.

Miles and Wood suggest that, until 1983 at least, the easiest explanation is that Omega and Rassilon are two different names for the same person. This is not a bad explanation, but it is wholly extra-textual, and, more to the point, seven years too new to count here. A more textual explanation exists. We know that two things occurred at the end of *The Three Doctors*, after all: Omega's black hole becomes a supernova, and the Time Lords utilize it as an energy source. Now, in *The Deadly Assassin*, we are told that Rassilon took the heart of a black hole to Gallifrey. By far the easiest way to account for this in the context of *The Three Doctors* is to assume that Rassilon obtained the heart of the black hole—presumably the Singularity—at the end of *The Three Doctors* when it exploded as a supernova.

The only problem this theory raises is it requires that a massive amount of time pass on Gallifrey between *The Three Doctors* and this story, but that's easy enough to account for even if you demand that the Doctor and Gallifrey age in sync. It's not that hard to assume a lengthy jaunt around the universe for Pertwee without Jo—he ran off without her in *The Green Death* and nobody thought anything of it, after all. Centuries can fall between *The Green Death* and *The Time Warrior*, or, for that matter, between *Planet of the Daleks* and *The Green Death*. And after the massive reconfiguration of Time Lord society that *The Three Doctors* implies, it presumably doesn't take that long for the civilization to reconstitute itself according to a completely new order of things. The ancient past of Gallifrey doesn't have to be nearly as ancient as people tend to assume. 1976 is already ancient history today, after all.

We also should, in thinking about all of this, deal with *Genesis of the Daleks,* in which the Time Lords opt to sneak around and try to destroy the Daleks in their past rather than meet them head-on as a threat. The Time Lords subjected the Daleks to history there. Why, then, would we be surprised when the Time Lords are themselves subjected to history? Far from a strange anomaly unique to *The Deadly Assassin*, this seems the point of the exercise. Following *The Three Doctors*, the Time Lords have been cast down into the gristle of history.

Vincent-Rudzki moves on, declaring that "the next blunder was the guards," specifically their existence given the supposed omnipotence of Time Lords. Again, however, we saw that omnipotence broken in *The Three Doctors*, with the Time Lords abandoning Omega's black hole for a new source of energy. The easiest assumption is simply that this new form of energy renders the Time Lords in need of guards. But all of this ignores a larger issue with *The Deadly Assassin*— the strong sense that eventfulness of this sort is profoundly rare on Gallifrey. Never mind the degree to which the guards undermine the past sense that "the Time Lords were supposed to be very powerful." Regardless of how necessary the guards are to deal with any given threat, what threats are they actually there for in the first place?

Again, there's a relatively easy explanation that alters very little: the guards, like almost everything else we see, are a matter of ceremony. This is, after all, wholly familiar to a British viewer, where the phrase "guards" can readily be linked to the ceremonial Changing of the Guard, said guard having essentially no practical role other than being changed periodically for the benefit of tourists. The scarlet clothing of Gallifreyan guards even seems to evoke the Queen's Guard. The Guard are, like everything else on Gallifrey, the empty repetitions of past historical moments.

Vincent-Rudzki next objects to the nomenclature of the TARDIS, specifically that it is identified as a "Type 40 TT Capsule" whereas previously it was a Mark 1. Well, first of all, here we have the benefit of better record keeping than Vincent-Rudzki enjoyed. Properly, it's the dematerialization circuit that is described as a "Mark 1" in *Terror of the Autons*. All we know is that the Master's TARDIS uses a Mark 2 circuit, and that the Monk's TARDIS in *The Time Meddler* is a

"Mark 4." Nothing, in other words, suggests that the Doctor's TARDIS as a whole is a Mark 1.

At this point it may appear that I'm just picking nits, but there are two important points here. The first is simply to expose the absurd speciousness of discussions of canon in general. The second is that Vincent-Rudzki, in poking holes that don't exist in the story, is missing the actual point. He asks why there is only one Type 40 TT missing, but that's not a question. It's an answer: the Doctor is unlike the other renegades we have seen as well. We knew his TARDIS was older than theirs, but we had no idea that it was so old as to be overtly obsolete and no longer in use. We assumed that the TARDIS was a pinnacle of Time Lord technology—and indeed, in *The War Games* this seemed overtly to be the case. But now we come to understand that it is, in fact, a completely crap TARDIS.

I will skip most of the bits in which Vincent-Rudzki complains about the seemingly-depowered Time Lords, as I've already proposed that treating *The Three Doctors* as a turning point in Time Lord history makes sense of all of this. I will similarly leave be his assertion that the problem with Holmes's CIA joke or with Time Lords who have bad hips is that "there is a time and a place for humour, and this wasn't it" as a simple aesthetic difference instead of a factual one. But I will finger his claim that "Time Lords are aliens and do not need to conform to human motivations whatsoever," a fact he believes to have been supported by *The War Games* of all stories.

First of all, let's note the obvious thing about Time Lords: as non-human species go, they sure look like humans. Sure, plenty of aliens do, but equally importantly, plenty don't. In the iconography of Doctor Who, true alienness is defined by monstrosity. But more than that, the Time Lords have always appeared as a race with an inherent tie to human culture, if not to humanity itself. They're the guardians of history and were first set up on opposition to the guardians of war. These are concepts that are only meaningful in a human-esque cultural context. To treat the Time Lords as completely alien is fundamentally absurd. To be truly alien they would need to have no understanding whatsoever of basic human concepts like "time" and "war" and "history."

Vincent-Rudzki next complains about a variety of anomalies surrounding the Doctor. Again, however, Vincent-Rudzki finds inconsistency where none exists. The overall point of everything he identifies—that the Doctor has premonitions where other Time Lords don't, that he scoffs at how primitive Time Lord technology is, and that he has seemingly been forgotten by most of the planet—is that the Doctor is in some sense special. Bewilderingly, Vincent-Rudzki manages to complain about the exact opposite, complaining that the Doctor should be better known because "it's very rare for a Time Lord to leave Gallifrey." But this is the entire point! The Doctor is here shown to be, if I may cheat and borrow a phrase from the future, far more than just another Time Lord. After all, the strong sense is that his fight with the Master is, at this point, bigger than Gallifrey—that this isn't a case of the Doctor being caught up in Gallifreyan affairs, but one of Gallifrey being caught up in the Doctor's affairs.

Again, this is not inconsistent with what has gone before. The Doctor has never appeared like an everyday member of his society. But notably, he's never seemed notorious either. Consider his initial descriptions: he is "cut off" from his people, and he says to the War Chief that he had "every right" to leave. His granddaughter was seemingly unusual in her psychic abilities, although he thought of returning to his home world to help her develop them. And of course there is *The Mind Robber* and its implications, if we want to go in that direction. But since Vincent-Rudzki says the reason the Time Lords should know who the Doctor is because he saved their bacon in *The Three Doctors*, let's just take our explanation from that story and remember that we are, with the Doctor, dealing with someone who broke the first law of time.

Surely anyone who is committed to the idea of a consistent Doctor Who continuity in 1976 would be struck by the potential ramifications of that phrase. If we are to treat *The Three Doctors* as some sort of monolithic continuity event that *The Deadly Assassin* is remiss for contradicting, surely we must treat it with considerable attentiveness and seriousness. (I, of course, have little desire to treat *The Three Doctors* that way, much preferring my Blakean fantasia (see Volume Three), but if we are going to play this game, let's play it.) In which case, we have to admit *The Three Doctors* constitutes such a change to what the Doctor is that there are few assumptions that one can still make about his relationship with the Time Lords. Not the first law of the Time Lords, but the first law of time itself—a fundamental principle of the universe—has been violated. At this point presumably all bets are off.

And again, this is borne out. After *The Three Doctors*, we basically don't see the Time Lords again until *Genesis of the Daleks*. (The only exception is K'anpo, who is a renegade as well.) And in both that story and *The Brain of Morbius* (where we as good as see them), they act profoundly different. Vincent-Rudzki admits this: he cites both stories as ones that "go very much against what has been done before." Yet this cannot be considered a problem when both the Time Lords themselves and the Doctor were shown in *The Three Doctors* to have gone through a transformative change. The Time Lords had the entire technological foundation of their civilization thrown into reverse and the Doctor violated the most fundamental law of time. If the Time Lords' next appearance in *Genesis of the Daleks* had been completely consistent with everything that had gone before it, that would be far more dismissive of *The Three Doctors* than *The Deadly Assassin* was. I wasn't cheating in the least when I did a mad Blakean fantasia for that essay: *The Three Doctors* plunged Doctor Who into complete chaos by any continuity standards.

Which brings us to Vincent-Rudzki's next sequence of objections, involving the question of why the Time Lords appear bounded in what they can see in time. To some extent this is simply a restatement of principles we've been applying to the Time Lords since *The Curse of Peladon*. If we treat the Time Lords as we have—as guardians not of history in the sense of an ordered and fixed set of events, but of history as a process that is continually in operation at every moment in time—then the powers Vincent-Rudzki wants to ascribe to them would be the absolute last ones they would have. "Why need the brain machines to predict the future?" Because the future is determined by the Time Lords' stewardship of the historical process. This has always been how the Time Lords appear to work after all: they foresaw a time when the Daleks would be the dominant life form. They foresaw the key moments of history on Peladon and Solon that required the Doctor's intervention. They clearly don't have a perfect record of all that has happened. (This also explains their somewhat torturously baroque approaches to interference in, for instance, *The Mutants*.)

Or, to put it another way, if there is such a thing as a planet of the Time Lords upon which a thing can happen in the first place, the Time Lords clearly do not exist sufficiently outside of time to be all-knowing. The possibility of having anything "happen" to the Time Lords requires that they have a sense of the present. And the present only makes sense as the moment that is accessible directly, as opposed to all other moments of time, which can only be understood through either imagination or memory. This has to work both ways: the present is not just a threshold beyond which we can only predict, it is equally a threshold beyond which we can only remember. Thus we answer, at least thematically, Vincent-Rudzki's next question: why don't they use a time scanner to learn exactly what happened at the assassination? We'll return to the practical matter later.

It is at this point that Vincent-Rudzki makes his most nonsensical statement. I quote, "Another fact forgotten is that Time Lords are immortal. In 'War Games' the Doctor said they could 'live forever barring accidents'." These two sentences are in direct contradiction. If they can only live forever barring accidents, they are not immortal. If you're allowed to bar causes of death, anyone can live forever. Having something that can kill you is called being mortal. The obvious assumption, once we reconceptualize the two face-changes the Doctor has made as "regenerations," is that this is the process by which Time Lords handle accidents. They get a regeneration cycle of twelve regenerations that allow them to survive mishaps. Barring any mishaps, each regeneration is immortal. Not only is there no contradiction when you look closely at the episodes, there's not even a contradiction when you look closely at Vincent-Rudzki's words.

Vincent-Rudzki then inadvertently raises one of the great misses of continuity in Doctor Who history: the world's most reasonable fan theory. Here we must give him credit—he gets it spectacularly wrong, but his case is impeccable. Remember how in *The Brain of Morbius*, Morbius shows us what give every appearance of being pre-Hartnell Doctors? Well... there are eight of them. Then Hartnell, Troughton, and Pertwee. So eleven. That would make Tom Baker the twelfth Doctor, and thus, as Vincent-Rudzki points out, this means that whoever his successor is must be the final Doctor.

Vincent-Rudzki is, of course, completely right—this is, by the standards of anyone trying to impose a "canon" of facts about Doctor Who, clearly the intent of the program. It makes sense: the Doctor and the Master are contemporaries. If the Master is this close to death, surely the Doctor would be as well. The evidence is even better than Vincent-Rudzki thinks it is: both *The Brain of Morbius* and this are Robert Holmes scripts, but *Morbius* was under the pen name Robert Bland to handle the fact that it was a heavy rewrite of a Dicks script. It's clearly the intention that whoever writes the story in which the next Doctor dies will have to kill him off forever.

Vincent-Rudzki continues, coming back to his insistence that Time Lords should look at the past obsessively with time scanners. Clearly they don't do things like that in this story. So why does Vincent-Rudzki obsess on it so? It is in fact worth noting that in none of the four stories we have seen in which scenes are set on Gallifrey has anyone mentioned anything called a "time scanner." The sole appearance of a time scanner is in *The Moonbase*, where it's used to provide a teaser of *The Macra Terror*, and there it attempts to demonstrate the threat of the Macra by showing a single giant claw, which suggests that the scanner is capable only of metonymy. The closest thing to a fully functional "time scanner" that has ever appeared in the show before was the Time-Space Visualizer, and that became an agent of narrative collapse. (And let's get around to interpreting the Time War in light of *The Chase* some day, shall we?)

But these devices are integral to Vincent-Rudzki's entire objection to how the Master is able to tempt Goth with knowledge. Yet again, the problem Vincent-Rudzki identifies disappears upon close observation. Here it's worth pausing to identify an outright theme of problems—one Vincent-Rudzki ultimately identifies as well. The Time Lords are seen to be able to be tempted by the devil in exchange for knowledge. Aside from being a straight lift from Faust, this combines with the next big point that Vincent-Rudzki raises: why don't the Time Lords know their own history?

The cheeky answer is, "because they don't." This alone should have been evidence that these time scanners he thinks they have don't exist, given that there's no actual evidence for the blasted things. But here I'm being a bit unfair. Goth would not have had to use a "time scanner." He could, after all, have used a TARDIS. I mean, even if the Time Lords don't watch history, we at least know that they go and visit it to observe it in person.

Don't we? Let's stop just a moment—we've only actually ever seen three TARDISes in Doctor Who: the Doctor's, the Master's, and the Monk's. We've actually never seen any other Time Lords travel by TARDIS. The bowler-hatted one from *Terror of the Autons* and K'anpo both appear to teleport. In *The*

War Games, we pointedly see SIDRATs on Gallifrey, and they're used to send Jamie and Zoe home, not TARDISes. It's worth noting, after all, that the total number of Type 40s ever in use were 305. That is, for a populated planet, extremely small. If that is an entire model of TARDIS, TARDISes must be extremely rare items. (In fact, the only people we've ever seen with them are renegades.)

This clarifies Goth's position considerably. If we assume that Time Lords spend most of their time on Gallifrey in their present, the very fact that he was traveling and on Terserus in the first place suggests a Faustian nature to him. Knowledge is tempting precisely because the Time Lords seem to allow themselves so little of it. The point that Vincent-Rudzki doesn't raise but should have, given his other objections, is to the idea of storing the brainwave patterns of dead Time Lords in the first place. What does death even mean to time travelers? If you want to meet a dead person, you go back in time and do it. But instead the Time Lords obsessively archive their brains. This suggests that, rather than valuing huge, sweeping overviews of history, they value the material experience of it—a claim that's very much consistent with the larger arguments of this project. The Time Lords, for reasons wholly consistent with what we know of them, appear to engage in sketchy historical record keeping. Indeed, they seem unwilling to commit much of any history to anything beyond memory—the prospect of something being stolen from their files was unusual in *Colony in Space*, after all.

I will skip Vincent-Rudzki's extensive complaints about the ending: they again seem like aesthetic complaints rather than those of content. This leaves, by my reckoning, one major point to deal with: how to reconcile the seemingly partial knowledge the Time Lords have of the Doctor with their lack of knowledge of their own ancient history, and, in turn, how to reconcile the fact that the Doctor had heard of Omega while apparently having no knowledge of Rassilon. Vincent-Rudzki proposes something close to the solution we've been moving towards—that *The Deadly Assassin* takes place in the far future of Gallifrey—but rejects it because of the problem of the Doctor being only hazily remembered.

Here it is worth simply summarizing our responses to Vincent-Rudzki's points. We have already observed that the doubling of creation myths to include both Rassilon and Omega (with Rassilon's accomplishment of removing the Singularity seeming much more impressive than Omega's of nuking a star) sets up an apparent problem. Likewise, we noted that the most straightforward way to resolve this problem is to observe that Time Lord society is radically transformed at the end of *The Three Doctors*, and that Rassilon's story took place after that story. We do not know how long after, though we are forced to conclude that it's been a while.

But not, apparently, so long that the Doctor is out of sync with Gallifrey's history. People still remember him. But curiously, he is not remembered as the hero of the Omega situation. He's remembered only for his exile to Earth and for his schoolboy antics. Much of this discrepancy, however, begins to disappear if we understand the Time Lords in terms of memory. As we observed, all evidence is that the Time Lords keep extremely shoddy records of everything but the minds of past Time Lords. The implication is that their society works entirely according to memory. This is not surprising—few concepts are more fundamentally allied with time than memory. In which case all we're actually being asked to believe is that Time Lords would have hazy memories of the sudden restructuring of their own society.

This is not unreasonable. We are in a Robert Holmes script, as Vincent-Rudzki states repeatedly, seeming to believe this is a bad thing. Holmes is exactly the sort of writer who would create a civilization that completely forgets their history after restructuring their society. (Ironically Vincent-Rudzki probably had seen the next story, which deals with this exact theme of cultural memory and its foibles.) Porting the conclusions over here is not unreasonable. Miles and

Wood give us opportunities to do so as well, observing the similarities between the resignation ceremony and the State Opening of Parliament, an ancient and tradition-steeped ceremony that, at the time *The Deadly Assassin* was written, was a whole 124 years old. The idea that the Time Lords have a short memory for their own history is, in other words, completely consistent with everything we see. Indeed, their tendency to rewrite history is displayed in this story, as Borusa casually decides to cover everything up and write a false history. And yet we're supposed to assume this wasn't done after *The Three Doctors*? Surely the opposite makes more sense.

As for the Doctor, as we said, he violated the first law of time. Why would we assume that someone who did something as horrific as violate the first law of time would be remembered in a society with a willfully selective memory? In fact, it seems far more likely that someone who violates the first law of time would be run off of Gallifrey and largely erased from the historical record. (Come to think of it, it wasn't just Pertwee's Doctor that violated the first law of time—it was Hartnell's. And we don't actually know from when in the Doctor's time stream Hartnell was plucked...)

But even if we don't decide to connect the dots and claim that the Doctor's exile from Gallifrey is actually caused by events in *The Three Doctors*, it's just not that hard to square all of this away. All it requires is a willingness to entertain ideas more creative than "Time Lords are generic godlike technocrats." The Time Lords rewrote their culture—which exists entirely as memory and oral tradition anyway—after *The Three Doctors* and, for obvious reasons, excluded the Doctor. Those Time Lords who knew him still remember him as the student he once was, but institutional memory declined to remember him. This is hardly surprising; it's far easier to rewrite political memory than personal memory. The Doctor, not having been on Gallifrey much lately, doesn't know the new history, but figures it out quickly, probably helped by the fact that he remembered *The Three Doctors* better than the Time Lords themselves did. Simple, consistent with everything we've seen, and, I would argue, a more logical interpretation of the events up to this point than the one that fandom settled on. (What the series settled on is a matter for another entry.)

The remainder of Vincent-Rudzki's objections are aesthetic, not factual, although as we're seeing, that critique really applies to all of his objections. In his concluding paragraphs, he first retcons *The Deadly Assassin* out of existence, declaring that this entire episode was just a crazy nightmare that shouldn't be considered part of Doctor Who canon before going on to bemoan the aesthetic horrors of the changes this story brought. He simultaneously rejects the idea that the story makes any sense and talks about how he hates what it means.

He is wrong, of course, that it does not make sense. We have at this point resolved most of the continuity errors he raises. This leaves only his aesthetic complaint: that "Once, the Time Lords were all-powerful, awe-inspiring beings, capable of imprisoning planets forever in force fields, defenders of truth and good (when called in). Now, they are petty, squabbling, feeble-minded, doddering old fools." Which is true—the Time Lords of this story are at times petty, squabbling, feeble-minded, doddering, and old fools.

Vincent-Rudzki then asks the following question, reprinted verbatim:

WHAT HAS HAPPENED TO THE MAGIC OF DOCTOR WHO?

Part Four

It's October 30, 1976. Pussycat remain at number one with "That Place Where They're Going to Define Fetuses as Human Beings." After two weeks, Chicago unseats them with "If You Leave Me Now," which remains at number one through the end of the story. ABBA, Rod Stewart, Wild Cherry, and The Who also chart.

In real news, Jimmy Carter defeats Gerald Ford to win the Presidency of the United States, setting off the American equivalent to the few years of relative social calm Britain is currently experiencing (relative, at least, to the government-felling upheavals of 1974 and 1978). Not much else happens.

Let us, then, take stock of what is on television.

The Doctor arrives on a fallen Gallifrey. But more instructive than the fact it has fallen is the nature of its fallen state. In the course of making sense of this story, we have found ourselves reimagining the Time Lords in terms of a radically different conception of time than what is usually assumed. We should note that this conception is not simply a high-minded and woolly bit of deconstructive theory, even if we did build it via a brazenly postmodern attack on what is basically just a thirty-five-year-old equivalent of a shrill Gallifrey Base post. It is relatively easy to conceive of the Time Lords as a functional society that works as I outlined above.

The basic idea makes as much sense as any other version of the Time Lords. If the Time Lords actually travel relatively rarely and maintain a primarily living memory, they are Lords not in the sense of being masters of a fixed map of history, but rather in the sense of being masters of an eternal present. They alter the past and future as they see fit, pushing the universe at large towards their view of the arc of history, but they themselves are also subject to that arc. They do not set the agenda of history, but rather enforce it. They are not history's authors, nor its readers, but its grammar - its sentinels, if you will. In essence, they exist in the eye of history's storm, (an Eye of Harmony, perhaps) changing the past and future at will, but also being changed by their engagements. This is not a sign of their weakness, but of their ultimate commitment to this sort of history; they allow their own history to be nothing more than memories and stories, allow themselves to be subject to their own grammar.

This is, as I suggested, essential; the alternative "detached technocrat" view is antithetical to everything the series has shown us. If the Time Lords were, in fact, detached, disinterested, all-powerful beings who simply wrote history by fiat they would, in the language of the show to date, be evil. All-powerful beings who bend the universe to their own design are, after all, the archetypal villains of Doctor Who. Similarly, Doctor Who has always shown an awareness of the Faustian aspects of knowledge. That was the point of *Planet of the Spiders*, for instance: greed for knowledge is bad. Surely Goth's noting that the Master offered him knowledge must be taken in that vein. ("Knowledge" as the prize offered in an act of temptation is, after all, not so much Faustian as outright biblical.)

The Time Lords make far more sense as a race who understands time not as a map to be studied but as a phenomenon to be experienced—time as something that divides the universe into a past remembered and a future imagined, with the present a knife's edge on which the arc of history continually exerts its pressure. This race of ancient beings whose memories span millennia but who act in a continual, short-sighted present is, in a fundamental sense, a better understanding of time and of the series' ethics than the idea of the Time Lords being detached technocrats, which seem to amount to little more than assuming they're are a rip-off of *Star Trek*'s Guardians of Forever. (This captures one of the essential ironies of fandom—despite the fact that by any sane measure Doctor Who had been more successful than *Star Trek* had been up through the late 1980s, Doctor Who fans were by and large insistent that it should act more like *Star Trek*. They got their wish, and the show proceeded to immediately become as successful as *Star Trek* had been: cancelled.)

So the strange power visibly held by the Master and the Doctor makes sense. The Time Lords may be the living grammar of history, but those who travel with TARDISes are its writers. Note that the one non-renegade we hear about travelling is Goth—one of the highest-ranking Time Lords in existence. The implication is that travel is a symbol of power.

Given the potential consequences of time travel, this is perhaps as it should be. It explains fully the strange reverence that the Doctor and the Master are held in by the rest of Gallifrey: they are known to be travellers. The games they play are, as a result, far bigger than Gallifrey itself.

And the game they play is the Kennedy assassination. Or, at least, a repetition thereof. But, of course, repetition is never equivalent to the original event. The whiff of Camelot (itself a suggestive term indicating that the Kennedy administration is itself a repetition of some earlier and not-actually-American event) may circulate around this story, but reading it as allegory is impossible. For one thing, is the Doctor actually cast as Lee Harvey Oswald? Or is he on the grassy knoll? Similarly, where does the CIA fit in? Is Goth Lyndon Johnson, or is Borusa? Perhaps most significantly, what on Earth are we supposed to make of the fact that the cop who figures everything out and helps the Doctor clear his name is played by a Czech actor who has an Eastern European accent?

No, this is not the Kennedy assassination, but rather the memory of the Kennedy assassination. A dreamscape, if you like. Crucially, this falls somewhere between depiction and symbol. It is not simply the Kennedy assassination with a veil of allegory drawn over it, nor is it merely a symbol of the Kennedy assassination. It is a restaging—a reiteration. It is not the event itself but an echo of it—a distorted repetition.

Here the genius of Robert Holmes comes into play. He is the only writer thus far in Doctor Who who is capable of managing this story. Holmes's specialty, after all, is his grasp of the small. He is at home with stories like *Carnival of Monsters*, where the threat emerges from nothing more than a scheming old carny barker meeting up with some literally grey-faced bureaucrats. His genius in *The Brain of Morbius* was in his grasp of small absurdities, like having an all-powerful galactic conquerer be a suicidal vegetable envier. And here we see that genius in applied form. Holmes manages to perfectly capture the tone with which a crisis actually plays out—not with inspirational rhetoric but with political bitchiness and squabbling.

This introduces, in other words, a genuine materialism to this, a materialism *The Deadly Assassin* displays consistently. This is in many ways the primary appeal of reconceptualizing the Time Lords as a race ordered around the idea of memory: memory is the material form of history. The reiterated dreamscape of the Kennedy assassination is closer to the actual post-1963 human experience of the Kennedy assassination than any thorough and well-documented account of the event could possibly be. The Kennedy assassination is far more important as an idea than it is as a documentable and falsifiable event.

Here we get to the true and frankly sickening absurdity of Vincent-Rudzki's argument. What has happened to the magic of Doctor Who? It bothered to apply itself, that's what happened. It bothered to acknowledge a world in which history is accomplished by squabbling politicians instead of detached technocrats holding to absolutist ideologies of "truth" and "good." It bothered to be magic that affects the real world instead of magic that masturbatorily sticks to the world of ideas. Far from undermining the Time Lords of *The War Games*, this is the story where we finally see the Time Lords bound by the same focus on the material realities of history that they demand of the Doctor.

I mean, really. If we're going to talk about the "magic" of Doctor Who—and notably I didn't even pick that word this time—which of these two options appears more magical? A show in which the past and future are fixed and knowable events that can be casually looked up on a time scanner, or a show in which the very nature of the universe is continually in flux because a race governed by memory and imagination is continually trying to maintain the moral force of history even while they descend into petty squabbles?

If magic is to be considered valuable then it's valuable only as the bridge between the realm of ideas and the realm of the material. That is the revelation of *The Brain of Morbius*.

Claiming that alchemy is solved by material social progress is not an abandonment of magic, but a confirmation of what magic is and always has been. Magic is not an empty intellectual exercise—the mere understanding of an already determined universe—but an engagement with it. Magic is action, not theory.

This brings us around to one of the most incongruous moments of the story, in which the Doctor refers to Borusa's cover-up as his proof that "only in mathematics will we find truth." Here again, in the name of the fealty to the material past of the series that fandom so ignores in order to fetishize, we ought acknowledge our antecedents. We have, after all, already been told that the TARDIS is a Platonic device. Likewise, the claim that mathematics is an absolute form of truth derives from Plato.

Mathematics, in this view, is distinct even from science. After all, mathematics is not based on falsifiability, but on proof. The claim that 2+2=4 is not an empirical claim but one of absolute truth: two plus two will always equal four, must always equal four, and cannot possibly be understood as equalling anything other than four. "What would a world without gravity be like?" is a question that can be answered as a thought experiment. "What would a world where two plus two equalled seven?" is not. Indeed, the truth of mathematics transcends reality itself. The combination of atoms into molecules and reality is less precise than geometry itself. No mathematically true right angle exists anywhere in the world, yet we understand the properties of a right angle. Mathematics is the realm in which we manipulate Platonic forms—the truest realm of all.

Given the spirit of this claim—and it seems unmistakably what the script is gesturing at—the Doctor arguing that Borusa's coverup constitutes proof of this statement must be understood as a claim that the messy political reality that Borusa's coverup represents is as much an ordering principle of the universe as mathematics itself. It is worth repeating this claim, lest its sheer radicalness be obscured by the fact that it occurs over eleven thousand words into a grotesquely long book entry: human nature is as fundamental a property of the universe as mathematics.

This is, of course, a corollary of the nature of alchemy. But that does not make it any less radical, simply because it appears in a story in which we see the breadth of human nature. Human nature, after all, has always been a part of history in the sense that the Time Lords seem to represent. Human nature extends from our limitations: the fact that we are mortal, and that we are bound by the surface tension of the present, able to access eternity only through memory and imagination. If the Time Lords are to be understood as embodying time as experienced, they are also testaments to the fact that human nature exists and orders the universe. And if they are how time is ruled then human subjectivity is, in fact, an ordering principle of the entire cosmos.

We see here, then, the show's understanding of materialism. Because in crafting a dreamscape of the Kennedy assassination defined by its fealty to the squabbling pettiness of human nature, the show has engaged in the real world in a manner far more material than last story's faffing with a nuclear reactor. This is far more real and material than anything the show has ever done while earthbound. And this is the show's great radicalism, its stunning rejoinder to the "hard SF" crowd: the realm of stories and ideas is every bit as material as the realm of physical things. Engagement with memory and imagination is as real—perhaps even moreso— than engagement with technology and contemporary culture.

There is a messiness to this, although the mess is problematic only if you are the sort of person who wants Doctor Who to be more like *Star Trek*, or who is prima facie opposed to the idea of granting memory and imagination power over the empirical. After all, the same messiness underlies the problem of conspiracy theories. In a rudderless world governed by a mad spectacle of contradictions, where the false is the moment of the true, what defense is there beyond allowing our understanding of the world to be messy in turn?

Conventional wisdom argues for two phases of Time Lords in the classic series—one that begins in *The War Games*, and another that begins here. We have already seen that the disjunct between these phases is not as stark as one might expect. But in truth it is more than that. This is the story in which the show takes up the challenge offered by *The War Games*—a challenge that was itself offered up by the revolutionary spirit of the 1960s, by the flower children and Marxists and radicals of the world. There, I said:

But in another sense, this is the real endpoint of the 1960s. The revolution failed. However much we may have liked it—and for my part, I loved it, especially in the Doctor Who sense in which the psychedelic revolution is literally embodied in Patrick Troughton's Doctor—it failed. It's time to break up the band. It's time to face the reality that the bad guys aren't external monsters, but the people who want to send riot police to crush the sex deviants planting flowers. It's time, in other words, to face reality. This is the message every sane and useful mystic in the world will tell you. It's all well and good to journey among the interiors of the mind and at the furthest fringes of consciousness and reality. It's all well and good to face gods and demons and encounter the fundamental truth of the universe. But the real test is what you can bring back from those mystical realms to reality. The real test is how you can live as a mystic in the real world.

Here we finally see the Doctor understanding how to do this. Baker retains the mercurial dazzle of Troughton, peering out at the viewer, whether from screen or video box. This is once again a Doctor who trades in anarchy, who brings the Time Lords' world crashing down around their heads just by his presence. Who runs for President to get off on a murder charge, then kills his opponent in a nightmarish dreamscape created by his arch-nemesis. Who grins and swaggers and charms his way around, and respects no authority. Who is animated by nothing so much as a giddy sense of joy at the universe (whereas his arch-nemesis proudly proclaims his sense of hatred). From day one, that was what we said of Baker. He is a creature of pure charm.

And now he returns to face his jailers. In a perfect detail, Goth is even played by Bernard Horsfall, who Maloney previously cast as one of the Time Lords who sentenced Troughton's Doctor to exile) in *The War Games*. Now the Doctor returns to show them that he has learned to use his anarchy. That he has realized the world of stories and the world of men are one and the same. Now his jesting truly becomes détournement. His wanderings through space and time are revealed derivés. Now he mocks his way through history, aware of all its foibles and how they drive the engines of the world.

If this story is to be a gravestone for Doctor Who, then so be it. I do not say this because it is the best story, although I've no argument with any who say it is. No. Let it be a gravestone for Doctor Who for one reason alone. Because if we do center Doctor Who here, if we do let this be the rock of our canon and our fandom, then it does serve as a tombstone in one regard. It does mark where the magic of Doctor Who has gone.

It's gone into the world itself.

A True History of The Conspiracy

A commissioned essay for Eric Gimlin

In 1976, just as the individual editions of *The Eye in the Pyramid*, *The Golden Apple*, and *Leviathan* were being released in the UK, Ken Campbell, who later infiltrated and had cancelled the popular television program Doctor Who through the clever use of his secret agent, Percy James Patrick Kent-Smith, began a nine-hour stage show based on Robert Anton Wilson and Robert Shea's *Illuminatus! Trilogy*. However by any sane measure the plot began in 1972 with the transmission of *The Time Monster,* which completed Doctor Who's parallel construction to *The Illuminatus! Trilogy*, which we can refer to as The Atlantis Trilogy, Atlantis having been a primary concern of *The Illuminatus! Trilogy*.

It is surely not a coincidence that the original manuscript of *The Illuminatus! Trilogy* was composed between 1969 and 1971, meaning that it was completed around the same time as the second of Doctor Who's three Atlantis story, *The Daemons*, which, like *The Time Monster*, was written by Barry Letts and Robert Sloman. This points strongly towards the possibility that Letts was, like Shea and Wilson, involved in the Discordian Society, which means that any of Letts's decisions might be plausibly taken as contributing to the larger plot.

This brings us around to the matter of Tom Baker himself, who, at fifteen, spent five years in a Catholic monastery, making him, by any measure, the Doctor Who cast member most likely to be an Illuminati plant. However this raises its own set of questions, as it double-books Barry Letts as both a Discordian co-conspirator and as an Illuminati puppet master.

This, however, reflects the troubling complexities of a psychic landscape upon which the Illuminati/Discordian battle plays out. So many infiltrations and counter-infiltrations have taken place at this point that it is difficult if not impossible to meaningfully treat the sides of the conflict as being coherent entities. The canonical example here is Lee Harvey Oswald, who became so confused as to his own allegiances that he assassinated John Fitzgerald Kennedy on what he believed to be the orders of the Illuminatus, but what were in fact the route plans for a downhill bicycle race plotted out by Discordian mastermind J.G. Ballard, who was forced to hastily contact actual Illuminati agent Jack Ruby to clean the entire mess up and die of cancer.

Interestingly, it appears that the primary confusion was not over the basic outcome (Kennedy's assassination) but over the means and timing, with the issue being largely focused on how the Kennedy assassination would or would not interfere with the planned debut of Doctor Who.

This anecdote ought illustrate why question of whether Barry Letts is an Illuminati agent embedded amongst the Discordians or whether Tom Baker was a Discordian plant within the Illuminati is ultimately irrelevant. What is important is not so much the actual sides of the conflict so much as the processes of synchronicity by which the conflict advances itself. In practice "Illuminati" and "Discordian" are simply placeholders for the basic act of arbitrary and largely fictional conflict that fuels the ongoing engine of history.

Nevertheless, it is obvious that this opposition has crossed into Doctor Who on several occasions. The Ken Campbell incident, in which Campbell served as an overly extreme candidate that made his protégé, Kent-Smith, look palatable by comparison, is only one (Indeed, it's not even the sole casting invasion—original Campbell cast member Bill Nighy, for instance, appeared in the program in 2010 in a story explaining the Illuminatus assassination of Vincent van Gogh). A year after Kent-Smith's casting Bill Drummond and Jimmy Cauty, who typically recorded music under the name The KLF or The Justified Ancients of Mu Mu mashed up pedophile Gary Glitter's "Rock and Roll (Part Two)" with the Doctor Who theme for a joyfully cynical single entitled "Doctorin' the Tardis [sic]" under the name The Timelords, taking it to number one. The KLF/JAMs were, in their other work, overtly inspired by *The Illuminatus! Trilogy*, with numerous songs referencing the book. Their turn to Doctor Who is in many regards completely mercenary: an unapologetic grab for a number one hit that they described in detail in *The Manual*, their cheeky guide to doing just that. Nevertheless, it further highlights the significance of Doctor Who as a battleground for the conspiracy.

It is tempting to call all of these later psychic skirmishes aftershocks of the real conflict—the Kennedy assassination. After all, Discordian cofounder Kerry Thornley knew Lee Harvey Oswald, and wrote a book about his defection to the USSR prior to the Kennedy assassination. Thornley was deposed by New Orleans DA Jim Garrison, who was convinced the Warren Commission had gotten it wrong, and upon whose photocopier Thornley had created the original Principia Discordia. Garrison's theory—that a small legion of Oswald impersonators deliberately muddied the waters by creating false trails of evidence to distract from the real killer—amounts to the same sort of "it's all true" interpretation that *The Illuminatus! Trilogy* eventually applies to conspiracy theories in general, and that Lance Parkin and other Doctor Who writers typically apply to the series' at times tangled continuity.

In his landmark book on The KLF and their decision to set fire to a million pounds on the Scottish island of Jura,

JMR Higgs follows from Alan Moore's suggestion in *From Hell* that the Jack the Ripper murders served as an occult ritual to bring about the 20th Century and suggests that the torching of a million quid was "the magical act which set the scene for a global economic collapse and, in doing so, created the twenty-first century." This is a good theory that Higgs supports with ample evidence, but it ignores (or at least leaves relatively undeveloped) the fact that at the midpoint between these sacrifices sits the Kennedy assassination, or, rather, the larger nexus of events that constitutes the Kennedy assassination, the foundation of Discordianism, the deaths of Aldous Huxley and C.S. Lewis, and the creation of Doctor Who, which recorded the episode "The Survivors," the debut of the Daleks, on the day of the assassination itself. If the Victorian Ripper murders were the start of the 20th Century and the KLF's money burning marked the start of the 21st, what did this mid-century ritual sacrifice bring into the world?

Given the nexus of events involved, in no way surprising to discover that Campbell's Illuminatus! show debuted on November 23rd, 1976, exactly thirteen years after the debut of Doctor Who, and three days after Doctor Who finished its own symbolic reenactment of the Kennedy assassination in the form of *The Deadly Assassin*. Both *The Deadly Assassin* and *The Illuminatus! Trilogy* suggest the possibility of a lurking horror underneath the ordered and static accounts of history—the possibility that there are dread secrets underlying Gallifrey's past, or that Lovecraftian beasts and aeons-old sea monsters exist.

This comports with the supposed cultural role of the Kennedy assassination as the moment where the 1960s lost their innocence—that is, where the facade of post-War technocratic order finally cracked, revealing the cavernous depths of brutal violence within. The immanentization of the eschaton writ large, the Kennedy assassination was when we realized it was possible for it all to end: that underneath all of our millennia of history and culture and buildings might be nothing more than the splatter of upper-class Bostonian brains on Texan pavement.

(We might at this point remember that the writers of *The Illuminatus! Trilogy* and *The Deadly Assassin* are all named Robert, giving this narrative three Rs, RRR being the production code of *The Three Doctors*, the other story revealing lost and daemonic powers beneath Gallifrey, providing the secret fourth volume of the Atlantis trilogy.)

Doctor Who, of course, is a series about tearing down the world, whether by punching a hole through it and scarpering out of it or through the basic anarchic glee of dismantling an entire society. That it is born and defined in the wake of the Kennedy assassination is sensible, as they have the same essential psychic purpose—the aggressive dismantling of the idea that the world is stability and order. And with the first real aftershock of the Kennedy assassination unfolding in 1976 we have Doctor Who at last turning its focus on itself, reenacting the Kennedy assassination within its own narrative. No surprise, then, that this is the story that begins the chain of causality leading to the show's cancellation, that it attempts, even, to ensure the series's cancellation through its regeneration limit. This is the cavernous void within Doctor Who's establishment of order, the revelation of savage violence (the actual cause of Hinchcliffe's sacking) at its core, and the beginning of its long night of the soul.

But as the Hinchcliffe era, and for that matter *The Illuminatus! Trilogy* prophesies, nothing remains dead and buried forever.

Master Restitution

A commissioned essay for John Wirenius

It is often said that the Master is the Doctor's Moriarty, which is one of those truisms so close to accurate that it causes us to miss the forest for the trees. The Master is not, in fact, the Doctor's Moriarty—he's Jon Pertwee's Doctor's Moriarty. While it's usually all well and good to treat the Doctors as interchangeable and as basically the same person, it's important to remember that the Jon Pertwee era is by any standard an outlier in comparison with the rest of the series. Perhaps unsurprisingly, his Moriarty casts a complex shadow on the remainder of the series.

First and foremost, let us consider the character played by Roger Delgado in eight stories from *Terror of the Autons* to *Frontier in Space* separate from the larger character of the Master, since at no point did Roger Delgado play a single version of a larger character. Much like William Hartnell never played the First Doctor, merely the Doctor, Roger Delgado only ever played the Master: the whole of the character. Given that, what sort of character did he play?

On a basic level, Delgado's Master was defined opposite Jon Pertwee's "James Bond" version of the Doctor as a Bond villain, specifically as the svengali. The term "svengali" comes from an anti-semitic 19th century novel by George du Maurier, but has generally expanded to mean an evil and manipulative figure, often a hypnotist or mesmerist, and in particular with an undercurrent of implying that the person is foreign or "not like us." Delgado's suitability to the role was thus evident: the London-born son of a Belgian mother and Spanish father, full name Roger Caesar Marius Bernard de Delgado Torres Castillo Roberto, was frequently cast in similar roles, typically playing characters of what I have previously called Shiftystani identity—that is, untrustworthy characters who appear to hail from a nondescript "foreign" place.

This, of course, contrasts almost exclusively with Pertwee's portrayal of the Doctor as an aristocratic eccentric working with the government. Pertwee's Doctor was particularly British, not just, as with most other incarnations, in outlook, but in identity. He took on a civilian identity as John Smith and was, it appears, an actual British subject— something untrue of any other incarnation. And so in contrast to that his enemy is vaguely foreign, in much the same way that the strict and patrician Hartnell Doctor got the impish and bumbling Meddling Monk as his "evil Time Lord" and the mercurial Troughton got the militaristic War Chief.

But as the Pertwee era wore on it became increasingly clear that Pertwee's Doctor was not a straightforward action hero, but a slightly camp, glammed-up pastiche of one. Accordingly, Delgado began to tune his performance to more precisely match Pertwee's. In time the character shifted from being a general svengali to being one half of an almost loving rivalry. The Master became a knowing wink: a villain who supposedly threatened the world, but in reality was only in it to match wits with the Doctor. Before long he was putting the arch in arch-villain.

This sense that the Master was, perhaps, not actually the most terrifying threat the Doctor could possibly imagine was reflected in the plot that was originally intended to wrap up the character. In this, the Doctor and the Master were to be locked in an adventure transparently based on "The Final

Problem," in which the Master was to be revealed as a part of the Doctor's psyche. With no way of knowing how this would have worked out on screen, it's tough to criticize in any detail. The resolution, however, is in keeping with the lightly Buddhist tone of the Barry Letts era. The reintegration of the Master's troublesome id forms what is, in many ways, a more potent version of the Doctor's acceptance of his responsibility for what's going on in *Planet of the Spiders*.

Indeed, the reintegration of the Master into the Doctor's sense of self and the Master's planned self-sacrifice to save the Doctor would have, one imagines, provided a more satisfying resolution to the era than *Planet of the Spiders*. Certainly it justifies the fundamental problem underlying any sort of Moriarty figure, which is that they're still secondary characters in a story defined by a charismatic lead who's always going to triumph. You can't simultaneously define a character as "just as capable as the lead" and "always beaten by the lead." But by redefining the Master not as the equal to the Doctor but as a diseased reflection and fragment of him, his necessary status as the one who gets beaten by the Doctor makes sense. This is in keeping with the Buddhist conception of demons as aspects of our own personalities that we have to come to terms with, and while it may clash terribly with much of what comes after the Pertwee era, it does, at least, make a lot of sense within it.

Unfortunately instead of filming *The Final Game* Roger Delgado had the remarkably poor taste to die in a car accident in Turkey, resulting in the story being abandoned. Instead the Master returned four seasons later in *The Deadly Assassin* in what has been affectionately referred to as his pizza-faced incarnation. This, however, marked a major shift in the character. Delgado's Master, nor any character like him would never work in the face of Tom Baker's tendency towards mocking his villains: treatment like what the Doctor gives to the Zygons would shred the character. So instead the Master becomes another iteration of the classic Baker-era villain—the returning menace from the past.

In the course of this the character changes massively, so much so that it's almost ridiculous to treat Peter Pratt in heavy makeup as the same character that Delgado played. All of Delgado's suave panache is gone, and the Master is instead a deranged madman trying to destroy everything. He's no longer the Doctor's twisted reflection but a disinterred detail of his past. While this is compelling, it's also the same thing that every other returning villain represents. The pizza-faced Master solved the problem of no longer having Roger Delgado—previously the sole reason the Master worked as a concept—by simply turning him into the most generic threat imaginable.

It is in this form that the bulk of his remaining history plays out. When Geoffrey Beevers played the pizza-faced version in *The Keeper of Traken* it was once again a shadowy, lurking threat from the past. After that came the largely disastrous Anthony Ainley incarnation, which consisted of mimicking Delgado's performance opposite a sequence of Doctors who were not Jon Pertwee's Doctor, and who thus did not lend themselves to the dynamic that Delgado's performance was designed to fit into. Much like Delgado's Master would never have worked opposite Tom Baker, Ainley's never worked opposite…well, anyone, really.

Ironically, it was the Eric Roberts version of the Master who started to move things back towards the way they'd actually worked. Roberts's campy, over the top performance was, if nothing else, a reasonable counterweight to Paul McGann's manic enthusiasm. Just as Delgado and Pertwee positioned themselves on opposite ends of the "dapper" spectrum, Roberts and McGann both turned in impassioned performances, with McGann ending up on "romantic" and Roberts on "scenery-chewing megalomaniac." Other than being a completely terrible idea, this was not a completely terrible idea.

Similarly, when Russell T Davies surrendered to the inevitable and brought back the Master, by now defined as the eternally returning bad penny, he returned to first principles, having John Simm turn in a performance that was designed to be the psychotic flipside of David Tennant's charismatic and fast-talking Doctor. The result grated on purists who wanted to see the Doctor face down yet another Roger Delgado impersonator, but the sheer comedy of imagining someone standing opposite David Tennant and saying "I am the Master and you will obey me" ought make clear that this was the best of available options.

Still, in the end, it's hard not to pine for the unavailable option: that Roger Delgado had lived long enough to actually bring his character, the twisted shadow of Jon Pertwee's Doctor, to a conclusion. Every Master story after *Frontier in Space* is, to be perfectly honest, an attempt to tack on a conclusion other than the one that the character actually built to. Some are good, and even great in spite of this. But none of them have ever had the Master in them.

Pop Between Realities, Home in Time for Tea (*Children of the Stones*)

The Deadly Assassin essay is, as you've no doubt noticed, somewhat long. As the old joke goes, "I apologize for writing such a long letter—I did not have time to write a short one." Length, to some extent, begets length—the nature of a nearly 13,000-word entry is that it raises further points that require following up. To this end, because Season Fourteen of Doctor Who had an unusually long Christmas break that ran from late November 1976 to January 1977, this essay and the next are, if you will, a pause to expand on and tidy up some points from *The Deadly Assassin* before we dive back into the wreckage for the coda to the Hinchcliffe era.

In some ways, however, *this* is the coda to the Hinchcliffe era. *Children of the Stones*—which ran on ITV roughly concurrently with *The Face of Evil* and *The Robots of Death*, airing on Mondays, just after sunset, at a quarter to five— feels in a number of ways like a lost story of the Hinchcliffe era. It is a natural extension of and response to many of the ideas animating Doctor Who in this period, matching the era in tone, mood, and iconography. More, really, than any Pop Between Realities we've done, this feels like a case of covering something that is inextricable from Doctor Who than it is looking at what else is going on in the larger culture.

There are two basic ways to make very good British television. The first is to try to make very good British television and succeed. This is the way of the prestige project—the stuff that forms the meat of the British television export. *I, Clavdivs* is the archetypal example, with later examples being things like *Prime Suspect*, *Downton Abbey*, and, since 2005, Doctor Who. These projects work by getting multiple leading lights of the British television industry together on one project and giving them enough money to do it well. It's a very good system and it makes very good television; HBO reinvented American television, basically, by pinching this system for domestic use.

The second approach is one that characterizes the classic series of Doctor Who. In this approach, you slap together something to fill a timeslot on the schedule and shoot for nothing more than "be entertaining enough that people watch it." Then you miss horribly and accidentally hit "brilliant" instead. *Children of the Stones*, much like the best bits of classic series Doctor Who, is a perfect example of this approach. ITV Children's entertainment, a style of television generally expected to produce things like *Ace of Wands* and *The Tomorrow People*, inadvertently turn out seven episodes of creepy supernatural horror of such quality that it frankly forces us to reevaluate our expectations of what television is.

By all accounts, *Children of the Stones* was a landmark piece of television—one that children of the relevant generation were thoroughly spooked by. It's the sort of serial that gets Stewart Lee to make a half-hour radio documentary decades later about how creepy and brilliant it is. It's one of those true classics of children's media, in the tradition we talked about way back in *The Ark in Space*: the sort that are memorable because they go just a little further beyond where children are prepared to go, pushing them out of their comfort zone. That's what true classics of children's literature do—they present children with something that's hard to deal with. They require children to grow. How do you make a child into an interesting, thoughtful adult? Alchemy. Material social progress. Growth.

In practical terms, *Children of the Stones* manages an uncanny drift into creepiness. The first episodes are merely unnerving, but as the situation worsens the show gets considerably scarier, until in its final two episodes audience identification characters are getting mind-controlled and turned to stone while the dwindling number of good guys are under increasing pressure and running out of options. On top of that, it does an excellent job of nondescript creepiness, things like the eerie atmospheric chanting used for incidental music. While it's not something you can point at to say "that's really scary" in the way of Goth drowning the Doctor, it remains tremendously unsettling and effective. (Stewart Lee memorably describes it as the most inappropriate children's television theme ever.)

It is the sort of horror that's most effective—especially in children's media, but really in general: conceptual horror. Hiding bchind the sofa only works to avoid a scary scene. There's no hiding from a scary idea. The use of creepy sound—chanting and singing—instead of merely horrific imagery is similarly effective: it is easier to avert one's eyes than one's ears. And this is what *Children of the Stones* does so well. Even if you don't watch the scene in which the mother and daughter Margaret and Sandra are corrupted by Hendrick, and even if you're young enough that the creepier sexual overtones of the scene sail past you, you're still left with the idea that the kind of unsettling man who invites your family for dinner might unexpectedly brainwash you. Better yet, knowing this in advance won't even help you, since the real brilliance of that scene is that both Margaret and Sandra have a basic understanding of what's about to happen but are still unable to save themselves. That's deliciously scary in a way you can't look away from.

But the ways in which *Children of the Stones* serves as a sort of lost story of the Hinchcliffe era are more than just the fact that both of them were effective children's horror shows which aired at the same time. It's the specific content: the way in which the phenomena seen in *Children of the Stones* flit between magic and science, in which the scary thing is something returning from the past, and, of course, in which history is treated as a cyclic phenomenon. *Children of the Stones* doesn't just act like Hinchcliffe-era Doctor Who by being scary and refusing to talk down or make things overly simplistic for its audience. The two series have the same basic concerns.

These are concerns we haven't quite spelled out, even though we've been talking about them for a while. One of the things that's been noticeable about the Hinchcliffe era is the frequency with which its threats emerge from the past. All three Season Fourteen stories to date have dealt with this to some extent, as did half of those in Season Thirteen and two in Season Twelve. This is not a complete transformation: Pertwee, Troughton, and Hartnell all dealt with evils returning from the past at one time or another. But no era has embraced them to such a massive degree. We've seen, over the course of the last few seasons, a fundamental change in what the "default" mode of Doctor Who is.

One thing that *Children of the Stones* shows us, then, is that this change is part of something larger. The most obvious thing to say is that a focus on the past is the obvious response to the crashing and burning of the future that constituted the end of the 1960s. There's a sensible progression from the failure of revolutionary movements to treating the future with considerable anxiety to abandoning the future entirely in favor of the past. So in this period there's a general turn towards the past: one that, arguably, culminates in the rise of the extreme and reactionary conservatism that politically dominated the 1980s. We've been seeing its effects for some time: the revival of interest in rural Britain that fueled things like *The Daemons*, for instance, or the rise of glam rock, which both came out of that interest in the past and was, as the wise Chris O'Leary points out, rock's first nostalgia movement. (The parallels between glam rock and the rural British mythology are larger than they might seem: prior to becoming a glam rock star, Mark Bolan was part of a Tolkien-focused folk duo.)

And we'll see its impact in numerous ways, including in the rise of punk rock—there are perhaps no lines in music more focused on a relationship with the past than "No Future / England's Dreaming." But more to the point, punk music rose in part out of the pub rock movement, which was about reclaiming rock from the starry-eyed sci-fi nerds doing glam and progressive rock and taking it back to good old fashioned pubs. Punk's driving aesthetic has always been authenticity, and authenticity is an inherently nostalgic value.

But punk also highlights another aspect of a focus on the past. In a society focused on the past, utopianism is reduced to two basic strategies. The first is to become intensely reactionary, advocating for the rolling back of history towards some prior design. This, however, is unsuitable for our progressive purposes. Progressive utopianism, then, has only one option remaining: anger. It is left advocating for a "rip it up and start again" approach that serves to eradicate history, not in the sense of forgetting history or erasing it, but in the sense of destroying it—of leaving the past as smoldering rubble.

This brings us around to the problem of cyclical history—something we've talked about in passing for several entries now without quite defining. There are in essence two ways in which the past repeats itself. The first is simply through parallelism: human nature dictates that certain patterns of behavior will recur. The second is through a stubborn refusal of the past to die. This is the sort of recursion characterized by something like Enoch Powell's "Rivers of Blood" speech: a vicious piece of xenophobia that was decried as antiquated, racist thinking when Powell gave it. And which then proceeded to tediously influence people and be praised for decades and counting.

This latter form of cyclical history is particularly potent in Britain, a nation ruled, as we saw way back in *The Invasion*, from a palimpsest of a city. In a nation where dead history routinely abuts with living memory, the sense of an undying past that looms continually over the present has particular power. And both *Children of the Stones* and the Hinchcliffe era traded heavily on this fact.

But what the Hinchcliffe era never quite does is connect its two major themes. It never manages to have a story in which the persistence of material elements of the past causes specific types of events to occur. That's clearly the natural endpoint of the era, but it's not one that ever gets to actually happen on screen. So in that regard, *Children of the Stones* fills in a useful gap for the Hinchcliffe era. Because what's interesting about it is that the physical detritus of the past—the ancient stone circle—is also the cause of a recurring social event. The whole premise of *Children of the Stones* is that the events taking place in this village are part of an ancient, recurring pattern. But this pattern is linked to old, dead ideas in a more Lovecraftian tradition. It's a very neat little move, and one that draws an important parallel that underlies the Hinchcliffe era's ideas.

Indeed, this link helps clarify another recurring motif of the Hinchcliffe era: possession. Characters are finding themselves possessed and mind controlled with alarming frequency these days in the show. I mean, you always had the Master as a Svengali, but these days people are having their bodies taken over by alien presences like there's some sort of intergalactic corporeality shortage. But in *Children of the Stones* the possession angle finally snaps into place along with the other key elements of the Hinchcliffe approach. Here we have characters who are possessed by ancient forces, but the possession amounts to social conditioning in a way that harkens back to *The Prisoner*.

The result is oddly fortuitous for the Hinchcliffe era. Often when we talk about shows that are often mentioned in the same breath as Doctor Who, we end up talking about what amounts to cheap knockoffs like *The Tomorrow People* or *Space: 1999*. Finally here we have something that adds real depth and character to the era and that genuinely enhances the show. It also suggests, pleasantly, that the series has, *The Seeds of Doom* aside, for the most part not been overdoing things in terms of horror.

One thing that comes up in conversations about this project sometimes is the extent to which I actually believe what I am saying. Certainly I willfully and deliberately overplay my critical hand just slightly, pushing just a bit further than is quite justifiable as descriptions of the truth in favor of, shall we say, a more interesting idiom. In truth I don't actually believe that the writers of Doctor Who were consciously designing a sentient metafiction that would continually disrupt the social order through a systematic process of détournement. Except maybe David Whitaker.

But on the other hand, I view this as a slightly overly optimistic, slightly doting, slightly over-sentimental version of accurate readings of what's going on in the stories. My goal is, if you will, accurate criticism with the volume turned up just a little too loud. And *Children of the Stones* thus serves as a pleasant confirmation of the fact that, yes, this is still an argument about the actual material history of the show. Because the ideas I'm picking out in Doctor Who are picked up seamlessly elsewhere in the culture; these ideas are not a weird alternate history of British culture, but a thread that really is unspooling across the culture, with Doctor Who, if not at the literal center of it, at least central enough to serve as an adequate derivé for the larger cultural history of Britain.

So yes, I do think that there were plenty of people watching *The Deadly Assassin* in 1976 and getting many of the ideas and themes out of it that I discussed. Not necessarily in the obsessively and conspiratorially organized form I put them in, but in a broader and more general case Because here we have another show, also popular, that clearly does do many of those same things. More to the point, it does them with surprising complexity. *Children of the Stones* is, as the idiom now goes, massively timey wimey. This is a show whose existence and popularity should really shame into silence anybody who complains that Doctor Who is too complex. Children's entertainment has been doing elaborate plots about time loops since 1976 without any problems.

One consequence of this is that it tells us that, yes, children did watch television rigorously. Because for *Children of the Stones* to have worked, they would have had to have had good memories across weeks and the ability to think through and anticipate future developments of complex ideas. This is not television to watch inattentively. And that means that there were plenty of children who were watching Doctor Who with savvy eyes. Subtleties of the show were communicated. And as *Children of the Stones* teaches us, once these subtleties were made material in the culture, their influence can be made to recur indefinitely.

Time Can Be Rewritten (*Asylum*)

One more essay of dotting "i"s, crossing "t"s, and playing with some of the concepts from *The Deadly Assassin* before we reach *The Face of Evil*. Here I want to look again at the ways in which having an understanding of history and of the world more nuanced than the ones I critiqued in *The Deadly Assassin* essay (or for that matter in *The Masque of Mandragora* essay) makes for better writing than those of the hardline rationalist views, or mainstream fandom's limited views of the nature of time and history. And for that we have Peter Darvill-Evans' almost but not-quite excellent book *Asylum*, featuring the Doctor and Nyssa of Traken and set in the period between *The Deadly Assassin* and *The Face of Evil*.

The first thing that should be said about Asylum is that Darvill-Evans is a much better writer than he is a historian. While it's actually a relatively minor point within the book, he goes out of his way to have the Doctor endorse a particular historical view of Roger Bacon in which Bacon is not considered to be a meaningful figure in the history of science on the grounds that his overall worldview was insufficiently empiricist. I am not a medieval/renaissance scholar, and I am not going to wade too far into this debate, but Darvill-Evans's view amounts to a variation on the idea that the rise of science was a light switch that got thrown somewhere in human history in which everybody became an empiricist. This is, in practice, ludicrous.

The argument Darvill-Evans gives the Doctor for this is that Bacon's "main objective is to prepare the Christian world for the coming of the Antichrist, which he believes is imminent" and that "he believes the universe is governed by the idea of the self-generation of likenesses." The problem is that this argument would kick Isaac Newton out of the scientist club as well, since he was, after all, an alchemist who spent an awful lot of time predicting the date of the Apocalypse. And anyone who wants to rule Newton out as a scientist is a braver man than I am.

The thing is, the rise of science wasn't just a sudden thing. Science came out of an intellectual stew that included theology, philosophy, what we would now recognize as occultism, and a wealth of other disciplines. Empiricism— whether in soft or hardline forms—ultimately traces its roots back to forms of thought that we now consider deeply unscientific. There's really not a way around this, and drawing a fence around the development of science that rules out Roger Bacon fundamentally misunderstands both science and human development.

This is very clearly what Darvill-Evans does. He has the Doctor say that Nyssa's thesis is inaccurate. Her thesis is explicitly that Bacon is a proto-scientist and that an understanding of the "dawning of the technological age" should extend back at least as far as him, as opposed to merely to the twentieth century or the Industrial Revolution. To say that is flatly untrue is, well, flatly untrue. Whether or not Bacon ought be called a "scientist" proper is perhaps open for debate, but Nyssa's claim is that he has an important place in the history of science. To dismiss that is ludicrous.

This isn't quite nitpicking, but it highlights an important point about the relationship between art and criticism. Darvill-Evans is a pretty good writer, all told. I mean, he's not one of the greats of the English language, but as guys who writes books based on a ropey old cancelled sci-fi series go, he's got some real game. He writes a good story. And we know for a fact he was a damn fine editor, because he spearheaded the massively transformative New Adventures line for Virgin in the early 1990s.

That said, his critical essay at the end of the book is... well, see, I don't want to say rubbish. It's not rubbish. It is a good writer trying his hand at criticism and missing a bit. Because there is a relationship between the two skills. If you can write a good novel, you know enough about how novels write to do decent criticism. If you can write a good piece of criticism, you can probably bash out a novel if called to. But that doesn't mean they're the same thing; they're just closely related. Darvill-Evans writes an essay that is genuinely good for somebody who has no training in literary criticism, but it reads like the literary criticism version of the slightly dodgy first novel. Then again, if I were to bash out a Doctor Who novel, I'd probably manage some staggeringly basic screw-ups too. They're different skills.

So for example, you have in his little concluding essay the fact claim that "the fact that place names and even some buildings survive for centuries gives a misleading impression of continuity." Well, no, it doesn't. It gives a completely accurate impression of continuity: the fact that the present developed out of the past. What it gives a misleading impression of is stasis—the idea that the past is identical to the present, or that any given thing from it has survived. And so as a result he confuses "Roger Bacon is different from a contemporary scientist" with "Roger Bacon was not a predecessor to modern science."

And here we have the rub. Darvill-Evans has a great book here, but he doesn't quite have the know-how of theory and criticism needed to do the job he's trying to do. And so he gets that detail wrong. But what's interesting is that he gets it wrong in a way that is largely incidental. It's one specific detail he gets wrong in a book that has much larger ambitions and that ends up being a quite impressive commentary on and partial indictment of Doctor Who in 1976.

The comics writer Warren Ellis, for a while, knocked on fascinatingly about the idea of the unexploded bombs of the twentieth century: the unresolved detritus of history still recent enough to feel visceral but buried enough to feel forgotten. This phrase—unexploded bombs—necessarily has more power in the UK than in the US. In the UK, there is still the problem of literal unexploded bombs, mostly German-made ones from the war, lying around in places and waiting to maim or kill someone. This is the metaphor Ellis is going for: the lurking disasters of wars we thought were over. In this book, then, Darvill-Evans deals with the unexploded bombs of 1970s Doctor Who—the Baker era most obviously, but also and significantly the Pertwee era.

The most obvious aspect of this is the Doctor/Companion pairing. Nyssa, after all, is a companion who shows up in Baker's second-to-last story, and is mostly associated with the Peter Davison era. So the Doctor is still some four seasons out from actually meeting Nyssa, while Nyssa, in this book, has long since parted company with the Doctor. This is a carefully-chosen pairing; Baker's Doctor and Nyssa go together, but just barely. Add the detail that Nyssa is at the end of her story, however, and there becomes one fundamental problem: Nyssa at the end of her story really and in a fundamental sense doesn't go with Baker's Doctor. There's one very simple reason for this: Adric.

So, not to spoil the big surprise or anything, but there's this companion named Adric who shows up late in Baker's run, and he bites the dust towards the end of Peter Davison's first season in a big, moving episode with a silent credit sequence so that fans can properly hear the sound of their own delighted cackling. We'll do a more even-handed treatment when we come to it, but this is significant in that he's the only "proper" companion to die (Katarina and Sara both being marginal examples).

The thing is, Adric's death couldn't have happened in the Baker era. I mean, they thought about things like that: Leela, Sarah Jane, and the Brigadier were all, at various points, slated for demolition. But they never did, and there's an obvious reason for that: Baker, like Pertwee, is leading man. The leading man role is defined by a certain invulnerability. All of the Doctors since Hartnell have been played as highly charismatic figures, but Baker and Pertwee take it further in a particular direction than anyone else. Their Doctors are not only charismatic but particularly unchanging and imperious—to the point where Lawrence Miles's getting the Doctor dirty and having him shot in *Interference* was a big, transgressive moment. Pertwee and Baker are, in other words, safe.

This is violated occasionally, most particularly with Sarah's manic reaction to going blind in *The Brain of Morbius*, but for the most part there's not a frequent sense that real harm might come to the characters. Even when Sarah complains about her circumstances, she never quite complains about the danger, instead saying "I'm sick of being cold and wet, and hypnotised left right and centre. I'm sick of being shot at, savaged by bug-eyed monsters, never knowing if I'm coming or going or been." She's annoyed, not scared.

So what you have in *Asylum* is a Doctor who genuinely doesn't believe that any harm can come to his companions paired with a companion who knows better. Or, to put it another way, a companion who desperately wants to find somewhere safe and a Doctor who has no understanding of how bad he is at providing it. This, in turn, is paired with a thoroughly interesting overall plot. The novel consists of two prologues, seven chapters, and an epilogue. All of the overtly science fiction content takes place in the prologues and epilogue. The middle section could, for all practical purposes, be a historical in the classic Hartnell tradition.

In the prologues and epilogue, however, we get a story about alien refugees who, in a desperate bid to survive, send one of their number back in time to try to get Roger Bacon, the nearest thing to a scientist they can find, to whip up a decent elixir of life for them. While the events of the middle section are caused by this, it doesn't become apparent to the Doctor. For all he knows, he's having a historical adventure, albeit one caused by something futzing with history.

The result is a rarity in Doctor Who stories: a story where the reader knows far more than the Doctor does throughout the story. The Doctor never encounters the aliens. Which means he never saves them either. They fail—not because of the Doctor as such (their plan would never have worked), but in a way related to him. He drops into their world, stops their scheme, and leaves without ever realizing they're there or helping them. He misses this material suffering, and the worst part is, he doesn't even look for it, instead treating all suffering that happens in the past as necessary and thus not worth looking at or thinking seriously about.

Taken in parallel with its dismissal of Bacon, *Asylum* begins to look like an attack on the "great man" theory of history. This theory is itself something of an unexploded bomb: discredited among scholars and seemingly immortal among the laity. Its main point is pretty much what it says on the tin: historical progress comes from the intervention of "great men"—called "heroes" in the original formulation—at key moments. Attached to this is a sense of an objective history that can be described objectively as a narrative with convenient main characters, as opposed to as a subjective, messy narrative comprised of memories and conflicts. "Great man" history, in practice, is usually nothing more than a tool to erase marginal perspectives from history in favor of a perspective that's not even of the dominant culture, but specifically of those with power within that culture. And I'll go one further and suggest that fandom's typical view of the Time Lords as all-powerful technocrats overseeing history embraced by fandom is inexorably linked to the flaws of "great man" history.

To be fair, in 1976, Doctor Who cannot help endorsing "great man" theory for a simple reason: it's a show about a hero who goes around intervening in key moments of history all the time. This is, philosophically, a real problem. And the solution, such as it is, is eventually to raise larger ethical questions about the Doctor—to ask if, in fact, he is a great man driving forward the engine of history or whether he's a figure of destruction and calamity. The split of Nyssa and the Doctor being from opposite ends of Adric's death is, ultimately, about this. We have a Doctor who is unambiguously a Great Man and a companion who knows unambiguously that he's not, at least in the capital-letter sense of that phrase.

By misunderstanding Bacon, Darvill-Evans misses the opportunity to argue for an alternative model to this formulation, to show that even if the great man model is flawed, there's still a sense of historical development that comes out of the everyday messiness of human behavior. The result is a book that delivers an effective critique, but has nothing left in the tank when it's done beyond a variation on Terry Nation's appallingly cliché "the only alternative to living is dying" sentiment from *Death to the Daleks*. Whereas a book that had taken Bacon's transitional role in the development of science seriously while still showing the failures of treating him as the forefather of science, and in which the Doctor's didactic monologue had reflected this complexity instead of essentially bullying Nyssa with an "I'm a better interpreter of history than you" monologue would have, in every regard, been better than this. It would have offered a third way in which the Doctor is neither a Great Man nor a Great Monster but just a man, like any other, who muddles through the universe in a particularly interesting and appealing way.

The problem is ultimately one of insufficient theory. Darvill-Evans is playing with the right set of ideas, but ultimately doesn't quite know them well enough to build them into the story he wants to tell. The result is a story that shows us a lot of problems with how the show handled history and heroism in 1976, but that doesn't quite manage to move beyond them. But in the end, there's only so much one can criticize a Doctor Who book starring a past Doctor for failing to transcend the limitations of the show that existed in the era it was set in. Yes, Darvill-Evans doesn't quite show how to move from Doctor Who's frustrating reliance on great man history to a suitably messy and materialist view of the world. But then again, we're not going to solve that problem completely any time on the show soon either. *Asylum* at least manages to make the problem visible, which is more than most of the actual episodes of the era can say.

And He Is Me (*The Face of Evil*)

It's January 1, 1977. Johnny Mathis is at number one with "When a Child is Born," because apparently Christmas songs don't fall from the charts when you'd expect them to. It's not until the 15th that David Soul's "Don't Give Up On Us" knocks Mathis down to number two. Soul holds number one for the fourth week of the story as well. Stevie Wonder, Mike Oldfield, ABBA, Queen, and ELO also chart. Album charts also show that The Eagles have *Hotel California* out, Genesis has *Wind and Wuthering* out, and Queen has *A Day at the Races* out. The Sex Pistols have their first charting song, "Anarchy in the UK," fall out of the charts in here as well, having entered while the show was on break.

Since *The Deadly Assassin* aired, The Band disbanded, nearly four thousand people died in an earthquake in Turkey, and Patrick Hillery was elected President of Ireland. Bob Marley was shot in an assassination attempt in Jamaica, then, two days later, performed at the Smile Jamaica Concert, originally saying he would perform one song, but then giving a ninety-minute performance in which he displayed his bullet wounds to the crowd. He then withdrew to the UK for two years, where he would record the album *Exodus*. Also of major note is the Sex Pistols catapulting to notoriety after appearing on Thames Television's *Today* program with Bill Grundy and engaging in a profanity-ridden interview. This set off a good old-fashioned moral panic of the sort we'll talk about in a few chapters' time.

While during this story, Commodore demonstrates the first all-in-one computer, the PET, at the Consumer Electronics Show in Chicago. EMI sacks the Sex Pistols, much to their delight. Gary Gilmore is executed in Utah, the first execution in the US since the return of the death penalty. And Jimmy Carter takes office and immediately pardons Vietnam draft dodgers.

While on the bookshelf...

I mean, on television as well. But let's begin with the bookshelf. For me, specifically the third shelf down on the first section of the left-hand side of the center alcove of my parents' library. That was where their substantial collection of Target books, spanning highlights of the First through Fifth Doctors, resided. These books have moved on—these days the shelf consists of a miscellaneous smear of old detective/spy novels of the sort my parents read, the Target books themselves having passed into my possession, which means they're yet to be sorted into my library's organization.

I say all of this for two reasons. The first is that *The Face of Evil* is one of several stories from this period that I experienced first as a Terrance Dicks novelization. The second is that the continual focus on the material nature of history dictates this approach. Doctor Who is not just an idea but a set of material experiences: a real set of television broadcasts, videos, DVDs, books, and acts of viewing and reading. Attentiveness to the material conditions of Doctor Who is a part of its story. And the nature of Doctor Who is that these material conditions are only partially constrained by time. This story aired at the beginning of 1977, but since the publication of Dicks's novelization in January of 1978, the story has, in one form or another, existed continually. This is a fact that's always erased by the ritual of our entry beginnings here.

The period where I read Target novelizations corresponded to the period where I was limited to the Doctor

Who that my parents had taped. So we're still mainly in the fifth grade here. I brought the books to school with me, holing up in a corner of the room for a daily SSR. That's Sustained Silent Reading, a ritualistic daily period of reading. For the most part my reading focused on Tom Baker stories. Within that list I favored ones with Romana, which was an era my parents spoke warmly of but had no videos of (and one comparatively poorly represented on the early VHS releases—for a long time it was just *Shada*, and then, later *City of Death* imported from the UK). But I also read *The Face of Evil* then. It doesn't stick particularly well in the memory twenty years later, but I remember vividly the story's most interesting conceit: the idea that the Doctor is returning to a planet where he made a mistake in the past that he has forgotten.

Rereading the novel, the thing that strikes me most is the way in which so much of what we assume to be the Doctor's default characterization comes from the novels. Admittedly, this period of the show frequently features ideas and takes on things that later became the default. The new series frequently does episodes that are collages and remakes of classic series stories, particularly drawing on the Hinchcliffe era. For instance, *The Impossible Planet/The Satan Pit* two-parter consists of direct lifts of *Planet of Evil*, *Pyramids of Mars*, and *Robots of Death* put into a blender, while *The Unquiet Dead* is unabashedly a remake of *The Talons of Weng-Chiang*. This is also the point in the show that much of David Tennant's characterization of the Doctor is clearly drawn from, with Baker getting several moments a story that it is easy to imagine Tennant performing almost exactly the same way.

All of this just restates what we already know—that we are in the midst of one of the most remembered and beloved eras of Doctor Who's history. What I'm talking about is altogether subtler. Dicks fills in reams of details about the Doctor's thought processes, talking about how "he'd set a course for Earth. Or had he? Had his fingers sent the TARDIS to some other destination, guided by some impulse deep in his unconscious mind?" or reflecting openly on how the Doctor is lonely without Sarah there. There's also a distinct change in tone between passages giving insight into the Doctor and other passages. Consider the beginning of chapter two: "The trouble with forests, decided the Doctor, is that they are undoubtedly rather monotonous." Compare that phrasing, particularly the double qualification of "undoubtedly rather," with the more clipped prose Dicks uses when narrating a passage from the perspective of another character: "Calib stood silent, considering the information. Already his cunning mind was seeking ways to turn this incident to his advantage." The Doctor, in other words, is given a wordiness in all of his descriptions that other characters don't get, increasing the sense that he is in some sense an outsider to the narrative.

These strands are every bit as much a part of the evolution of Doctor Who as the ones we track more regularly. And for all that I use this book to establish counter-narratives and give alternative depths to stories, the dominant, default narrative of Doctor Who is real and has its material foundations as well. These narratives do not compete but compliment, creating further wrinkles and nuances to the vast gestalt that is "Doctor Who Canon," i.e. "everything ever written that isn't Enid Blyton's *Noddy* series, unless the Doctor was lying in *The Unicorn and the Wasp*." This is another reiteration of history's endless propensity for reiteration. The same story is told, across media and time, literally recurring and reiterating endlessly.

This frame of reference exists for every story, but it carries an odd potency with this story. Not only because in its first iteration this story follows the classic Doctor Who story with the single most complex version of this process of reiteration, but because this story is itself concerned explicitly with the reiterations of history. An interesting feature of the back four of Season Fourteen is that they end up oddly mirroring the first four/five stories of the series at large. We've already discussed how the Kennedy parallels make *The*

Deadly Assassin a reframing of *An Unearthly Child*. The next story, *The Robots of Death*, evokes both *The Daleks* in its play with the concepts of machines and identity, and *The Edge of Destruction* in its opening TARDIS scene about the function of the ship. And *Talons of Weng-Chiang*, for obvious reasons, evokes *Marco Polo*. Given this theory, here we have a strange mirror of *100,000 BC* (readers may remember that I argued for treating what is conventionally called the four-episode first story of Doctor Who as a one-parter followed by a three-parter).

The primitive tribes are, of course, different. *100,000 BC*'s Orb and this story's Xoanon are not the same gods. But reiterations always drift; the similarities are far more striking. The Doctor arrives at the height of a leadership dispute within each tribe. Each tribe worships a god that they visibly misunderstand. And, not to belabor the obvious, but each tribe is in fact a primitive tribe. And, of course, the Sevateem are a tribe the Doctor has visited in the past. In this case we have a piece of continuity that is thoroughly metaphoric, but it is nevertheless clearly present. Any primitive tribe that the Doctor has had a profound influence on the development of is, in an unavoidable sense, a reiteration of the Tribe of Gum.

In which case what this story sets up is truly incredible. But to get to that, we have to take a quick layover at cargo cults. Once again we have an idea here that is cropping up on multiple fronts almost simultaneously. Just as Foucault and Doctor Who seized on the idea of the Panopticon simultaneously, here, within about a six-year period, we have a couple major moments of fascination with the idea of cargo cults. Richard Feynman delivered his famous "Cargo Cult Science" speech in 1974, while the famed *The Gods Must Be Crazy* was first released in 1980 (though it didn't come out in English for five more years). Squarely in the middle of this we have *The Face of Evil*. So clearly there's something in the air around here.

Cargo cults, if you're not familiar with them, are a type of religious practice that spring up in populations that had contact with more technologically advanced civilizations that was then cut off. Usually this happened in the Pacific during World War II, as islands that were of strategic use in the war against Japan had huge amounts of goods shipped into them, and were then largely abandoned by the US after the war. On several of these islands the tribes quickly generated a new religion built around the idea of getting these goods back to the island and restoring the plenty that existed during the war. The cults are characterized by an inaccurate aping of the practices of the Americans (or whoever)—most famously building landing strips in the jungle and engaging in an imitation of the procedures for having a plane land in an attempt to get the cargo to return to the island.

Cargo cults are kind of doubly problematic. First of all, they represent an egregious bit of cultural violence due to colonialism—a sobering reminder of just how much the West just casually destroyed entire cultures and lifestyles without even meaning to. Second, however, there's an uncomfortable tendency among western cultures to treat cargo cults as a source of novelty—either, as Feynman does, using them as a self-evident metaphor for sloppy intellectual practices, or as *The Gods Must Be Crazy* does, as a source of comedy: look at the funny little bushman worshiping the Coke bottle. There's a real cruelty to this double logic. The cargo cult is bad in part because it's a deformation and corruption of existing cultures, but we also refuse to take it seriously because we recognize it as a silly misunderstanding of the West. And in doing so, we repeat the violence against the tribes in question, delegitimizing their culture twice instead of once.

In *The Face of Evil*, then, we have a truly strange phenomenon: a cargo cult based around the Doctor. There are a number of interesting implications of this. First of all, it marks the first real step since *Planet of the Spiders* to present the Doctor as thoroughly fallible, and the first time since *The Massacre* that his fallibility has been defined in terms of its consequences for the people around him. This is a first, tentative step towards the themes *Asylum* was wrestling with.

The Doctor completely ruined an entire civilization through his errors, and this story is him cleaning up a mess that is entirely his fault: not in the mere sense of "he brought this threat to Earth" that we get in *The Masque of Mandragora* but in the sense of "there are centuries of real destruction and death that have happened as a result of his actions."

Second, however, we are presented with, two stories in a row, a shadow version of Doctor Who as a whole. Just as the Matrix on Gallifrey is Doctor Who as written by the Master, here the Doctor is forced to deal with Doctor Who as written by people who do not understand anything about Doctor Who. To some extent this is the natural evolution of the general tendency of Doctor Who to be about ideas and stories that has been developing since *Genesis of the Daleks* and *Pyramids of Mars*. Eventually it had to hit the point in which the Doctor is inserted into the pre-existing story of Doctor Who.

The result is a fairly straightforward dialectic. The Doctor's version of Doctor Who comes into conflict with Xoanon's version in a way that renders them mutually exclusive. This is not merely a practical consequence of Xoanon's desire to kill the Doctor, but a fundamental one. Xoanon's entire conception of the universe is threatened by the Doctor, whereas Xoanon's existence as a failure of the Doctor's is a direct threat to the Doctor's ethical legitimacy: indeed, in Xoanon's worldview the Doctor is the very embodiment of evil itself. The story thus presents us with two seemingly irreconcilable positions.

The end synthesis, then, is Leela. On the one hand she is a character born out of Xoanon's society and out of the Doctor's failures. On the other hand, however, the Doctor takes her on board the TARDIS to travel with him, albeit grudgingly. By the end of the story, therefore, she is simultaneously a part of both the Doctor's version of the show and of Xoanon's. The consequences of this, of course, are going to extend far beyond this story, creating another iteration of the Problem of Susan. This time we are closer to the original formulation of the conflict between the companion's role as being subservient to the Doctor and the companion's own individual identity and existence separate from the Doctor.

In this case, however, we have the problem manifesting in an unusually literal sense. For really the first time since *The Silurians* the Doctor and his companion have an actively antagonistic element to their relationship. The Doctor wants to change Leela to be more to his liking, and Leela is resistant to being changed. And because of the Eliza Doolittle aspect of the plot, this conflict plays out in a way with profound material and social consequences. The show, in what is either a staggering feat of ambition or of hubris, is now playing the Problem of Susan out as an account of social and historical development. And this is, in its own way, a microcosm of the story's larger concerns. This is a story about the way in which the Doctor has traumatically rewritten another culture, and it leads to an ongoing plot line of the Doctor trying to aggressively rewrite someone's cultural upbringing. It's terribly clever and, more to the point, unsettling.

And on top of all of this, it's a good story. The Doctor has some great moments, Louise Jameson is a fantastic actress, the plot is full of creative ideas and great images like a spectral Doctor's face that kills people and the sublime third episode cliffhanger. Once again we have a series that is firing on all cylinders, matching ambitious ideas with fantastic stories in ways that justify the way in which the series and its individual stories persist uncannily over time. Indeed, this story's basic process of deforming Doctor Who and then reconciling the deformed version with the original itself serves as an allegory for the process of reiteration and complexly integrated variations that creates the larger cultural artifact of Doctor Who.

In other words, this story both represents the material process by which Doctor Who functions as a cultural force and performs that process itself as a successful and well-remembered piece of Doctor Who. Or, to use its own logic, it juxtaposes the representation and the thing itself, and then, through the very process it describes, synthesizes them into a single object. And it does so with a casual confidence that suggests that the show is not even reaching to do this: that this sort of dizzying and complex integration of multiple material frames of reference is now simply business as usual for the show.

Oh, It's a Robot! (*The Robots of Death*)

It's January 29th, 1977. David Soul continues to implore you not to give up on us. After two weeks, Julie Covington takes over number one with "Don't Cry For Me Argentina." As it happens, the truth is that Covington, who declined the title role in Andrew Lloyd Weber's *Evita*, had never left Argentina, though this is largely because she had also never been there. One week later it goes to Leo Sayer's "When I Need You." Also in the charts are Elvis and... things I have honestly never heard of. Let's try Heatwave, Barry Biggs, Rose Royce, and Harold Melvin and the Bluenotes.)

While in real news, between the last episode of *The Face of Evil* and the first episode of this the Massacre of Atocha took place in Madrid. Spain was still in the fragile period of transition between Franco's military dictatorship and a meaningful democracy, and this was basically the darkest day of that process. Neofascists, failing to find the communist leaders they were looking for, simply opened fire on whoever they could find, killing five and injuring four more. The gunmen, believing the government would protect them, did not even attempt to flee Madrid. In cheerier news, *2000 AD*, arguably the most important of the British comics magazines, publishes its first issue or "prog." More on that next book.

While on television we have one of the big classics: *The Robots of Death*. This is widely (and not unreasonably) cited as one of the greatest Doctor Who stories of all time, and was trotted out by the BFI to represent the entirety of the Tom Baker era. Certainly the video release supports that: it's another early story that every Doctor Who fan of a certain age has seen. But after establishing its classic bona fides, every discussion of the story these days begins with it: it's a shameless rip-off of Isaac Asimov's novels *The Caves of Steel* and *The Naked Sun*.

It's a minor complaint, to be sure. But that it's pointed out at all is strange. After all, anybody who is just now waking up to the Hinchcliffe era's tendency to do lifts of existing works of fiction should probably have a look at, oh, say, *Blood from the Mummy's Tomb*, *The Quatermass Experiment*, *Frankenstein*, and *The Manchurian Candidate*. And yet those stories aren't nearly as regularly talked about in terms of their source material as *The Robots of Death* is. This is a bit unusual, and it's worth looking at why.

A lot of it is, I think, simply that Doctor Who fandom— i.e., the people who write and read reviews of individual stories instead of just watching them like normal people—are largely sci-fi people, and thus know and adore Asimov. There's a peculiar sort of person to whom *The Caves of Steel* is better known than *The Manchurian Candidate*, and among them this lift jars strikingly. This relies on the assumption that Doctor Who is actually a closer cousin to Asimov than it is to the other sources: in other words, that it's a normal sci-fi show. Fourteen seasons in, we should know better. Even though during the 1980s it engaged in a (largely disastrous) attempt to reinvent itself as a cult sci-fi show in the *Star Trek* mold, that's not its default mode, and it's definitely not how its makers considered the show in 1977. This is family teatime entertainment for an audience that mostly wouldn't have heard of Asimov. So yes, the ideas are in part taken from Asimov, but surely repackaging Asimov for a mass family audience is a valid thing to do with a show with one foot in the world of serious science fiction and the other in mass appeal entertainment.

So even if this were just a straight repackaging of Asimov in the way that, say, *Death to the Daleks* was a repackaging of H. Rider Haggard or *Pyramids of Mars* was a straight repackaging of Hammer's Mummy films, there would be some sense to it. Asimov is worth repackaging. Furthermore, there's something to be said for precisely what Asimov is repackaged. The two Asimov stories most similar to this are, as I said, *The Caves of Steel* and *The Naked Sun*. Those two books, along with *Robots of Dawn*, published in the 1980s, form a set of stories following the crime-solving team of Elijah Baley, a human, and R. Daneel Olivaw, a robot. But the book most people think of when they think of Isaac Asimov and robots is *I, Robot*. So the first thing we should note is that there's a profound difference between *I, Robot* and the Baley/Olivaw books.

I, Robot is really a short story collection, and all of the stories in it are about robots. This may seem terribly obvious, but it's a telling point all the same. In *I, Robot*, Asimov invents his famous three laws of robotics and then writes a series of stories in which he explores the consequences of those laws. The stories read like little logic puzzles in which the trick is how the rigid laws of robotics interact with an idiosyncratic situation to produce an interesting result. They're quite good for what they are, but they fall into a particular model of science fiction story, and one that is rarely seen any more.

The Baley/Olivaw books, on the other hand, are something more interesting. First of all, they're something we're familiar with as Doctor Who fans: genre fusions. They mash together the sci-fi genre with the mystery genre. And in this regard, Asimov deserves a lot of credit, because he explicitly wrote them to prove to John W. Campbell that those genres could be merged, which opened a lot of doors for science fiction as a genre. But they also represent a move forward into a more complex sort of story. *I, Robot* is about how a set of rules invented by the writer work. It's interesting, but a limited thought exercise. The Baley/Olivaw books, on the other hand, are explorations of types of society in which

Olivaw is used to provide a detached outsider's perspective that can comment on the society. This is a fundamentally more complex sort of structure.

And, just to gesture at a theme that will play into this project heavily in the next book, this represents an important stage in moving beyond the limited "golden age" version of science fiction as a genre—a transition that is, as of February 1977, about three months out from its defining moment in the form of *Star Wars* (or ten months in the UK). As I said, I'm gesturing forward here, but thematically, in terms of the direction science fiction was going in 1977, the particular Asimov books that Chris Boucher is lifting from here are a significant and potent choice.

All of which said, I've been acting for six paragraphs like all *The Robots of Death* does is pinch some concepts from Asimov. Which isn't even remotely true. I mean, yes, obviously it does pinch some concepts from Asimov, but that's not all it does by a long shot. For one thing, there's a major difference in the sort of mystery stories that Asimov and Boucher are telling. Asimov writes Elijah Baley as a detective in the Hammet/Chandler noir tradition: the sort of detective described in Chandler's seminal "The Simple Art of Murder." That essay, which, if you've never read, you really should, attacks many other mystery writers, singling out the British tradition exemplified by Agatha Christie.

Boucher, on the other hand, writes what is a straight-up Christie-style mystery, with the production team falling into step behind him with a gorgeous art-deco inspired set that perfectly matches the Agatha Christie vibe. In terms of the mystery, this owes far more to *And Then There Were None* than it does to the Asimov novels, and certainly more than it does to something like *The Big Sleep* or *The Maltese Falcon*. This is a story about a killer among a small group of people, all of whom have at least one dark secret. It's vintage Christie.

So off the bat there's something to be said for the story taking repatriating Asimov's idea to the British idiom, showing that the British mystery tradition is just as good as the American one for matching up with science fiction. Indeed, he even takes a shot at Asimov—Poul and D84 are clearly analogues for Baley and Olivaw, and by the end of the story one is dead and the other has had a complete nervous breakdown. Far from imitating Asimov, Boucher goes out of his way to screw over Asimov's characters. This isn't just appropriation but a careful and considered response to the original text. (Similarly, the Doctor taking down the ranting mad scientist by making his voice squeaky via helium is very possibly the most beautiful defeat of an enemy to date in Doctor Who—a perfect example of the Doctor simultaneously winning by being clever and by refusing to take his enemies seriously.)

And on top of composing an effective response to two classic science fiction novels, Boucher further develops Leela as a character. One of the biggest problems with Leela is the way in which she gets pushed into the Eliza Doolittle role to the Doctor's Henry Higgins, thus troublingly reasserting a wealth of Victorian colonial ideologies, including many of the ones her debut story was in part a reaction against. All of this comes to a head in *The Talons of Weng-Chiang*, but for now let's just acknowledge the problem.

Given that, the needed counter narrative is fairly obvious. Leela, due to the nature of her origin, is simultaneously the product of the Doctor's actions and a reiteration of an older form of civilization. The words "savage" and "primitive" are problematic, but they capture a basic truth: Leela's civilization is at a much earlier level of historical development than any companion the Doctor has ever had before. But notably, her culture is also one that extends entirely from the Doctor's actions. She's not so much a primitive as the reiteration of primitive culture. She is, in truth, as much futuristic as primitive.

In which case the way forward is to combine those, using that disjunction to produce insights about the world that are at once savvy and based on her somewhat orthogonal relationship to other cultures. This role, in fact, is one very similar to the one Olivaw plays in Asimov's novels. She can provide, to use the more ideologically charged term, détourned understandings of culture. This is what has to happen for her character to work: she has to be able to outdo the Doctor at times by having a different kind of insight to his.

Boucher pulls that off beautifully by having her figure out what's going on with Poul episodes ahead of everyone else, only to be unable to frame her insight in terms that everyone else understands. It's not until in the end, in which body language and human nuance turns out to be central to everything that we understand that Leela has spent the entire story ahead of the game. This is exactly what Leela needs to have happen on a regular basis in order to work as a character. Inevitably, of course, she, like every other innovative companion, regresses from the cleverness of these early stories into a more generic role. But here, at least, we see exactly how she's supposed to work—by showing that the reiteration of history contains a form of truth and knowledge and by complicating the notion of "progress" itself.

This also brings us to the otherwise strange explanation of how the TARDIS works at the beginning. The Doctor engages in an explanation of how the interior of the TARDIS can exceed the size of the exterior by framing it in terms of how objects that are closer look larger than they do when far away, then making a comment about how "If you could keep that exactly that distance away and have it here, the large one would fit inside the small one." This is total nonsense even as technobabble goes. In particular, it doesn't jibe at all with the part of his explanation that ultimately gets adopted as the standard explanation—that the interior of the TARDIS is a different dimension than the one the exterior exists in. That's perfectly sensible: the door is a dimensional portal. We've seen those before in various forms.

But the explanation the Doctor gives is ridiculous. The differing sizes of objects at different distances is purely a phenomenon of optics and the human eye. It's a matter of interior human experience, not an actual physical property of objects. The comparative difference in size exists only as an illusion in the human mind, based not on the objects themselves but on the light bouncing off of them into the human eye. Thus what the Doctor says about keeping an object at a distance and having it here to fit objects into one another is complete nonsense—a piece of technobabble that simply does not cohere to reality on a meaningful level. But crucially, Leela calls the Doctor out on it, accusing him of being silly. Which he dismisses, but this ignores the real point of the scene: Leela is right. The Doctor has obviously just BSed an explanation to try to shut her up. (Or, alternatively, the TARDIS is purely a phenomenon of mental perception as opposed to an actual object. Which is closer to the style of interpretation I usually pick, and delightfully compatible with the understanding of Time Lords I proposed for *The Deadly Assassin*.)

More than anything, *The Robots of Death* is a strong validation of the Hinchcliffe approach. It's not one of the most spectacularly ambitious stories of the era. In fact, by almost any measure it's the second simplest story of its season. But even in a comparatively simple mode we have a story that uses genre fusion to comment on and subvert a classic of science fiction while simultaneously continuing to develop the series' ongoing themes about historical progress in new and interesting directions. And it can do it while telling a cracking good adventure yarn. The sheer potency of this show's poetics right now is blinding. May it continue like this forever.

Time Can Be Rewritten (*Corpse Marker*)

Chris Boucher is a tricky case for Doctor Who. He only wrote three stories—all four-parters—that aired within a one-year period. But he's something of a big name in the larger scheme of British science fiction television by dint of being script editor for *Blake's 7* for a while, and, perhaps more importantly, all three of his Doctor Who stories are held in fairly high regard.

That these stories also make up two-thirds of the post-*Deadly Assassin* portion of the Hinchcliffe era adds to the tension. It's clear that Holmes and Hinchcliffe were in the process of dramatically revamping Doctor Who in the latter portion of Season Fourteen, moving away from a structure still grounded in Earth and towards something ... ah, but there's the rub. The Hinchcliffe era is most associated with its "Gothic" tone, but of the post-*Deadly Assassin* stories only *The Talons of Weng-Chiang* feels entirely like what we expect from the Hinchcliffe era. The other two stories, that is, Boucher's stories, are much more overtly science fiction than anything since *The Ark in Space* or so.

More to the point, they're science fiction in an almost Golden Age sense. *The Robots of Death* is an Isaac Asimov riff, and *The Face of Evil* is concerned with Golden Age sci-fi topics like secularism and artificial intelligence. But it's impossible to tell whether this was representative of what Holmes and Hinchcliffe planned to do prior to Hinchcliffe's sacking, simply because they're only by one writer. Even Leela isn't entirely representative: Holmes and Hinchcliffe intended her to be used for a three-story arc and written out in *The Talons of Weng-Chiang*, and it was only Graham Williams's desire to minimize the amount of stuff he had to deal with coming in that kept her onboard.

In other words, what we often take to indicate where Holmes and Hinchcliffe were headed next is, in practice, just the particular interests and focuses of Chris Boucher. Nevertheless, as the previous two essays reveal, Boucher was very good. And so it's not surprising that when he came back in 1998 to write for BBC Books's Past Doctor Adventures line it was something of a big deal: one of the lost greats of the classic series returning. Free pints for all, the prodigal son returns.

There's always a risk in a return like this. The Hinchcliffe era and Boucher had both been gone for a quarter-century. The latter had matured, while the other remained trapped in amber as the seeming peak of Doctor Who before the show went steadily downhill towards until, in 1999, it was merely an obscure line of novels seemingly destined for extinction. Boucher was going back to what was, by consensus, the holy and sacred Last Great Era of Doctor Who, and thus the series' absolute apex. Notably, that show was not actually what he'd written for at the time. The Hinchcliffe era was well-liked at the time, but it's only the decade-long stuttering collapse of the series after Hinchcliffe's sacking that really cemented him as the producer of the series' glory days. And so the weight put on Boucher's shoulders was, in practice, ridiculous: he was expected to show what the series could have done that would have prevented cancellation.

Boucher was damned if he did, damned if he didn't. If he simply tried to pick up where he left off, then his novels would feel like old hat. If he innovated too fiercely, then he would fundamentally frustrate the fan base's underlying desire for the return of a classic writer. So it's hardly a surprise that Boucher's novels proved controversial.

Let's set aside, then, the question of quality. Suffice it to say that *Corpse Marker* is an entertaining read that captures Baker's Doctor well, and that Boucher is one of the handful of writers to use Leela to her full capacity. It's a briskly paced sci-fi thriller that doesn't overstay its welcome. And it falls squarely between the two extremes that Boucher could have gone to—it's recognizable as a Boucher story, but it's also clearly not written in the mid-1970s. It reads like what it is: the return of a writer to a franchise after twenty-five years.

What's more interesting about *Corpse Marker* is the degree to which it serves as a reflection on the way in which Boucher was an odd fit for the Hinchcliffe era. In one sense the novel is the archetypal Hinchcliffe story: an old threat from the past comes back. But, of course, Taren Capel isn't back, having thoroughly died in *The Robots of Death*. The frame may be the Hinchcliffe standard, but the contents aren't. Rather, the contents are straight science fiction.

Unfortunately for Boucher, science has shifted a bit. Artificial intelligence and robots aren't the most gripping conceptual read for the world of 1999. They're firmly one of those futures that never arrived: a dead end, along with space travel, where science fiction diverged from actual technological progress. And so what would have, in 1977, been a terribly clever alternate version of the Hinchcliffe era instead falters. Taren Capel doesn't quite work as a dead threat returned, nor does his real identity as mad robot SASV1 quite work as a sci-fi concept: by 1999 Capel is no longer an image of the future, but of the past's future.

This isn't inherently a problem. Plenty of Doctor Who stories have gotten away with playing in the rubble of abandoned futures—it's arguably the most sensible approach to the task these days. The problem is that Boucher doesn't really play it this way. Instead, he seems like the sort of person who still thinks that science fiction about robots has a lot to say about the human condition.

But there's a larger issue here. As suggested, the Hinchcliffe era isn't all that invested in science fiction. It did plenty of sci-fi stories, but even those tended to be sci-fi takes on horror that owed more to HP Lovecraft than Isaac Asimov. The actual business of Golden Age literary science fiction—commenting on the implications of technology—just wasn't something the show was ever particularly interested in. The Hinchcliffe era's interest in the future was typically just as a canvas on which to paint distortions of the past.

And given that *The Face of Evil* fell into that category, as did his Season Fifteen script *Image of the Fendahl*, it was easy to assume that Boucher fit into that mold. But *Corpse Marker* suggests that, no, he's actually firmly a sci-fi writer in an almost classical sense. Because *Corpse Marker* is about the business of structuring society and controlling it.

This is, in many ways, odd territory for Doctor Who, and it's telling that after bringing down the existing structures of society the Doctor and Leela just bugger off and allow technocratic authority to prosper. The book's major interest is in criticizing cults and fanaticism, and it seems to ultimately go back to the ethics dominant in the Hartnell era—that scientists were reasonable types who, if you let run the world, would probably do a reasonable and good job of it.

To say that this is an odd fit for Doctor Who in 1977, let alone 1999, is an understatement. Doctor Who, for the most part, prefers to bristle with anarchic and revolutionary energy, typically suggesting that the best solution to a given problem is to burn down the fundamental tenets of society and then go running off into the night to find something new.

And yet despite all of this, Boucher's take feels like a road not taken. Not to get ahead into the next volume, but the incoming producer after Hinchcliffe, Graham Williams, does focus the show more on the science fiction, although still not in a Golden Age style as such. But there's a narrow window here: one of the earliest events in the next volume is the release of *Star Wars*, which, as you might imagine, changes just about everything in terms of expectations surrounding science fiction on television. One of the things it did was prompt a final and decisive turning away from the Golden Age model, which is part of why *Corpse Marker* feels so strange coming over twenty years after that.

We can, if we want, just about imagine a world in which David Maloney and Chris Boucher, the team who would, starting in 1978, oversee *Blake's 7*, instead took over Doctor Who, creating a last great moment of Golden Age science fiction that existed right as the book was being closed on that approach. Such counterfactuals are, of course, perpetually hypothetical; there's no way to know what that future of Doctor Who would have looked like. *Corpse Marker*, written in 1999 as a novel and not as an episode of a television series, doesn't tell us about alternate 1978s at all.

But equally, it puts the lie to the idea that there is some inevitable historical development that took place in Doctor Who—that the Hinchcliffe era could only have been followed by one thing. There were other directions. *Corpse Marker* is one of them. That may be all we can know, but given that the story of Doctor Who becomes one of decline very soon after this point in its history, it's still worth knowing.

Philip Sandifer

Time Can Be Rewritten (*Eye of Heaven*)

Among the most stereotypically overdone debates in all of Doctor Who fandom is the debate that took place over the so-called wilderness years of the 1990s between the so-called "rad" and "trad" schools of novels. This was a proper debate, and thus characterized by each side considering the other's position to be self-evidently silly and essentially unworthy of discussion, and of everybody actually advocating a middle road between two parodies of extreme viewpoints. Proponents of the "trad" school—short for "traditional"— favored novels that closely hewed to the approach and aesthetics of televised Doctor Who. They tended to view the "rad" school's preference for more radical and experimental novels, as being indicative of a strange sort of Doctor Who fan who was only fond of Doctor Who when it wasn't much like Doctor Who. The "rads" on the other hand largely viewed the traditionalists as unadventurous sticks in the mud who failed to appreciate that anything considered traditional Doctor Who now was, at one point or another, radical Doctor Who. (The other 99% of fandom just read books and enjoyed some while not enjoying others.)

As is usually the case with a divide like this, the truth of the matter is that both sides of the debate are rather silly. We've already seen over the past three volumes how "trad" novels can be subversive and challenging to the aesthetics and approaches of their eras. And we've followed the progress of the series closely enough to know that the idea that all changes are radical shifts is nonsense. The series has often improved incrementally, with "normality" being established through small shifts. The Hinchcliffe era really only did a dramatic revolution of a story twice: once with *Genesis of the Daleks*, and even that's still 80% just "generic Terry Nation story done really well" and would probably have qualified as "trad" in the wilderness years by dint of having Daleks in it. And then, of course, once with *The Deadly Assassin*, which is unquestionably "rad." Still, one example doesn't change the fact that even in an era full of iconic stories, not much is actually radical in televised Doctor Who. And so in this regard we recognize that in fact the very act of writing a Doctor Who novel means that you're signing up to try to do radical and interesting things within a prescribed form—a tradition, if you will. And that criticizing "trad" novels while extolling the virtues of "rad" ones is the height of idiocy. Right? Good. Moving on.

Here we begin to see the other side. Jim Mortimore is one of the archetypal "rad" writers, which should surprise nobody who has been reading this series from the beginning, since one of the first Time Can Be Rewritten essays was on his novel *Campaign*. Unlike with that novel, here he manages to avoid casually reconfiguring reality every chapter via an Aristotle-infused video game being played on the TARDIS. Instead he tells his story through two distinct sequences of alternating chapters in which even and odd-numbered chapters each tell a different part of the story. This is not, to be clear, just perspective jumping. The first half of the book is almost all written from Leela's perspective, but alternates between telling one portion of the story in the odd numbered chapters and a second, chronologically earlier portion, in the even numbered. A similar structure is used in the back half. The result is akin to what would happen if you watched the first two episodes of a story, alternating between them every five minutes or so, and starting with Part Two. And yet despite the ostentatious structure the book is by and large a solid fit with the tone of the show in this period, following the basic structure of a Hinchcliffe-era story (at least once you put the bits in the right order). Plus it's actually quite good to boot. So here's the obligatory celebration of going completely nuts in a Doctor Who novel.

First of all, let's put the kibosh on one of the central lines of critique that books like this get: unintelligibility. I admit that I, being an English teacher and all, am one of the least sympathetic ears imaginable when it comes to the complaint that something is hard to read or hard to follow. Sometimes books are hard. The usual complaint—"it didn't make sense"—is ludicrous, and in essentially every case where you're talking about something that is remotely widely read— let's draw the line at "professionally published" for the sake of argument—simply wrong. Books that don't make sense don't get published. More to the point, a fair number of people have read *Eye of Heaven* and found it to make sense. Saying it doesn't make sense is thus more than a little silly. But nobody wants to say "I was too thick to understand it," so they blame books and authors for their own intellectual shortcomings.

Let's also note that *Eye of Heaven* just isn't that hard a book. It only alternates between two points in its narrative timeline, and tells each individual part of the story in order. The chapters alternate back and forth. The prose is crisp and clear, with only its tendency to shift among viewpoints and occasionally leave the reader spending two or three pages trying to figure out what's happening proving tricky or difficult. And if you, as a reader, are complaining that you sometimes have to go a few pages before the context of something starts to settle... jeez. I mean, that's one of the most fundamental tools of writing you're rejecting there; the idea of revealing key points of context as you go is as basic a literary technique as exists. If you have trouble with it on an inherent level...that's a problem with you. And, I mean, this is more broadly true. I've read an awful lot of Doctor Who books in my life, and anyone who is complaining that they are difficult and hard to understand must break down into a gibbering mess when confronted with James Joyce or William Faulkner. Heck, they must be terrified by Alan Moore or Iain Sinclair. Or, like, this book. I mean, I'm surely preaching to the choir here, having long since scared everyone else off.

But fine. Let's pare this attack on *Eye of Heaven* of its more unfortunately anti-intellectual aspects and try for an approach that doesn't lend itself to complete dismissal. Clearly treating the narrative complexity of *Eye of Heaven* as an inherently bad thing is ludicrous, and clearly you don't want to argue that the book is unintelligible. But like cleverness, complexity is merely something that can be used well, not something that's inherently good. There is such a thing as overkill. The question we should be asking isn't "is *Eye of Heaven* too complex?" but rather "is its complexity appropriate for what it does?"

There are two aspects to this question. The first is whether the book's complexity contributes significantly to what the book has to say. Or, to put it another way, is there a point to all of this, or is it just Mortimore showing how clever he is? The second is whether its complexity is in line with the expectations of its genre. After all, even if we reject the idea that *Eye of Heaven* is particularly hard as books go, if there is a compelling reason why Doctor Who books shouldn't even be that hard, that's a valid criticism.

We'll start with the first. There are, of course, tons of reasons why one might pick a non-chronological narrative style. Most of them fall under the broad heading of breaking the equivalency between story and plot. The easiest way to explain the difference is in terms of a mystery story. The plot of a murder mystery begins with the murderer killing someone. But the story of a murder mystery ends with that. That is to say, the murder is something that happens early on, but in terms of the order things are revealed to the reader, the murder happens late. I use this example because it should make obvious the way in which it is often important to distinguish plot and story: because the order in which the reader learns things is a separate narrative logic to the order in which they happen.

In the case of *Eye of Heaven*, Mortimore is able to simultaneously approach key events—the ones that happen at the end of the even numbered sections—from both ends. For instance, at the point chronologically between the plots of the even- and odd-numbered chapters in the first portion of the book, a major new character is introduced. By interleaving the two sections Mortimore is able to simultaneously build to the character's arrival and show the consequences of her arrival, with the moment of her arrival and the ultimate explanation of who she is coming only when both of those have been explored sufficiently. (A near-identical narrative technique is used in the opening parts of *The Wedding of River Song*, and Moffat uses the technique frequently in his pre-Doctor Who shows. Other adept practitioners include Aaron Sorkin.)

But there's a complexity to this book that exceeds what can be accounted for this way. When time-jumping techniques are used on television they're usually accompanied, at least at the start, with helpful captions saying something like "Four months earlier..." or some other clear signpost as to the relationship between the two timelines. Mortimore makes no such concession, jumping back and forth between his two timelines with no explanation as to how they relate or to who is narrating a given chapter.

This makes sense for what he is doing as well. *Eye of Heaven* is thoroughly steeped in the intellectual tradition of the Hinchcliffe era that it's supposed to embody. This is a book explicitly about the repetitions of history and the nature of memory, and so a structure in which one is forced to engage with the story via idiosyncratic chronology is wholly sensible. For a book about odd and impenetrable legacies of the past, having odd and inexplicable past events that are nevertheless hugely important to what's happening at any given moment adds obvious dimensions to the story.

All of this is also tied in with Mortimore's unusual decision to narrate the novel from various first person perspectives, the most common of which is Leela. (There are also two sections narrated from the Doctor's point of view that are widely criticized in reviews. These criticisms miss that Mortimore is clearly borrowing the narrative voice used on *The Pescatons*. It's a perfectly fair way to sidestep the question of how to narrate a story from the point of view of the Doctor: use the way it's already been done to nobody's particular alarm. It's also very funny.) His decision to use this particular era for this particular story is in no way incidental. This story fills a major thematic gap for Leela that the series itself was never going to (and really should never have given the limitations it would have faced doing so on its budget) by juxtaposing her with indigenous people of the sort that her character was based on. This book exploits the obvious question posed by a character who is a futuristic member of a "primitive" tribe: what happens if you put her opposite a "primitive" Earth culture?

I've been putting "primitive" in scare quotes here because there's a whole nexus of issues with Leela that I've been dancing around and should quickly flesh out. I've complained about the whole "civilizing Leela" tone of stories without really digging into what's wrong with this. At the most basic level, it's just a bit of good old lefty cultural relativism on my part. The implicit value judgment in saying that a civilization with less advanced technology than ours is inferior to ours is obscene. So when the show dips into creating a value judgment around Leela in which the reason she is "less" than the Doctor is that she's a primitive or a savage, it's problematic. And I use that word in its real sense instead of in the generic academic "I am hedging because I want to condemn something but opt out of the moral judgment" sense; it's an interpretive problem. Because there are, of course, ways in which the Sevateem or the Rapa Nui are inferior to the Doctor. They are less good at chemistry and yo-yos. It's not, in other words, that every time the Doctor makes a negative judgment of Leela it's bad. Nor is it that it's bad when the Doctor objects to how violent she is, because that's a moral judgment. (Correspondingly, it would not be bad if Leela objected to how cowardly the Doctor is because of his nonviolence.) But on the other hand, sometimes it is bad—the way in which the Doctor makes dismissive jokes about Leela being a savage while visibly liking her less than he liked his previous companion is... tough to get around the implications of, even if you do know that it's really Baker declining to hide his own dislike of the character/actress/fact that other people appear in his television show.

This gets worse when, as we'll see happen in *The Talons of Weng Chiang*, Leela's "savagery" gets equated with class prejudice. Again, this is the difficult point in which there exist value judgments that can be made, but where an absolute value judgment is horrific. And the show manages to tie those two together, which, of course, isn't that hard because of the fact that education, poverty, and race are correlated due to systemic biases and discrimination in human culture. So this is, basically, one of those really shitty situations that make literary critics want to crawl back into bed instead of writing decently nuanced analyses.

And where all of this gets horribly nasty is that nothing I've said in the last two paragraphs is actually news to anybody. Which means that when we get our political correctness party going and ramp up the discussion of privilege-denial and negative tropes, what we encounter is usually not frothing lunatics who rail against the fundamental moral inferiority of other cultures or of poor people, although you will find plenty of those too.

More often we find cases where people, aware of how horrible it would be to treat another culture as inherently inferior to your own, throw a couple of bones to the "primitives." These bones may range from the horrifically meager (black people sure are good musicians though!) to the exceedingly complex (the subgenre of movies about brilliant minority kids overcoming the odds to succeed), but what they end up doing is creating a cultural norm that reinforces systemic bias. For instance, teaching minority kids that their lives are miserable and hopeless cesspools that only one or two exceptional geniuses will ever rise out of has a disastrous effect on every single minority kid who isn't an exceptional genius. In effect this scenario promotes the idea of a cultural lottery, where some lucky few will transcend the circumstances of their birth and the rest will, in theory, be pacified by the hope that they might get lucky.

What's really tough is that any given "brilliant minority kid succeeds against long odds" movie is in fact made out of a sincere desire to help inspire at-risk kids into doing what it takes to improve their lives, and is based out of a whole host of completely reasonable and understandable and sympathetic and, no, let's go all the way here, ethically good decisions about how minorities have lower graduation rates which trap them in lower-paying jobs that sustain the vicious cycle of poverty. But that doesn't erase the fact that it's feeding a larger cultural stereotype that badly undermines everything that a given movie is trying to accomplish.

What I'm getting at in this somewhat torturous digression is that Leela is always a very difficult character to do anything with. Because on the one hand there are genuinely interesting things to be learned and said about how different cultures interact. And these things get very, very interesting and profound when you start running into things that imply some sort of cultural element that exists in some form in all human or even perhaps in all intelligent cultures. That's the sort of thing that science fiction and fantasy were made for as genres. So in that regard, Leela is a goldmine for the show—a vast trove of amazingly interesting stories.

Except that she's also slap bang in the middle of a host of cultural stereotypes of the sort that make a few concessions to the ethical value of the "savage" while still declaring that they need rich white people to swoop in and save them. So the show is constantly walking this horrible line between brilliant science fiction about the nature of humanity and cratering failures racism/classism. And if you find a critic who says that they enjoy picking through the smoldering ethical rubble of crap like this, know that they are liars and you should not play any games with them for money.

In any case, connecting Leela with some of the tribes whose culture she was based on is really interesting too. There's a really lovely idea in the heart of this book about how truly and horrifically oppressed cultures—ones that are oppressed into extinction or virtual extinction—survive and propagate. And the idea is framed in terms of the Rapa Nui, a culture that had very nearly been driven completely extinct in the time period the book is set in, and of Leela—whose culture was destroyed before her eyes by the Doctor. Indeed, not only was her culture destroyed by the Doctor, so was an entire previous culture whose destruction caused hers to be created. So Leela serves as a nexus of problems of oppression that are less dramatic than what the Rapa Nui suffered, but that are nevertheless truly harmful. So a narrative structure that distances the reader slightly from the action and forces them to feel like cultural outsiders to the story puts the reader in the exact right frame of mind to connect with this larger idea of how dying cultures cause their history to reiterate and survive, for better and for worse.

Which brings us at (far too) long last to the second aspect of our question about whether *Eye of Heaven* is appropriately complex—is this the correct level of complexity for Doctor Who?

The fun answer is: "Well it sure as hell would go over Mary Whitehouse's head."

The larger and more serious answer is that of course it is. I mean, it's not one of the best Doctor Who novels of all time. Mortimore is better at coming up with narrative devices than he is at using them—a problem that anyone who generates a large number of clever narrative devices runs into eventually. (I certainly have some essays in future books where I am not entirely convinced of my own complex structure.) There is a constant sense that he is hitting the exact wrong amount of trying the reader's patience—that if he'd lengthen his leash and really screw around he might have something really special, and that if he reeled it back and tried to take a little bit of the edge off of the alienation of the reader, he might have managed something more effective, but that instead he fell between two stools. But, look, if you're going to criticize Doctor Who novels for not being as adept at narrative experimentation as Alan Moore or William Faulkner, you're doing it wrong. The narrative faults of this novel are solidly in the range of what is acceptable for a Doctor Who novel, and it's only because writers as good as Paul Cornell, Gareth Roberts, Russell T. Davies, and Lawrence Miles wrote Doctor Who novels that Mortimore's novel even looks imperfect in comparison.

Unless , of course, we want to attempt to stray into the much uglier question of whether there's something wrong with making Doctor Who too weird or too hard. Or too anything. I mean, let's just go with the broad question of whether Doctor Who is an appropriate venue for aesthetic extremism. To some extent it is difficult to take anybody who says no seriously. "No" mainly seems like a boring and intellectually uncurious position of the sort that I just don't have the life expectancy to deal with. So let's treat this like the idea that Doctor Who endorses a hardline rationalist position and just look at the best possible form of the argument, figuring that if we shoot that down then all the inferior formulations will go down with it. And any way, given where this book is going to end, tackling the avant garde in Doctor Who makes sense, given that this is in some ways its last stand until 2011 or so.

In many ways, the best possible version of this argument is one of crass commercialism: if you push the show too far towards the avant grade you lose too much of the audience. Even when the show is a niche set of novels, you can only maintain that via the good will of the existing audience. You don't want the novels to become so weird that the line goes out of print. And weird is harder. You lose readers to not getting it and then blaming the book. That's just life. And so you don't want to be too weird unless you're funded by a model that doesn't depend on having a lot of fans.

But there's a moral dimension that can be made here too. Doctor Who is amazing in part because it moves back and forth between the cultural avant garde and the mainstream. It's a show about the point of contact between the normal world and the world of the completely strange. Whether you go back to its original educational mandate, its current "let's have a nice big wholesome cultural event" mandate, or its alchemical mandate, this is very much what the show does. Alchemy through material social progress. This means that it actually can't go too far and still work. If it crosses the line into the completely avant garde, it stops doing one of the things it's there for.

On the other hand, it's a fine line between that observation and "if you act less smart, people will like you more." Which, incidentally, I was told in fourth grade, the year before I discovered Doctor Who. By my teacher. Just to keep that theme in the mix while we discuss this.

It comes down to the fact that Doctor Who is an anthology show. And to the fact that underlies why a bunch of well-meaning movies about smart minority kids become a harmful racist stereotype. Doctor Who novels would be bad if every novel were weird and experimental like *Eye of Heaven*. Just like movies about minorities are bad because every one is about smart minority kids triumphing over adversity. But notably, not every Doctor Who novel is like *Eye of Heaven*. Indeed, hardly any of them are.

But crucially, the entire line would suffer, and in all likelihood suffer even more if none of them were like *Eye of Heaven*. You can't mediate the space between the avant garde and the mainstream without pushing against the lines. Anthology shows triumph in part because they can pull back from any mistake immediately by just not doing that sort of story again. It's hard to do long-term damage with a poor aesthetic decision.

And one thing that we will eventually discover in the back portion of the classic series is that if you fail to push against the limits of experimentalism and ambition occasionally, the show as a whole will wither badly. Very soon the show enters a period where its aspiration is to be comforting instead of challenging, and it goes quite poorly for the show. *Eye of Heaven*, as a story, is set in the last moments before that happens, and it honors that era well.

Time Can Be Rewritten (*The Valley of Death*)

To tip our hand just a little bit, the next story is the last one of the Hinchcliffe era and, by extension, the last one of this volume. Hinchcliffe is, as we've discussed, sacked from the program due to complaints from Mary Whitehouse. To tip our hands a little bit more, the story he goes out on, *The Talons of Weng-Chiang*, is a problematic number because of some rather vicious bits of racism towards the Chinese. Furthermore, it's not the only racially problematic story of the Hinchcliffe era: *The Pyramids of Mars* has some dreadful portrayals of Arabs.

I mention all of this because there's something of a pattern that forms when you look at those two stories alongside *The Valley of Death*, an actual Hinchcliffe-penned story. Some caveats are necessary; first of all, this was not written for the Hinchcliffe era itself. It was a rejected script for Season Seventeen, although About Time claims it would have been used to open Season Fifteen if Hinchcliffe hadn't been sacked. The version we have—a Big Finish release from 2012—was rewritten by Jonathan Morris for audio, a rewrite that must have involved substantive changes since it went from being a script featuring Lalla Ward's Romana to one featuring Leela. On top of that, Morris has been roundly criticized for a xenophobic streak in some of his other writings, most notably his audio *Flip-Flop*.

Blame, in other words, is at best nuanced here. Nevertheless, blame is clearly required. We have here a story in which aliens whose defining traits are that they are little and yellow are discovered by a Victorian expedition, eventually come to contemporary London, and promptly try to take over the world after initially appearing to be nice and friendly. And where the military flat-out says that all aliens are hostile, to no particular objection from the Doctor. It's a dreadful story in this regard.

Some of the defenses wheeled out for *The Talons of Weng-Chiang* and *The Pyramids of Mars* work here as well. The first two episodes are a straight up H. Rider Haggard pastiche, firmly situated in the "lost world" genre. There's not really any way to do Haggard without some racism, because the genre is based on the idea of enlightened western cultures (really just the British empire) encountering unenlightened but wondrous "primitives." It's a genre based around a racist imperial fantasy, and there's not an easy way to untangle that. *The Valley of Death*'s main twist—that the lost city has been duped by aliens—is characteristically Doctor Who, but doesn't really do anything to change the underlying racism of the story.

And when this is combined with the second half of the story, which is a fairly straightforward alien invasion plot with aliens pretending to be nice, the result is unfortunate to say the least. At best what can be said is that any racism seems terribly confused, with "South American savages" colliding with "short yellow manipulators" in a way that at once drips with stereotypes and seems utterly incoherent.

The larger problem affecting *The Valley of Death* is that it is, simply, not very clever. The H. Rider Haggard stuff is interesting, but it's clear that Hinchcliffe loses interest in it after a few episodes. The latter material, on the other hand, is just *The Claws of Axos* mashed up with *Terror of the Zygons* in a banal rendition of "bog standard alien invasion tropes." The villain is a generic cackler, the supporting cast is wooden, and nothing interesting happens after a clever joke about the aliens using Television Centre. (And that joke's already done in *Remembrance of the Daleks*.)

It is, in other words, not a stunning advertisement for Philip Hinchcliffe, a creative figure that is, outside of this, difficult to judge. The entirety of the Hinchcliffe era, after all, coincides with the zenith of Robert Holmes's influence on the program. And Robert Holmes is quite easy to judge on his own terms: we have Holmes stories from the Troughton era up through the end of Colin Baker's tenure. Figuring out what Hinchcliffe brings to the table is thus tricky.

But it appears that the answer is, at least in part, a reliance on standard tropes. Hinchcliffe is praised for the "Gothic horror" tone of the program, but what this means in practice is that the best stories of his tenure were the ones that ripped off Hammer Horror films. Certainly *The Valley of Death* has no particular connection with Gothic horror—it appears to be aiming for comedy, which is consistent with Season Seventeen (in which it was supposed to go) but which works against any argument that Hinchcliffe had a style.

Or, rather, it works against the idea that his style was something other than skillful imitation of other work. Because while he had a lot of gothic horror in his sixteen stories, other stories involved straight-up lifts of *The Avengers*, Isaac Asimov's Robot novels, *The Manchurian Candidate*, and an extended run of recycling classic Doctor Who stories to get things started. This is not a criticism—pilfering the larger culture is one of the things Doctor Who does best. The demonstration of this is straightforward: look at the Hinchcliffe era itself, which is one of the series' absolute high points.

But there's a peril in this sort of approach. It works when you have writers good enough to make the pilfering interesting and not just slavish recreation. And Hinchcliffe was consistently blessed with this in Robert Holmes, a supernaturally good writer who had no real problems with rewriting the bulk of the season to his own tastes. This meant that his apparent strengths—a strong visual sense and an understanding of one particular formula—were allowed to shine.

But it also means that Hinchcliffe's weaknesses were seemingly covered over. His sense of what to pastiche was limited, and he was apparently not particularly concerned with the details. We have a tendency to call this period of the program the Hinchcliffe era, because it creates a nice, clean division between Seasons Fourteen and Fifteen, and because we rather like delineating eras by producer. But this isn't some period of Doctor Who defined by a solitary visionary. Hinchcliffe oversaw the best work by several of the greatest creatives on Doctor Who: Tom Baker, Lis Sladen, Louise Jameson, and Robert Holmes. But on the evidence of his own script and how it compares to his era at large, he's not so much the visionary behind his era as the secret sauce that somehow holds it all together.

The Lion Catches Up (The Talons of Weng-Chiang)

It's February 26, 1977. Leo Sayer is at number one with "When I Need You." Two weeks later The Manhattan Transfer take over with "Chanson D'Amour." It lasts for three weeks before ABBA play us out with "Knowing Me, Knowing You." ABBA, ELO, Elvis, Bryan Ferry, and David Bowie also chart. Bowie with "Sound and Vision," off of *Low*, the first album of his Berlin trilogy, recorded, predictably, in France. This trilogy, in many ways, amounts to a sort of public rehab stint after the excesses of the Thin White Duke era of *Station to Station*, especially with *Low*, which is basically Bowie's "quitting cocaine" album.

There is a weary familiarity suffusing this album. Its title is suggestive enough. The ever-fantastic Chris O'Leary describes one song in terms of "the idea of Bowie's LA life as having been a time of samsara, a cyclic period of endless suffering and no advancement; a pointless life, one equivalent to getting into a different auto accident every day (but in the same car, of course, so even that variety is lessened)." There is, in this, a grim flip side to our old concept of reiterated history. No pattern captures the idea of history repeating itself quite like that of the addict, perpetually in recovery, fighting the continual downward progression of their cravings. The materialism of reiterated history indeed.

An earthquake in Bucharest kills 1500. Queen Elizabeth opens the New Zealand and Australian parliaments. The rings of Uranus are discovered. Focus on the Family is founded. Hay-on-Wye, an odd sort of success story in the depressed coal mining economies of Wales, declares independence from the UK. This is, of course, a publicity stunt, but it is a brilliant one, devised by Richard Booth, the self-proclaimed King of Hay. Booth, a Hay native who went on to Oxford, wanted to try to find a way to save failing towns like the one he had grown up in, and toured America with strapping young Welshmen to obtain scads of books from closing libraries, shipping them to Hay to open a wealth of bookstores. His proclamation of independence was another step towards this revival—a deft pastiche of the comedic stereotypes of rural Wales.

The calmness masks a transition seeping along in the background—one discussed towards the end of the Pertwee volume. I suggested then that we had, for most practical purposes, exited the Long 1960s, and were beginning to approach the Long 1980s. Here, at last, we enter them. For Doctor Who purposes, at least, this story is the transition point. It's an odd sort of transition: one expects to see the Long 1980s begin with the start of something. But for the purposes of Doctor Who, I think there's a strong reason to set it here, at the end of the Hinchcliffe era. Because in many ways, this point marks the beginning of the story of Doctor Who in the 1980s. And in many ways, the story of Doctor Who in the 1980s is a story of slow and often agonizing collapse.

None of this should detract from the fact that we are, once again, dealing with a story widely regarded as a classic. This alone is worth noting. In less than three seasons, one of which was abridged, Philip Hinchcliffe has overseen no fewer than nine stories that reliably show up on lists of the greatest Doctor Who stories of all time: *The Ark in Space*, *Genesis of the Daleks*, *Terror of the Zygons*, *Pyramids of Mars*, *The Brain of Morbius*, *The Seeds of Doom*, *The Deadly Assassin*, *The Robots of Death*, and now this. This is, by any measure, a jaw-dropping success rate. Even if one or two of those aren't to your taste (they're certainly not all to mine), the sheer number of hits—half of the eighteen stories he produced—is striking. And in the eyes of many, this story the best of the best.

As I said before, though, I hadn't seen *Talons* before watching it to write about it. I got it on VHS for my eleventh birthday in 1993—a birthday memorable mostly for the fact that I'd come down with chicken pox a few days earlier and was in miserable agony. (The chicken pox were a gift from my sister, who wasn't even one yet. Her birthday presents have consistently improved since then, including the years where she forgot to get me anything.) And, well, I really just wasn't in a state to make it through a six-parter edited into movie format. So I somehow never got around to it.

Here, then, is one of the endings of my childhood. The last four years of Tom Baker's tenure were ones I knew only from novelizations for quite a while, all of them having been relatively late to VHS release in the US (and indeed at all). When the Doctor Who that I was ten or eleven for returns in these books, it will be the Davison era, and there's virtually nothing from *Castrovalva* to *Survival* that I haven't seen at least once. So *Talons*, in that sense, is the last hole in the Doctor Who of my childhood; the last time I can experience that version of Doctor Who fresh.

There is, of course, no way to really watch this story fresh. I know too much. We all do. Especially since I inadvertently acquired a reputation for attacking *The Celestial Toymaker* for being racist anti-Chinese trash. Leading up to posting this essay on the blog I got three separate commenters, plus a few e-mails speculating about what I'd say when I got to it. Because my criticism of *The Celestial Toymaker* was at least somewhat novel, whereas this is a story that absolutely everybody knows is racist and Sinophobic. So it seems that I have some expectations upon me.

I won't lie, it was an odd experience watching the story given this, and the knowledge that, given that *The Celestial Toymaker* essay remains controversial, someone, somewhere, is almost certain to try to abut that essay with this one and conclude hypocrisy if I dare do anything but condemn this story as racist trash. Whereas if I do dismiss this story for its racism I'll get equally pilloried by its many fans. And so the already conflicted idea of "finishing my childhood" becomes more vexed when bound to this sort of intensive scrutiny - the sense that my watching of this story must be impeccable and perfect, and that I am in some sense obliged to a higher standard than usual.

There are, of course, defenses to be made of this story. The strongest—and I mean that in terms of the extent of what it excuses, not in terms of the quality of the argument— is that the story is in fact a satire of racism and is not racist in and of itself. Or, more properly, it's a satire of Victorian colonial attitudes. Under this argument everyone in the story is a stereotype, the English included, and so the stereotypes of the Chinese have to be taken in that context. The entire story, in this view, is told through a blinkered, Victorian perspective, and that's part of the joke.

This defense, however, is pathetic. First of all, it egregiously ignores the fact that there is no way for a show made by British people to be an equal-opportunity offender between the British and the Chinese. We know Doctor Who is British, and we know it's ideologically British. Even if it's poking fun at British attitudes, that will always come off as just that—a loving poke at history. Whereas the anti-Chinese sentiment in this story comes down to the fact that every single Chinese character is playing off of Fu Manchu-inflected yellow peril stereotypes and treated as a villain based purely on the fact that they're Chinese. And the fact that the main Chinese character, Li H'sen Chang, is played in yellowface. And this is the difference. Jago and Litefoot may be bumbling comic relief, but they're lovable bumblers played by actors of the same nationality as their characters. The Chinese have their biggest role played in yellowface, and are treated as a bunch of menacing criminals. There's no good way to equate those.

But more to the point, even if we give this story a pass on the grounds that everyone in it is supposed to be a dated stereotype, this defense would fall down for the simple reason that the Doctor and Leela display the same attitudes about the Chinese as everyone else. The Doctor describes the Chinese men who attacked him as "little men," and generally acts as though he broadly agrees with everyone else's characterizations of the Chinese. And Leela refers to Chang as "the yellow one." This is problematic in the extreme. It's one thing for the supporting cast to be stereotypes bound by the attitudes and conventions of the time and genre they're playing in. But the Doctor and Leela are supposed to transgress against the conventions of the settings they land in. That's the point. When even they're spouting racist slurs, it's pretty hard to say that the problem is one of satire.

We are forced back, then, to a less all-encompassing defense. A two-pronged one, if you will. The first is that this story is problematic in a way that we know Robert Holmes has been problematic before. He is a writer praised repeatedly for his cynicism. It's unsurprising, then, that he falls afoul of good taste. whether it's by treating Sarah Jane's feminism with condescension or by tripping over some anti-Arab sentiment, Holmes has never been careful about staying on the right side of the line with regards to good taste. So when he writes a Sherlock Holmes vs. Fu Manchu pastiche he doesn't really stop to think about the consequences. Unlike *The Celestial Toymaker*, where the racial coding is arbitrary, there's at least a reason why this story is about the villainous Chinese. So it's covert racism, which is at least some defense compared to *The Celestial Toymaker*, which seemed to go out of its way to offend.

The second prong of the defense is that the story doesn't suck. *The Celestial Toymaker* wasn't just racist, it was bad: its plot was non-existent, it treated the star with utter contempt, and it mainly consisted of watching a rigged game show with no actual rules. It was lousy television that, for good measure, was also racist. *The Talons of Weng-Chiang*, on the other hand, is good television that is also racist. And racism doesn't erase that. It makes it problematic and it gives us a lot to discuss and it is a distinct bad part about the story, but it doesn't erase clever characterization, great set-pieces, witty dialogue, a sense of adventure, or any of the other plusses this story has.

Inasmuch as I am willing to cede any ground to those who whine about excessive "political correctness," a term that more often means "basic politeness," this is a real and important point. We do too often treat problems of bias and discrimination as totalizing issues, such that someone who displays overt racist or sexual bias suddenly has this become their identity: they are a racist or a sexist. Racism is horrible and appalling, but it's not a human identity, and reducing someone to it renders their sins irredeemable in a way that impedes any actual progress towards social justice. And if we treat racism as something that invalidates every other aspect of something, making it a label that erases every other detail of a person, we do real harm.

Or, to put it another way, nobody disputes that *The Adventures of Huckleberry Finn* is racist, but that doesn't mean it's not also a triumph of American literature that is rightly assigned in numerous American literature classes. If it's being taught well, the racism is acknowledged and accepted as a part of what the book is. But, crucially, as a *part* of what it is—not as the last word on it. *The Talons of Weng-Chiang* is racist, yes. But before we decide that it should simply be condemned, we need to at least ask what else it might be.

Yes, there is much here to like. That old saying applies— works of art are wrongly forgotten, but never wrongly remembered. All that we have loved thus far in the Hinchcliffe era is in play here, and then some. *The Talons of Weng-Chiang* is a dizzying genre pastiche that, as mentioned, merges not just Sherlock Holmes and Fu Manchu but a wider constellation of images. The disappearance and death of women in the vague vicinity of Whitechapel (which is mentioned in relation to Magnus Greel's hideout) cannot be taken as anything but an allusion to Jack the Ripper. The

Philip Sandifer

reliance on the buried River Fleet as a plot point evokes the vast palimpsestual history of London. This is the densest nexus of ideas to date.

But really, why bother? Yes, of course there's a dizzying array of literary and cultural references that leads to this being a stylish and clever invocation of a huge swath of Victorian culture. At some point, no matter how clever these panoramas of cultural pastiche are, they become a crutch every bit as much as the base under siege did. So we have a kaleidoscope of intertextuality. We excused being clever for its own sake back in *The Pyramids of Mars* because Holmes was revising an existing script and because it was opening a new door. At this point, however, just being clever isn't enough. It can't be. The show has demonstrated its ability to be so much more.

But is something rotten in the story: a festering wound at the heart of it. Whatever else it is, it doesn't lose this dark undertone. A dark undertone that, in its own strange way, infects the whole series. Consider that the third episode of the new series—Mark Gatiss's *The Unquiet Dead*—is nearly a straight lift of this story, with entire sequences being nothing more than light reskins of this. Even Sneed and Dickens seem like an attempt at a 21st century Jago and Litefoot. And, of course, *The Unquiet Dead* was pilloried, not entirely without reason, for its supposed xenophobic attitude. When we move beyond racism to the rest of the story and don't draw the angry "not canon" line we drew for *The Celestial Toymaker*, there is a price that we pay.

We've spoken before about the growing problem of Baker's arrogance after Lis Sladen's departure. Here it begins to become a genuine problem. One of the first consequences of Baker's increasing tendency to bully his colleagues is that the Doctor stops being vulnerable. Back in *The Pyramids of Mars* there was both literary pastiche and an effective stab at horror accomplished by having the Doctor be truly terrified of Sutekh and, eventually, enslaved by him. Now by this point the Doctor doesn't get hurt or scared. He might get knocked out for a bit, but nothing bad is going to happen to him. And that drains a lot of tension out of the story, increasing the risk of mere cleverness.

Then again, that phrase always got my hackles up. "Nothing more than clever," as if clever isn't a valid end in itself. Surely being smart is a good thing. I mean, here I will invoke my childhood. Because, look, let's admit something about American Doctor Who fans prior to about 2008. We were the freaks at the freak table. And if you were foolish enough to be an American Doctor Who fan in, say, 1993, in the sixth grade? You were going to get pure hell.

And so in that sense, Doctor Who is, for me, endlessly intertwined with the idea of bullies.

"Too clever" is a bully's phrase. As if it's possible to be too intelligent. As if being challenging and requiring your audience to think is a bad thing. Cleverness, in and of itself, is a valid aesthetic goal. No. More than that. It's a good aesthetic goal. A story shouldn't need more than cleverness to be judged well. Unless it has other overt problems, cleverness should constitute a defense. Not every story needs to be better than everything that's come before.

But, of course, there are other overt problems. The story is racist. And while cleverness is a virtue, it no more erases everything else about a thing than racism does. Indeed, cleverness is an easily corrupted virtue. Clever racism is worse than stupid racism because clever racism can appear compelling and alluring. There's something worse about dressing racism in the trappings of quality. Not for nothing is the evil genius a better villain than the evil moron.

Still, there's no reason to cede the point that cleverness is all *The Talons of Weng-Chiang* has to offer. Let us turn to the aspect of the Hinchcliffe era which has, of late, been paying the most fascinating dividends: the reiteration of history. This, after all, is the aspect of the Hinchcliffe era which offers the most effectively materialist aspect. This is where its alchemy arises.

Philip Sandifer

The Talons of Weng-Chiang adds a fascinating new wrinkle to this approach. Magnus Greel is, superficially, an iteration of the standard issue Hinchcliffe era arch-villain: the once-great threat back from death with lots of snarling rants. There's one detail that's profoundly interesting. Greel is from a futuristic dark age. This obviously parallels significantly with Leela, but it also introduces a strange new sort of causality. In one sense this is an inevitable consequence of the observation that the past reiterates. If history repeats itself, so too must the future.

Let us repeat that so that we grasp the magnitude of it. The future repeats itself. In this regard, the future affects the past—and not just in the sense of time travel. The Doctor is adamantly clear that the "zygma" technology Greel used to travel through time was a dead end—a wrong decision. It's the philosophic dimension of this idea that's most interesting: not that Greel has traveled through time, but that the source of his disfigurement and monstrosity is the existence of a futuristic dark age. He is, after all, apparently a Chinese god. He is a mythic being who hails from the dark ages: a classic Hinchcliffe villain in this regard. But his dark ages are those of the future. This is a show that has been going on at such a variety of lengths about the survival of the past into the present. And now it extends that trend into the future, reminding us that the survival of the past also means that the future is in a real sense present—accessible and ready-to-hand.

Which brings us back to Leela. The interesting thing about Leela is, as we saw last time, the way in which she is at once futuristic and primitive. In this regard she prefigures the larger idea of a futuristic dark age. But here the ugly flip side we've been putting off about her finally rears its head properly: the Eliza Doolittle aspect of her character. Because there's a real and ugly kick in the teeth in this story that's fairly horrific. We already noted that Leela is a particularly extreme form of the Problem of Susan in that the tension between her subservience to the Doctor and her

independence as a character gets played out materially, as a commentary on the nature of social development. Boucher, in his two stories featuring the character, more or less successfully walked this line by finding ways to give Leela her own strange power over the narrative.

More to the point, Boucher did this in a way that set up the interesting implications of the future recurring. If the past reiterates into the future then any notion of progress must assume the reuse of past elements—this is the basic logic of détournement. By giving Leela insights beyond those of other characters Boucher shows this viscerally. It's an astonishing concept for a companion.

Were it that the streak continued. But it doesn't. Leela becomes almost completely subservient to the Victoriana in this story, alternately used as an excuse to show off a new period dress and stripped down to soaking wet white dresses that are even more revealing than her usual leathers. She is chloroformed and captured, and even gets her first proper scream as a companion. The climax of the story hinges on her being used as a peril monkey. She is completely beaten down by the story.

And in that context, the horrific colonialist implications of "civilizing" Leela rear up horribly. Here she becomes the full-out Eliza Doolittle figure. Her entire nature is shown to us as flawed and in need of changing. Her major contribution to the story is to provide comic relief in the form of her failures to understand Victorian England. And these failures are generally not clever ones in which she comes off as possessing some secret insight on the era. Her jokes revolve around her failure to use plates and glasses, not in her ability to savvily deconstruct Victorian excess.

At least the Doctor still gets in plenty of deconstructions. Even if we lose Leela—and I'm not denying that it's a nasty and ugly moment—we still have Baker at his imperious best, stomping around and delightfully mocking and subverting everything in sight. This is a story in which it's easy to just sit back and delight in the anarchic glee of the Doctor, revelling in his most mercurial elements as he tears down everything he can find. Even the structure of this story is borrowed from Whitaker: the steady colliding [cohering?] of elements into set pieces as the story builds towards the inevitable marquee confrontation is right out of *Enemy of the World*. This alone should satisfyingly undermine the Victorian tradition and give Leela at least some cover.

But surely at some point there just becomes too much to excuse. We now have a story that is racist, sexist, and, due to the nature of *Pygmalion*, classist. So the Doctor gets some good lines off and the plot is fun. At some point you've got to say that's not enough. That the story is, at its heart, just a cynical piece of dreck. Yet even here the story seems to offer a defense of itself. After all, cynicism is supposed to be what we love Robert Holmes for in the first place.

That's a cop-out though. Cynicism isn't a virtue. If we're going to declare that history reiterates, at this point we have little choice but to reiterate the message of *The War Games*. If the Doctor is only good for anarchic tearing down without any attempt to construct something new, then he must be punished and cast down. If all the show offers is cynicism, surely its fate must be the same. Cynicism is, after all, self-defeating. Look at the ruin it's left in its trail within this story. Untethered from a belief in progress, the urge to tear down and destroy becomes mere cruelty.

Let's return to the original problem here: the racism. The Doctor, early in the story, refers to being attacked by "little men": a nasty little moment of stereotyping. But not, to my mind, the nastiest. Later on in the story, the Doctor is ambushed by Greel and his servants and has a glib comment about how he loves "little surprises." I strongly suspect, of course, that Holmes did not mean this line to be a racist jibe as well. It's a perfectly ordinary Tom Baker line that one can imagine him saying in any story when the bad guys surprise him—a standard example of him refusing to take the enemy seriously.

But in this story, surrounded with such careless bigotry, there becomes no way to completely avoid the negative implication. That's the problem that this utter and unfocused cynicism leaves us with. Because the story is being so gratuitously careless with its politics everything—even light moments of banter—become tainted with... you can't even say malice. No. Condescension. That's what this is. There's an ugly, arrogant condescension to this—a refusal to care what you're saying as long as you're being clever.

And there's the word that does it. The word that brings the entire defense of this story crashing down around our ears. The thing that has been floating around in Robert Holmes's writing since *Carnival of Monsters*. Recall Vorg's bit in that story about how "our purpose is to amuse, simply to amuse. Nothing serious, nothing political." But we know better. There's no such thing as "nothing political" when wandering through time and reiterating it endlessly. *In Carnival of Monsters* it seemed that Holmes was joking—that he understood that Vorg, by his very nature, becomes political when thrust into the world of Inter Minor, and allowed Vorg's protests to mask the revolution lurking within.

Here we have a dark mirror of that interpretation, in which the insistence of apoliticism isn't so much a joke as it's an ignorant denial. Now there's the sense that Holmes just doesn't care about the politics. The goal of amusement feels like a fig leaf to avoid confronting the political implications of the story, so that Holmes doesn't have to worry about things like not perpetuating racist stereotypes or demeaning the working class. It's all in good fun. He can just be clever and witty and everything will be good. Just like Baker can be. Just like the whole show can be. There's an arrogance here that's demoralizing. A sense of the show flying too close to the sun. A sense that it must be cast down.

(This is where you should be imagining the "sting" sound effect and a fade to a cliffhanger.)

Pop Between Realities, Home in Time for Tea (Mary Whitehouse)

It is, above all else, a profoundly stupid way to go down. Philip Hinchcliffe, after three years of making an enormously compelling case for why he is the best producer of Doctor Who since Verity Lambert, is told during rehearsals for *The Robots of Death* that he's being sacked at the end of the season in order to appease Mary Whitehouse, a sanctimonious prude of the worst sort. Three years of dark fairytale postmodernism with a flair for the cynically epic end because of the incessant complaints of a crazy woman. Not with a bang but a whimper.

There's an odd justice to it, though. If the one aesthetic crime we can firmly get to stick to the Hinchcliffe era is hubris, there becomes a poetic justice to the era being taken down by a deluded fool with the visual literacy of a donut. It's oddly fitting that a show that has become so cavalier about the material consequences of what it does should go down to a hack who should have been trivial to refute. Doubly so for it to happen under Robert Holmes, who isn't sacked here, but whose hatred for the banal evils of the world makes the show getting brought down by Whitehouse on his watch a particularly savage irony.

Let's discuss some facts then. One of those people who spent almost her entire working life as an old lady, Whitehouse was a high profile campaigner in the UK since

1964 on the issue of excessive sex, violence, and moral depravity on television and elsewhere. An outspoken and evangelical Christian, her initial battle of choice was with Hugh Greene, the Director General of the BBC when Doctor Who was created. It was under Greene that the BBC took its most concrete and visible steps towards a model of appealing to all of Britain, instead of imposing the ideology and worldview of "establishment" Britain. Most concretely, this manifested in the production of things like *Z-Cars* or *Cathy Come Home* (see first book). Whitehouse hated this; she believed that Greene was "responsible for the moral collapse" of the UK, that he spread "the propaganda of disbelief, doubt, and dirt... promiscuity, infidelity, and drinking," and that the correct role of the BBC was to "encourage and sustain faith in God and bring Him back to the hearts of our family and national life."

It is possible, and many have done this, to consider the nature of this argument to be an art versus commerce debate. This does not even involve ignoring the obvious theocratic implications—the UK is, after all, technically a theocracy, though it manages its condition well through a long-term regimen of secular democracy and keeps acute attacks of theodicy to a minimum.

(Yes, the UK is technically a theocracy: its titular head of state is also the Supreme Governor of the Church of England, which is a state religion. The line between this and destructive theocracy is, in the case of the UK, one of active and continual choice not to do anything unseemly with the fact that they are ruled by a monarch who is also a religious figure. I don't even note this as a fault in the nature of British government—clearly they do just fine with this setup. Complain all you want about the fundamentals, the thing works. In practice, the US has more of a problem with theocratic lunatics than the UK does, so it's not like fundamental separation of church and state is a panacea or even, for that matter, particularly effective. My point here is really just for American readers: the claim that the correct role of the BBC is to bring God back into national life has a different relationship with the structure and principles of British government than it would with the structure and principles of the US government. You're not arguing against the grain of the Constitution there, in no small part because the UK doesn't have a written Constitution.)

Art, after all, in its more Enlightenment-infused senses has always been about the divine, with art being a tool that reveals aspects of the divine to humans. Even in the more secular versions of Enlightenment thought, this tends to be fairly close to what art gets valued for. (Or at least, it seems to be, because let's face it, secular versions of Enlightenment thought are, for good reasons, not the place most people go for aesthetic advice.) From this viewpoint, the problem with Greene's BBC is that he is turning away from the production of art and towards mass-market commodities. This is the view that you get if you start pairing Greene off against the so-called Reithian model of the BBC (named after its first director). Wikipedia—I'll admit openly that's what I'm using here—describes the Reithian model as valuing "an equal consideration of all viewpoints, probity, universality and a commitment to public service."

There is a philosophical landmine here that we are going to have to pause on for a moment. Because that list of four values does not cohere. "Equal consideration of all viewpoints" and "probity" are necessarily in opposition. If you hold to a specific moral code, you necessarily consider some viewpoints—namely those antithetical to that moral code—as unequal in stature. That's by definition not equal consideration. Liberal democracy does not hold totalitarianism in equal consideration, at least not unless you dress it up in the rhetoric of self-advancement. There is no such thing as complete cosmopolitanism. And this point underlies the fundamental difference between two visions of liberalism that have been quietly (and at times loudly) coming into conflict throughout the period this book has tracked. For that matter, these two visions are still pretty much the big headline, because philosophical shifts take place over decades and we're still playing this game.

The first of these two ideologies is Enlightenment liberalism. In this model, the application of human reason leads towards truth. Diversity of viewpoints is valued because of the belief that when the ideas are pitted against each other the right one will rise to the top. Democracy works because it will produce the best solution—the aggregate power of human reason is viewed as the best decision-making process available. So long as every viewpoint gets a chance to be heard, the right one will, seemingly inevitably, win out.

Postmodern liberalism, on the other hand, rejects this idea. At its most basic level, it rejects the sort of hyper-sanitized purity of it. Democracy doesn't work because it picks the right option, it works because anything else is even crueler. (Which is, of course, basically the content of Churchill's famous line about democracy being the worst system of government. The transition from Enlightenment era to postmodernism was not a light-switch event any more than the transition to science was. For one thing, you had to go through modernism.) Moral rightness does not inherently rise to the top: it certainly doesn't do so with anything near the effectiveness that money and power do.

And so Enlightenment liberalism tends to mistake the desires of those with enough money and power to win elections for an inherent moral authority. The positions that are given "equal time" are really just sanctioned oppositions—there to be argued down and kept on the margins. Ultimately only those with access to the tools of reason—which, mysteriously, always keep being the tools of the upper class—wield actual power. This is the end problem with Reithianism: in the end, it sustains social inequity by continually making class judgments.

The response is Greene's BBC. And this is where the art vs. commerce angle falls down on this debate. Because, in hindsight, we have to realize that Greene's BBC was putting out some of the best art ever to be made for television, and thus that criticizing him for embracing commerce over art is nonsense. Yes, he embraced commerce in ways previous heads hadn't, but in no way did he do this in opposition to art. Greene arguably moved the BBC towards a more postmodern sort of liberalism. He actually took seriously the idea that the BBC should equally consider all viewpoints and made television that came from multiple viewpoints. That's the whole idea of social realism: it gives the audience viewpoints they wouldn't be exposed to and shows them aspects of the world they didn't know about. Television, under Greene, isn't a device to show The Truth but rather a device to show more information, more perspectives, and more things in general. In this regard the idea that Doctor Who would develop under his watch seems like the most obvious thing ever.

There is still an embrace of cosmopolitanism here, but there's a fundamental difference in goals. Enlightenment liberalism embraces cosmopolitanism because it believes that a single "best view" will bubble up to the top. Postmodern liberalism embraces it because it believes that given a sufficient critical mass of views, the worst views will wither and die, and that this is about the best you can hope for in terms of social progress. It recognizes that progress is not about approaching a defined goal of the future but about clearing away the reiterated fossils that litter the present; that the march of history is not about the oncoming rush of the future but about the steady killing of the past. The production of new ideas and new perspectives is the material fuel that enables this, and is thus valuable. Postmodern liberalism values cosmopolitanism because cosmopolitanism breeds the conditions in which decaying ideologies are sped to their deaths.

But just as history repeats itself, as we've learned, so does the future. This finally brings us around to the earlier point I made about this moment being the start of the Long 1980s. It's not a big spoiler that the 1980s, in both the US and UK, were dominated by conservative politics. But there's a particular model of conservatism that we see here: one that's still enormously powerful and is still recognizable as what things like the Occupy movement are reacting against. What's particularly insidious about this sort of conservatism is that it's in many ways the logical endpoint of Enlightenment liberalism.

In America this fact has become completely explicit, with a segment of the political right fetishizing to the Constitution in a large part because they want to pretend that no significant developments in moral or political philosophy have happened since 1787. The Enlightenment is, in this context, unambiguously treated as the last word on politics. (There is, of course, an odd fundamentalism to this—a decaying ideology reverting to its original form in a last, choking stab at purity of reiteration.) But more broadly, the right wing trades on an Enlightenment model of individual liberty. And for a variety of reasons, the most obvious ones being that the Enlightenment model of individual liberty was created by rich white men who naively assumed everyone else was basically like them, this model itself is corrupt. It's not a matter of misusing the model. Rather, it's one of utter fealty to the model. Libertarianism is little more than a proof by contradiction starting with the premises of Enlightenment liberalism in which everybody forgot what to do after you find the contradiction.

It should be no surprise that Whitehouse was, in the end, an ally of the Thatcher government. They shared, after all, a commitment to Enlightenment liberalism. The evangelical Christians that took Whitehouse seriously were part of Thatcher's base. They were not allies as such—in truth, Thatcher's ideology was always more economic than social. But they shared a hatred for postmodern liberalism, and a reliance on the idea of the "silent majority," a concept first developed by that great statesman, Richard Nixon.

There are few concepts more insidious than that of the "silent majority." This is true for one very simple reason: silence is already antithetical to postmodern liberalism. If social progress is understood as the demolition of the past via the continual acceleration of new forms of thought then there is nothing more toxic to that than the idea of people who simply refuse to engage with the creation of new forms of thought. Silence, in the context of the silent majority, is nothing more than a refusal to play—a complete rejection of the idea that you can be challenged in the first place. If there is one point of view postmodernism is very, very clear on, it is that you should make a lot of noise. Preferably obnoxious noise.

Again, then, no surprise that Whitehouse's arguments, based as they were on appeals to this silent majority, were appallingly incompetent. She had been targeting Doctor Who since about *Genesis of the Daleks*, with her most famed line being a description of the show as "teatime brutality for tots." But the fuss she raised that ended up bringing Hinchcliffe down was due to the episode three cliffhanger of *The Deadly Assassin*, in which Goth drowns the Doctor. The director, David Maloney (who, sadly, never returns to the series following *The Talons of Weng-Chiang*, having been working on it off and on since *The Mind Robber*), opted to do that cliffhanger with a freeze frame on the Doctor's submerged head. Whitehouse flipped out, claiming that children would believe that the Doctor's head was underwater for the whole week and would be terrified by not knowing if he survived, while simultaneously claiming, in what seems like something of a contradiction, that they would all try to drown their siblings. Which, I mean, you can kind of find some way of connecting those, I suppose, in which the show is teaching kids that you can hold your breath for a week, but, well... seriously?

I took a shot at this kind of thinking way back in the Hartnell volume, but let's be clearer here. Even if one grants some set of claims about the harmful effects of violence in the media on children—and notably, these claims have generally failed to survive any scholarly scrutiny—this position is indefensible for the simple reason that it's based on normalizing bad readings and sloppy thought. The failure to understand freeze-frame only makes sense if you assume viewers who don't think at all about the technical properties of the medium in watching it. It relies on a naively immersive model of media in which television is a literal representation of things.

But look, we know it isn't. We know that camera angles and editing are part of how storytelling works. We know, in fact, that it's impossible to make sense of drama if you don't understand the conventions of visual storytelling. To say that a freeze-frame suggests the Doctor's head being held underwater for a full week would require thinking that narrative time and audience time pass at the same rate, an assumption that can't even be taken seriously. It requires that you think of a cliffhanger as a genuine source of danger for the character, and thus to think of Doctor Who not as a television show that exists in a real cultural context but as, to borrow a term from Gayatri Spivak, gossip about imaginary people: a look into the lives of people that could, in fact, simply die at any moment. It requires that the audience watch Doctor Who as found footage of real life as opposed to as a story. None of these are sensible things to do.

And these are not subtle, advanced issues. The "kids don't understand any of that" argument doesn't wash. These are fundamental aspects of how the medium works. This is basic visual literacy, not some advanced value-added extra. People learn this stuff instinctively. As I understand it (and I should note that developmental psychology is not my field), it's actually older people who have the most trouble with new-ish techniques like freeze-frame because they've already learned visual literacy and thus have trouble with adding new dimensions to their understanding. Kids, as I understand it, pick this stuff up fine. Most people do, actually. It's only when they're misled by moronic zealots like Mary Whitehouse that the sense of functional visual literacy they develop by reading/watching is overwritten by idiotic aesthetics of "immersion" and "realism." Even if the episode three cliffhanger of *The Deadly Assassin* was a terrible thing that would deform children for years, it sure as hell wasn't for the reasons Mary Whitehouse said it was.

This, more even than the censorship, is what I, at least, find so horrific about Whitehouse's arguments. It's not merely that they attack a show I love, one that provides what I think is a real social good. (Though I think in the end Whitehouse was either implicitly or explicitly aware of the degree to which the show's ideology was opposed to hers. Simply put, it's difficult to believe the idea of someone who watches and pays attention to a lot of Doctor Who ever agreeing with Mary Whitehouse.) It's the fact that she's doing it by mainstreaming visual illiteracy. It's the fact that on the way to "censor the violence" she insists on stopping off at actually and overtly endorsing uncritical and bad reading. If she had the integrity to actually accuse Doctor Who of being a left-leaning postmodernist show with Marxist influences, that would be one thing. Instead she just engaged in the narrative equivalent of climate change denial, peddling incompetent practices as something that should be taken seriously.

But, of course, the silent majority is absolved of all responsibility for this. Being silent, their views must be respected without argument, for no argument is possible. You can, of course, try to argue. Every viewpoint must be given fair representation, after all. But the opposition viewpoints are minority viewpoints. They occupy defined roles on the margins, existing only to be rejected in favor of the enlightenment of the majority, which need not argue its case when it can simply win elections. It doesn't matter how clever you are or how good your argument is, because in the end, you're talking to a brick wall.

This viewpoint was toxic enough when it was used to justify tuning out the counterculture in 1968. But in the 1980s it finds itself wedded to existing structures of power in the worst ways possible. This is, as is becoming increasingly clear, the real horrific legacy of the 1980s: the way in which neoliberal economic policies created the conditions for a media that actively propped up particular forms of ignorance when they benefitted those with power.

This is also where Whitehouse's and Thatcher's ideologies part ways. There is no serious way to think that Thatcher's government, profoundly media-savvy as it was, actually believed the incompetent critiques offered by Whitehouse. Whatever one might say of the Tories in the 1980s, they were not stupid people. And there's ample evidence that Thatcher had little actual fondness for Whitehouse and her views. Unlike Whitehouse, Thatcher was invested in the art vs. commerce debate and, unlike Whitehouse, she recognized Hugh Greene's BBC as art. It's just that in the art vs. commerce debate, Thatcher sided definitively with commerce, as she did in any "vs. commerce" debate. But Whitehouse was useful in that she could draw crowds, and thus corral the silent majority, which was a useful 10% or so of the population to have on your side. And as long as Whitehouse directed her ire at mutual enemies like the BBC, Thatcher's government was happy to have her around regardless of whether she made a lick of sense.

(I'd treat Whitehouse as a victim in all of this, but I can't bring myself to. She was a bigot and an idiot who understood nothing about television and wasn't going to let that get in the way of her crusade. She and Thatcher share their commitment to Enlightenment liberalism. Hers was, in the end, less devastatingly effective than Thatcher's, and so Thatcher won. As she usually did, unfortunately.)

The real point is that there's an ugly logic to this that is chillingly familiar: the use of power to sidestep the messy materialism of the battle of ideas, treating the fact of victory as an argument for the legitimacy of the victory. Which brings us back to that most inseparable of concepts for me with Doctor Who: bullying.

There are moments in life where you have a sudden and striking realization of just how fucked-up a person you are. I had one about a month ago. I was driving past my old middle school—the school I was attending the year I got chicken pox and *The Talons of Weng-Chiang*. Sometime in the decades since I left there, an annual tradition of a scarecrow competition began. Around Halloween, some class or another within the school makes big, colorful scarecrows and sets them up on the front lawn of the school. The scarecrows are generally in the form of recognizable pop culture icons: Spongebob or Spiderman or the like. This year, there was a Dalek. And I found myself choking up at the sight of it: not just the first time I drove past, but every time I drove past. It was a flawless impression of the presumptuous pathos with which adults view "It Gets Better" ads. (Those being bullied tend to view them with an air of "so stop screwing around with the webcam and make it better, jackass.")

I talked last time about the degree to which being an American Doctor Who fan in middle school in 1993 was a miserable experience. And we'll eventually get to 1993 and play that story out right alongside the Doctor Who I was reading. But I should perhaps stress the depth of the crap that I waded through. On two separate occasions people stole Doctor Who books from me and defaced them. Once the torn-up remains were shoved in my desk; the other time I got to see them kicking the book around the hall. The defense was predictable: that these people, who had been mocking me for months for liking this weird Doctor Who thing they'd never heard of, were somehow unaware that the Doctor Who books they were destroying were mine. Because, I mean, there were lots of other people they might plausibly have belonged to.

My middle school had, while I was there, an overt policy called "restitution" which, instead of handling misbehavior punitively, ruled that the two sides of a dispute should come to a mutual understanding and that someone who does something to hurt somebody else shouldn't be punished but should have to make it better. On paper this all sounds very nice. In practice, it was a disgusting system that served bullies above all else. For one thing, it was toothless—even if the school had the authority to, say, make students replace the destroyed books (i.e., to actually make the harm better), importing obscure sci-fi books from the UK wasn't something anybody in Newtown knew how to do in 1993 besides my mother. In practice, nobody even tried to make them offer restitution in such a materially useful sense. What restitution actually meant was that both parties would be forced to apologize to one another regardless of what actually happened.

But even if they had actually attempted to make it right, the idea that bullying can be undone is farcical. Even if the immediate damage is subsequently undone, the real damage of bullying is the longer-term knowledge that people are going to hit you. They're going to hit you because they don't understand you, or because they view your intelligence as a threat, or maybe just because they feel like hitting you. And no restitution undoes that lesson.

And so I choked up at the sight of a Dalek scarecrow outside my old school. Because the idea that over the course of nearly twenty years my popular culture actually won out, to the degree that it's possible to have a team of four middle-schoolers build a Dalek in art class and don't get the shit kicked out of them for it, was... somehow just too much for me. I was utterly overwhelmed by it.

So for a fucked-up lunatic like me, it's impossible, in 2013, not to see the vicious extent to which the ideological legacy of the 1980s is one of bullying. There's no other explanation for news stories about a bank specializing in foreclosures holding a Halloween party in which their employees freely mocked the people they were busily throwing out of their homes. There's no other way to read a description of police pinning nonviolent student protesters to the ground and forcing pepper spray down their throats. There's no other way to read yearlong jail sentences for stealing bottled water during the London riots while ignoring the poverty that led to the riots. In every case there's that familiar overexertion of power—the need to demonstrate it for its own sake. And of course there is. Why settle for the banality of evil when you can have the probity of evil. The decent, hardworking middle-American cops of New York City can be trusted to beat socialist hippie dirtbags exactly how they deserve to be beaten.

And, of course, bullying is in its own ways intertwined with the excessive brutality of fan politics, within which there are too many stories of unconscionable acts of sheer nastiness to even sort through effectively. This is a legacy that spills into the modern show, from the utter hate-fests that review threads on forums turn into right up to, say, a fifty page thread that exists somewhere devoted to how much a particular Doctor Who blogger (nobody you'd have heard of, I'm sure) sucks, where he's described as "an ignorant knobhead," "fcuk [sic] stupid," and suggest that it would be nice if he were beaten up. None of this is new, of course— I'm not saying that bullying was invented in the 1980s. Rather I am saying that it is impossible to understand the 1980s without understanding the way in which bullying works.

Let's start with a definition. At its most basic level, bullying is the use of power to cause harm when the power is not being used in accordance with the purpose (if any exists) for which it was granted. That doesn't mean that breaking up an illegal protest is bullying. It does mean that holding a nonviolent protester down and pepper-spraying them is. Let's further add a few clarifications. Bullying specifically means the use of force, whether social or physical. Inasmuch as it explains why the person being bullied deserves negative treatment, the explanation is generally based on who they are as opposed to what they've done—they're a nerd, or they're gay, not "they insulted me for being dumber than them" or "they triggered my own neuroses about anal penetration and that made me angry." And bullying carries with it the threat, implied or explicit, of future punishment. The nature of this last point varies heavily based on who's bullying. A sixth grader's threat of further punishment amounts to little more than "and I'll hit you tomorrow too." When you get into powerful political figures making bullying comments, on the other hand, the threat becomes much broader and more ambiguous. But this ambiguity does not keep it from being clearly understood by its intended audience.

This, rather than the actual aggression, is the worst part of being bullied. In the moment, there is enough adrenaline to distract you from a proper consideration of the situation's horror. No, the worst moments are the long amounts of idle time you get to spend constantly formulating escape plans. What seat on the bus gives the driver the best view of you? Which piece of playground equipment is least likely to have anyone bother you? What do you say that gets him not to hit you? It's the way in which your world re-orders to be about avoiding getting punished for existing in it. So that the existence of people who want to hurt you is just something you assume.

Then come the lessons. That there is no reasoning to be done with the people who want you to suffer. That in the end, they want you to suffer because they can make you suffer, and because they can get away with it, so that means it's OK. Whether because the laws that govern it are soft enough to make it de facto legal—as bullying under restitution basically was—or because they have the ability to lie effectively. When raw wealth owns the entire media then it is far too easy to say that you didn't know whose Doctor Who book it was, or that people might think a cliffhanger lasts an entire week diegetically, or that the proposed health care bill contains death panels.

These are the legacies of the 1980s. An economic ideology that fostered profits above all else created a world in which power justifies its own use and where the maxim that history is written by the victors becomes a moral principle instead of a cynical observation. Were these the legacies on display at the start? No. We'll get to the Winter of Discontent and the circumstances that brought Thatcher to power in the next book. But as Magnus Greel revealed to us, the future recurs as well. To go into the Long 1980s pretending that their consequences were other than what they were is foolish.

And this is what makes the Hinchcliffe era falling in an early skirmish of that larger culture war so sickening. Whatever the flaws of the Hinchcliffe era—and there were, as we saw last entry, many—for it to be brought down by feckless bullies is just crushing.

Of course, it's only the Hinchcliffe era that gets brought down. Doctor Who survives. Gravely wounded, yes. And arguably, as I've said, you can trace a direct narrative of Doctor Who's cancellation starting here: a chain of creative decisions and reactions against past creative decisions that ends with the show finally losing all support at the BBC. But then, other shows Whitehouse took on (*Till Death Do Us Part*) got cancelled outright under her assault. Doctor Who survived another twelve seasons, then came back for another run of, to date, at least eight. Whitehouse lost. We won. The Dalek went up outside the middle school.

But how? This is, after all, the real question. Because one thing that quickly becomes clear when dealing with the conservative ideology that stemmed from the 1980s is that Enlightenment liberalism is completely unsuitable to the task of resistance. This is because, as I said, what arose in the 1980s was not, in fact, opposed to Enlightenment liberalism but was the logical conclusion of it. Like any ideology surviving past its time, it becomes malignant. New ways forward are necessary. Or, to put it another way, there's no way to fight back against bullies within their rules. That's the other big lesson. The rules are never going to help you.

This is the other story of Doctor Who in the 1980s. Not a replacement for the story of how a great show finally slips and lands in it, but a counterpart to it. A story about learning how to fight bullies; a story about surviving. If the first four volumes of this series—the Long 1960s—were about the history of utopian ideology as told through a British science fiction series, then this is, at its heart, the history of the marginalized and the counterculture as told through the same series. This is a history of freaks and weirdos of various sorts, whether self-identified or mockingly identified by the people who hate them: Punks, homosexuals, goths, fanboys, women, racial minorities, and nerds, to name just a few. It's a history of how marginal culture works, and of how it finds ways of wielding power. And of how marginal culture gets steamrolled, kicked, and beaten down.

Here, then, is our first tool. Because even after everything that could be found to criticize about *The Talons of Weng-Chiang*, when watching it some part of me, fresh from choking up at a paper mâché Dalek, was busy bringing an eighteen-year long wait to a delighted end. For all the deep-seated cynicism of that story, there is also a sense of manic glee to it, a telltale whiff of mercury, if you will. A refusal to slow down or to allow boredom to happen. A driving mania. It is giddily, madly, delightfully fun to watch. It's screamingly obvious why it's been ripped off so many times. It's funny, it's exciting, it has a wonderful and friendly clever wizard who runs about being brilliant. It is so blessedly fun to watch, and fun to love. This in and of itself has power. Once one accepts a position on the margins, one of the most savagely effective moves one can make is to have the unmitigated gall to enjoy yourself there—to act as though one would rather be there.

And then there is also the same thing we began the Hinchcliffe era looking at: fear. As I have said before, there are few purposes more fundamental to children's fiction than completely screwing up children for life. The best children's fiction disturbs and unnerves. And for all its flaws, *The Talons of Weng-Chiang* does. Heck, the cackling, snorting madness of Mr. Sin is unnerving even as an adult. But it is, oddly, its ending that's the most satisfying in this regard. The climax of the story is a straight lift from the first episode of *The Ark in Space*—an attempt to hide while something shoots laser beams at you. It's an odd sort of symbolic unity for the Hinchcliffe era, with its first and last episodes each using the same plot point. It serves as a reminder that, in this regard, the era put its best foot forward, establishing from the start the thing that would really shape its legacy—a sense of giddy, terrified suspense that guaranteed that it could not be forgotten, not completely. And as we know, if something can be remembered...

History repeats itself. And now the dizzying, endlessly complex horror of the Hinchcliffe era is history, freed to happen again and again. Held in the memory of a generation of freaks, waiting patiently for their time to come.

Now My Doctor: Tom Baker, Part One

When I was writing the William Hartnell volume, I titled the final essay, a reflection on the Hartnell era as a whole, "Now My Doctor." Partially this was because of my existing naming convention of using quotes from Doctor Who for all my titles, but also because I really liked the implications of the title. The idea for these essays is that I make the case for why each version of the Doctor could be "my Doctor," as the phrase goes, moving through them in turn. And for Hartnell, at least, that was a change—I've never listed the Hartnell era as one of my favorites, and so it really was a case of deciding, OK, now I'm going to make Hartnell my Doctor.

But at last we come to one that requires a different approach. Because as I've said throughout this book, Tom Baker really is my Doctor—the first one I fell in love with, and the one who formed the largest chunk of my childhood viewing. That's not to say this is my favorite era outright: at least three more of these essays will have completely legitimate claims to being "my Doctor," but the point stands: to write about why I love Tom Baker requires no imagination.

Actually, Tom Baker presents a different problem, in that I have two of these to write, although this is not as big a problem as it might seem—the stark difference in the way in which the Hinchcliffe and Williams eras were treated in VHS release means that I do have very different relationships with the two eras. My history with the Williams era is based on my inability to access its stories, whereas my history with the Hinchcliffe era, once you get past the first few months of my Doctor Who fandom, are based on the fact that well over half the era was easily available on video in the US when I was buying Doctor Who VHS tapes in the US.

This is, of course, because the Hinchcliffe era was massively popular among Doctor Who fans, which raises the question of whether it's possible or, indeed, desirable to separate the Hinchcliffe era from its popularity. This is widely considered the definitive era of Doctor Who. And it's tough to argue with that. Not impossible—the claim that the Hinchcliffe era is overrated certainly exists—but even its detractors can, broadly speaking, see the appeal of the era. It's got a lovely mix of humor and scariness, has one of Doctor Who's best-ever writers overseeing everything, has the iconic Doctor, and has a strong case for the most iconic companion. You've got one of the best Dalek stories ever, the definitive Gallifrey story, and a host of other classics. What's not to love?

Well… we might admit that the legends of the Hinchcliffe era's searing terror are perhaps overstated. There are some good moments—I'll freely admit to *The Ark in Space* creeping me out a bit—but if what you really want is effective horror, the fact of the matter is that you can usually do better than Hinchcliffe-era Doctor Who. Including the Hammer horror films they're often riffing on. Nor is it the era in which Tom Baker is funniest: he's let off the leash in the Williams era, and many of his best comic bits are there. (Although to be fair, it's possible nothing is ever quite as funny as *Terror of the Zygons*.) Indeed, there's no one thing that Hinchcliffe-era Doctor Who straightforwardly does better than any other era. Even Robert Holmes, although he writes some corkers here, is largely more defined by his other material. When fans praise Holmes it's usually for his dark humor and his railing against bureaucracy, but these are the two things he really doesn't do much of while script editor.

"real psychological trauma" when you're paired with Tom Baker's giant scarf and similarly-sized grin.

This comes closer to an understanding of the era's alchemy. On one hand you have Holmes and Hinchcliffe pulling towards gothic horror and darkness, and on the other you have Tom Baker, who makes just about everything look fun. And who, equally importantly, is capable of selling fear when he has to: *The Pyramids of Mars* is a frighteningly generic script enlivened largely by the degree to which Tom Baker sells the fact that even the Doctor is afraid of Sutekh. So you have an era of Doctor Who that contains terrible and awful things, but that feels like the Doctor is having more fun than he's had in years.

Much of this book has talked about the value of being scary and a little too adult, and we should admit that while the Hinchcliffe era is not exactly what a grown-up horror fan is likely to turn to, it is reliably scary enough to unsettle children. But it pairs this fear with a sense of wonderful excitement. It makes fear fun. The cliché response to fear in Doctor Who is the whole "behind the sofa" business, which is almost certainly exaggerated, but which captures an essential truth. The idea of hiding behind the sofa is that you are in control of what you see—you can hide from the image or peek up over the sofa and see it.

Within the Hinchcliffe era, Tom Baker serves as the sofa. Because one massive grin and a quip is enough to take the tension out of any scene, the sofa is almost unnecessary. The show controls its own fear, using the Doctor as a hedge against things ever getting too scary. It's easy to treat Baker as a Patrick Troughton clone, but it's worth noting how different an approach this is. Troughton's comic antics often masked a real sense of danger. Especially in his earliest stories, the Doctor's clowning around wasn't reassuring—in *The Power of the Daleks*, in particular, the Doctor clowns about to make the story more scary, not less. Troughton offered an unpredictable Doctor.

What the Hinchcliffe era does, really, is manage to be all things to all people. It's funny, scary, intelligent, has some of the best design in series history, and is generally lacking in any obvious flaws. But this doesn't constitute a reason to adore the era. What's key isn't that it does everything reasonably well. Let's look at a specific story, *The Brain of Morbius*, because it's one of my absolute favorites. What's appealing about it isn't the lack of things wrong with it, but the fact that it has such a wonderful mix of things. It's at once deliciously and cheekily low-rent, featuring as it does a vegetable-envying madman as its primary villain, a skillful horror story, a tremendously literate story, and one with a real epic heft to it. What appeals isn't that the story is all things to all people, but that it successfully mixes such a heady set of concepts and images.

It's also worth noting that *The Brain of Morbius* contain one of the era's most unnerving scenes, namely the on where Sarah visibly has a bit of a nervous breakdown over th terrible things that are happening to her. On one level th feels like the logical endpoint of a certain perspective on wh Doctor Who is or should be—really scary, horrible, ep stuff. On another, it feels like a real threat to Doctor Wh Doctor Who works because nothing too awful happens the main characters. Even in the early days, when the sh was about how Ian and Barbara wanted to get home, tl were only ever put in scary situations. They were ne completely broken down and psychologically tortured. C of the basic ethics of the series is that going on an adven with the Doctor is the most wonderful thing ever.

And even though *The Brain of Morbius* pushes Sarah to brink, it ultimately stops there and remains on the pos that traveling with the Doctor is terribly fun. And Tom B is particularly good at making it seem fun because he al always seems like he's having fun. The rest follows from Even Sarah's near-breakdown comes off more as her hav bit of a rotten day because she's gone blind and not a psychological trauma. Because it's hard to have any id

Baker's Doctor isn't unpredictable: he retains the steady invulnerability of the Pertwee era. It's impossible to imagine anything truly bad happening around him. (Indeed, the first story of the next book demonstrates this with particular aptness—everybody gets slaughtered, and you hardly notice because the Doctor is having so much fun.) It's easy to miss it, because it's by now become the most standard-issue concept of who the Doctor is: he's the most fun person in the universe. But it's really Tom Baker who establishes that.

And that's why I fell in love with him as a child, and, through him, the entire series. It's why I still love him. Because he's just devilishly fun. In almost every story of the Hinchcliffe era, Tom Baker is having a tremendous amount of fun. So much so that it risks becoming overpowering, which, again, is an issue for another book. But under Hinchcliffe, paired with gothic horror plots that contrast meaningfully with his sense of fun, the series absolutely shines. It becomes one of the best things on television, ever. Even for an adult audience the mixture of fun and terror sparkles. But for a childhood audience for whom Tom Baker really is one of the most fun characters they've ever seen and the scary bits really are unsettling, it's like nothing else. It's a rabbit hole that pulls you right down, and even now, twenty years later, I'm still in it. Yes, Tom Baker is no longer my only Doctor.

But he'll always be my Doctor.

About the Author

Philip Sandifer lives in Connecticut and writes about both Doctor Who and British comics.

He blogs at philipsandifer.com.

Printed in Great Britain
by Amazon.co.uk, Ltd.,
Marston Gate.